a bit of
Heritage
for you.

*January 17, 2006*

*For my Beloveds, my Grandsons,*
*Sam and Rob.*
*Love, Grandmother*

# Jesse Stuart
## THE HERITAGE
### A BIOGRAPHY

David Dick *[signature: David Dick]*

Foreword by Wade Hall

Afterword by Thomas D. Clark

First Edition, January 1, 2005

Copyright by
Plum Lick Publishing, Incorporated
P. O. Box 68
North Middletown, KY 40357-0068

www.kyauthors.com

Dust jacket design and book production
by Stacey Freibert Design

Front cover photo by Thomas V. Miller, Jr., *The Courier-Journal*

Endleaf photo by Wade Hall

**Other books by David Dick**

*The View from Plum Lick*
*Follow the Storm (Original Edition)*
*Peace at the Center*
*A Conversation with Peter P. Pence*
*The Quiet Kentuckians*
*The Scourges of Heaven*
*Follow The Storm: A Long Way Home*

**Other books by David and Lalie Dick**

*Home Sweet Kentucky*
*Rivers of Kentucky*

Portions of "The Brotherhood of Minstrels"—Copyright © 2002. Courier-Journal &
Louisville Times Co. Reprinted with permission.

Portions of "Here Is Writing That Touches the Heart" have appeared
previously in *A Literary History of Kentucky* by William S. Ward,
Copyright 1988 by The University of Tennessee Press. Used by permission.

ISBN: 0-9755037-0-7

Library of Congress Control Number
2004108929

*In Memory of*

*Naomi Deane*

# CONTENTS

Foreword
Acknowledgments

Afterword
Chronological list of books

## "The Writin' Man From W-Hollow"
### by Wade Hall

Writing is surely the most autobiographical of the arts. Despite disclaimers, writers are supreme egotists. Their lives are spent spinning out pieces of themselves for public consumption. Kentucky's late author Jesse Stuart was driven to write. Even in the shadow of death, he was plotting new poems and stories. Throughout his life, he was supremely self-confident of his ability to compose worthwhile poetry and prose to share with his readers. Lest you think I have come to damn my favorite Kentucky author, I should quickly add that, on the contrary, I have come to praise him. I am merely clearing the air. Jesse was a supreme egotist. He was simply sharing himself with others. Isn't that what, in one way or another, we all want and try to do? Jesse believed that he had something valuable to share. Indeed, he did.

May we say that Jesse was self-affirming? Of course, he was. He liked himself. He liked what he did. He was impressed with his rise from extreme poverty in Greenup County, Kentucky; and he loved the fame and acclaim that he achieved and, he believed, he so rightly deserved. Indeed, he did.

But Jesse was more than an egotistical author and self-admirer. He was also an altruist. Because of his self-confidence, other people's successes did not threaten him. He loved and valued all people. Once, when a friend and I were eating dinner with Jesse and his wife, Naomi Deane, in the Jesse Stuart Lodge at Greenbo State Park, I saw his enthusiasm and affection for other people spill over. We had just arrived and were ordering our food when an old man suddenly appeared at our table and said, "Mr. Stuart, I just want to shake yore hand. I want to be able to tell my grandchildren that I shook the hand of Jesse Stuart." Jesse jumped up and began talking with this retired coal miner who probably had never read one of Jesse's books. Fifteen minutes later, Jesse was still talking with him as if he were the most important person in Kentucky. Indeed, at that moment and for Jesse, he was. Ten minutes later Jesse finally sat down to eat his cold food. I realized suddenly that, whether you were a poor Kentucky coal miner or the Kentucky governor, it didn't matter. Jesse loved other people and gladly gave himself to them, in his books and in his person.

Moreover, although he wanted desperately to be accepted by the literary establishment, he did not feel threatened by the success of other writers. He was free with his encouragement of young writers and free with his praise when his peers won prestigious awards. Jesse was doing his work the best he could, and they were doing theirs. There was room for everybody at his table.

Like most of us, I became acquainted with Jesse Stuart when I read his stories in high school English classes. Jesse even saved my career when I was a nineteen-year-old English teacher in a small town in south Alabama. One Friday I decided that I was having more problems than I could handle, and after school was out, I moped over to the library to find, I suppose, either a loaded gun to end my misery or something to read that would save me. The librarian, Mrs. St. John—yep, that was her name—came over to where I was pouting and looking disconsolate. "Honey," she said, "what is wrong? You look like you've lost your best friend." I said, "Oh, Ms. St. John, I think I'm a failure as a teacher." She smiled and said, "Wade, you are too young to be a failure at anything." Then she added, "Wait a minute. I have just the book for you to read this weekend. It'll make you feel a lot better."

I said to myself, "That's what she thinks. It's only October and I have to get through a whole year as a first-year teacher with unruly (so they seemed to me) students who were simply not interested in either Shakespeare or Salinger." In a couple of minutes she returned with a worn copy of *The Thread That Runs So True*, and said, "Take this book home and read it. It will lift your spirits and inspire you." I didn't believe her, but I took the book and trudged over to my small apartment. After supper, I took up the book, opened it to the first page, and read:

> *Monday morning when I started on my way to school, I had with me Don Conway, a pupil twenty years of age, who had never planned to enter school again. I was the new teacher here at Lonesome Valley and I didn't know what kind of brains he had. He had left school when he was in the fourth grade. But I did know that he had two good fists and that he would be on my side. All day Sunday while I had worked at the schoolhouse, I was trying to think of a plan so I could stay at Lonesome Valley School. I knew I had to stay. I knew if one had to go it would be Guy Hawkins. I might have to use my head a little but that was why I had it.*

Four hours and almost 300 pages later, I finished Jesse Stuart's account of his first year of teaching in a Kentucky backwoods school when he was seventeen. His book had saved my career—maybe even my life. It was the beginning of a vocation and an affectionate relationship with Stuart that lasted for more than forty years.

After I had done time in the U.S. Army and in a couple of graduate schools and was teaching with my freshly minted Ph.D. at the University of Florida, I met Jesse Stuart in the flesh. The head of the English Department asked me if I would drive over to Jacksonville to pick up Stuart, who was coming to read and lecture our students on writing. Although I was nervous about being alone in a car with a world-famous writer—what would we talk about, for Heaven's sake?—on the trip back to Gainesville, I accepted and invited a friend to go along for company. At least, I thought, we could talk to each other. I shouldn't have worried. Before we got Jesse in the car, he and I had bonded, and he was calling me Wade and insisting that I call him Jesse. En route, I noticed that Jesse was writing down something in a small feed-and-seed tablet. I said, "Mr. Stuart—uh, Jesse—are you working on your lecture notes?" He said, "No, you've just given me an idea for a new short story."

After I told Jesse about my experience with *The Thread That Runs So True* at Opp High School, and what an inspiration it had been for a novice teacher, he said, "Wade, let's stop at a bookstore. I'll get you a new copy of the book and sign it for you." And so he did. He wrote: "For my new friend, Wade Hall. It has been such a pleasure to meet you. Your friend, Jesse Stuart." Little did I know that I would be moving to Kentucky within a year and would be able to know Jesse Stuart, the man, as well as Jesse Stuart, the author. For more than twenty years, Jesse and I were friends. I visited him and Naomi Deane many times at W-Hollow. I reviewed his books for *The Courier-Journal*, and I wrote essays and articles and gave speeches about his career as Kentucky's most beloved writer. Finally, I helped to celebrate his life and works at his funeral in Greenup on February 20, 1984.

Now I have met Jesse Stuart again—this time the complete man and writer, fully fleshed, warts and all, and talking through the words he wrote and the words of his family, friends, and readers. It is not the usual academic biography. It is the kind of familiar life that Jesse would have loved—unorthodox, up-close, slightly ragged and irreverent. Imagine any other biographer describing Jesse's mother giving him birth: "August 8, 1906. Martha Stuart felt the surge of pounding pain of the birthing of her second child. She took to her bed in the fifteen-foot by fifteen-foot one-room cabin of hewn half-dovetailed tulip poplar logs. She triangulated her long legs and dug at the tick bedding with her heels at the foot of the bed. She seized the sideboards with sun-hardened hands. She bit down hard the way a land turtle snaps at a piece of sniffing dog that gets too close for comfort."

David Dick uses a variety of strategies in putting together Stuart's life. At times he is an omniscient Appalachian bardic narrator who sees outside and inside Jesse and his people. Sometimes he is the indefatigable researcher who comes up with a forgotten or unknown letter or remembered tale. Sometimes he sounds like D.H. Lawrence, the great English author who wrote not only *Lady Chatterly's Lover* but also the brilliant, staccato analysis of America and American writing in his *Studies in Classic American Literature*. Sometimes Dick presents his research in a conventional, staid and scholarly manner. He seems to say, "Jesse Stuart was too large a man to be contained in one way."

For techniques and presentations, Dick has drawn on his own rich and larger-than-life life and career as a broadcast journalist to create a mosaic of many pieces that make up a rich and busy life. Or rather, it is more like a Kentucky patchwork quilt, with pieces of a worn life well lived and worth admiring all recycled into a new portrait of Kentucky's revered Bard. Reading this book by David Dick has been an experience I will never forget.

Dick has created a portrait of Jesse Stuart that is many layered and textured, containing even more dimensions and facets than the Jesse I knew or have read about in other books. In these pages Dick has captured Jesse's talent, his compulsion to write, his vitality, his love of life and his struggle to live long and productively. Here is a book that embodies a great writer who was an even greater man than the sum of his works. It is a delight to read, with surprises in content and style at every turn. Here is a man of humble birth with big ambitions and big achievements. Here is a man who is as much the archetypal American writer as Mark Twain. Here is a man I will never forget. Neither will you.

## ACKNOWLEDGMENTS

An inner voice kept whispering:

*listen to the wind blowing in W-Hollow,*
*go looking for Cedar Riffles,*
*walk in the cold rain on Seaton Ridge,*
*step inside "Old Op's" cabin,*
*hear the thunder in Plum Grove Cemetery.*
*Nay, don't sell Jesse down the river.*

My thanks, first and foremost, go to Jesse, who believed his life, both as writer and as teacher, could make a difference.

My gratitude goes also to CEO and Senior Editor Dr. James M. Gifford of the Jesse Stuart Foundation in Ashland, Kentucky, for permission to use Jesse's pictures and intellectual property.

Profound thanks to archivists Clara Keyes and Teresa Johnson at Morehead State University, as well as Larry Besant, Director of Libraries at Morehead State, archivists Leanne Garland at Lincoln Memorial University, Ernie Bailey at Murray State University, Delinda Stephens Buie and George McWhorter at the University of Louisville, archivists William J. Marshall and James D. Birchfield, and librarian Robert A. Aken at the University of Kentucky, the Special Collections staff at Vanderbilt University, and columnist Bob Hill, archivist Amy Inskeep, and senior librarian Sharon Bidwell at *The Courier-Journal.*

Thanks to Dr. Jack D. Ellis, retired pastor for the United Methodist Church, for his historical perspective leading to the establishment of the Jesse Stuart and James Still Rooms at Morehead State University.

To Greenup County reporter G. Sam Piatt, I say Jesse was a good judge of reporters. Every community newspaper deserves a Sam Piatt.

My editor, Georgiana Strickland, has again been masterfully painstaking, and I am deeply grateful for her unwavering, wise, and patient corrections.

Stacey Freibert designed the book and gave it a strong simplicity, which Jesse would have admired.

On the eve of his one-hundredth birthday, Kentucky historian laureate

Dr. Thomas D. Clark drove from Lexington to Estill County to lead the search for one-room log cabins. He was unfailing in his belief that a popular biography of Jesse Stuart was an important task to be completed. Dr. Clark's afterword adds an essential historical context.

David Palmore, elementary school principal, collector and foremost authority on Stuart books and memorabilia, was unselfish and untiring in his dedication to the idea that his hero should not be forgotten. Mr. Palmore spent many volunteer hours reading the manuscript from the earliest to the final revisions. He provided the "Chronological List of Jesse Stuart's Books," and he graciously opened and shared his priceless collection of Lena Wells Voiers letters.

Wade Hall was supportive at crucial moments, provided new insights, and in the foreword brings to the study of Jesse Stuart a fair and critical judgment.

H. Edward Richardson's superb, comprehensive biography of Jesse has been invaluable. Frank H. Leavell's dissertation stands out for brevity and clarity.

Dr. John Holmes's knowledge of advances made in cardiology during the past half-century was indispensable.

At the annual Outloud Festival at Thomas More College, Dr. Ray Hebert was unwavering in his belief that Jesse Stuart's words deserved to be heard by a new audience.

Thanks to: George Brosi, Editor of *Appalachian Heritage* at the Berea College Appalachian Center, for timely encouragement and excellent criticisms during the final rewriting; Chester Powell for friendship and warm-hearted honesty; Dorothy K. Griffith, Greenup County Librarian/ Director for hospitality and assistance; Ethel McBrayer for inspiring the dedication of the finished work to her friend, Naomi Deane Stuart; Roy Jack "Todd" Preston, president of the Magoffin County Historical Society and Pioneer Village for glimpses inside early eastern Kentucky log cabins, and David Skinner at the Kentucky State Nature Preserves Commission, who helped me to walk the walk.

My soul mate, Eulalie, will have more love as a result of the writing of this narrative, for which she brought unfailing inspiration. She explored the archives, called attention to invaluable pieces in our joint effort to produce a faithful accounting of the essence of Jesse Stuart, and she insisted that there be even-handed storytelling. Just as Naomi Deane was Jesse's anchor, Eulalie has been mine. Without her, there would be no book for which I now can say, here it is, a gift to the friends of Jesse and Naomi, a volume for which I accept full responsibility as to accuracy and intent.

David Dick
Plum Lick, Kentucky
September 1, 2004

# IN THE BEGINNING

*He sendeth the springs into the rivers;*
*which run among the hills.*

*The Book of Common Prayer*

*Listen!*

It's 1906, the summer of Jesse Stuart's birth.

A northeasterly wind gathered itself, blew stronger with each lonely mile of watershed, moaned around the big bend from Firebrick toward South Shore, past the mouth of Tygarts Creek, and on upstream to Little Sandy River.

Devilish, heat-driven, dog-day storms washed up the Ohio Valley, and pitch-black clouds streaked a Highland baby's appointed window of time on Earth. The massive squall line swooshed past Coon Den and Shinglemill Hollows, then, in fierce swirls, engulfed W-Hollow hills of double-butted oak, hickory, and tulip poplar.

Did Jesse Stuart have a preference in the matter of when and where he'd first see the light of day?

If he'd had a choice he'd still have taken his chances and lived out his years upon the laps and land of his mothers and fathers—the Hiltons and the Stuarts of the spirit-spiked "dark hills" of Greenup County, Kentucky. This was his home for the present and for all eternity.

This wedge of Cumberland Plateau of the Appalachian region lies downriver from the mouth of Big Sandy, about four miles over the Highlands from the mouth of Little Sandy, which brings in the branch waters of Whetstone, Dime, Wolfpen, Tarkiln, and Archie Creeks. One hundred years ago the area was cut off, isolated, gorged with natural wonders, hanging by fingertips on scar tissues of memory—and in time past, home to the strong, the wary, and the feverish.

Storytelling was a tolerable way to hold tight and make it through what the Good Lord had laid upon His kin. Speaking the truth as best the truth be known—touched and tasted, with a stretch here and a pull or two there—was good medicine for aching hearts. The tradition of giving an exaggerated account of the Highland people of Appalachian Kentucky was a form of much needed amusement, generously laved upon with a flurry the way butter be slathered on steaming hot biscuits straight from the oven.

The hour of another childbirth had arrived, and it was the wind god Zephyrus who announced the day and place—W-Hollow—breathing sweet new life inside a plain, unselfish mountain woman's womb. It was the water god great Neptune who refreshed the seed nestled there in poverty, destined for plowboy's poetry.

The Good Lord knew what He was doing because He operated according to the way described in the Book of Luke: "Neither shall they say, Lo here! Or, lo there! for, behold, the kingdom of God is within you." This idea of "the kingdom within" was something Highlanders understood and practiced throughout their lives—that is to say, whenever the strongest push came to the baddest shove. It was something that kept a man and a woman *alive*, and when rain swept up to Plum Grove Cemetery, up where the ridge spirits laughed and cried among the Stuart markers, there came a cleansing, a wiping away of mortal miseries.

August 8, 1906.

Martha Hilton Stuart felt the surge of pounding pain of the birthing of her second child. She took to her bed in the fifteen-foot by fifteen-foot one-room cabin of hewn half-dovetailed tulip poplar logs. She triangulated her long legs and dug at the tick bedding with her heels at the foot of the bed. She seized the sideboards with sun-hardened hands. She bit down hard the way a land turtle snaps a piece of sniffing dog that gets too close for comfort.

The crop-rented home place—ramshackle, slapped-together, teeter-totter—was situated a short ways up from Cedar Riffles, a trickle becoming a runnel flowing into Little Sandy River, where other timeless rivulets roll into streams—Old Town Creek, East Fork, Shackle Run, Raccoon Creek. These waters eddy, tumble, and sometimes raise a tumult as they pass their pitched way to the Ohio—Mother River—then twist miles to the Mississippi and finally to the Gulf of Mexico.

The perpetual miracle—precipitation, percolation, and evaporation—wheeled the great water cycle, causing moisture to be born again in the Highlands, where it had "begun." As 'twas said in the Book of Revelation:

> *I am the Alpha and the Omega, the beginning and the end. To the thirsty I will give water as a gift from the spring of the water of life.*

There was another proverb that couldn't be washed away:

> *All the water that's here now was here in the beginning, and all the water that's here now is all the water there'll ever be.*

Still, for many a Highlander, 'twas be born by a throw of sixes and sevens, live a hard, stormy, uncertain existence, finally be buried for unfathomable time, way down deep in crumbling family ground.

Might be a lively romp or two to the fiddler's call—

> *Elbow Jim and elbow John,*
> *mule ran away with the harness on.*

might lead to romance 'round the fodder shock yonder side the low ridge.

> *Promenade and circulate,*
> *swing your lady,*
> *like swinging a gate.*

Martha's husband Mitchell, known as "Mick" throughout Little Sandy country, had sent hasty word over the tousle-treed, jet-black ridgeline to a doctor, any doctor—*somebody*—didn't they know, a woman's time would soon befall? But, no, it didn't do a particle bit of good.

No, *Sir*.

No telephones, no fauceted water, no electricity, no automobile, and you never knew for sure if a midwife, apron pinned to ample bosom, would be handy 'nough to granny-frolic up the holler to fetch a baby falling. The Stuarts were so poor they rubbed their coins together until they shined.

They thumbnailed so as to sharpen the edges of the creases of their greenbacks, and they saved all the soap but the squeal. Mick and Martha, as 'tis said, were too poor to paint, too proud to whitewash.

By nightfall, old Neptune was heaving rain in sweeping sheets, like John Henry driving steel, turning dirt roads into waterlogged wagon wheel hub-huggers. The wind was testing the chinking of those eighteen-by eight-inch tulip poplar logs in the one room where air was stale, heavy with the bittersweet smells of puccoon and the sweet-sour sweat of August labor.

Birthing odors too.

Martha Stuart's brow was bright with beads of sweat, when she — swooooo — felt the breaking and the cutting loose of her woebegone bag of waters. Contractions squeezed closer now, engulfing her, reminding her of wee flash floods on Little Sandy.

Oh, Lord, Lord! Don't let me lose my mind, don't let me be swept away to your mighty, mighty ocean. No, not now. Oh, Lord, not now! Be with me, please don't leave me, Lord. Come on and help me. You hear me, now!

Mick was present, face puckered tight, lips forbidding useless words, knowing it was his God-directed portion to attend to Martha's moment of difficulty. Nay, no time for jibber-jabber. His was a Highland man's proud moment. Time for abiding silence. Brag and Talk Big were good dogs, but Believe It and Hold Fast were better.

Sophia, first born, barely knew what was happening. She might stand and stare, and twist to trouble her ribboned hair. For everybody present, it was a moment about to be washed away down Cedar Riffles to a disremembering sea of unrecorded history. No one was keeping and saving a journal, no one was writing down words or painting pictures for the pleasure of future biographers and a passel of tall-tale tellers. Some historical traipsers might happen along later and do some guesswork, surmising, wetting a finger and holding it up, taking an honest stab at what actually happened.

Not quite four years old, Sophia probably had grown used to her mother and father's night sounds — Sis accepted the hullabaloo and the hustle, same as the way she saw Gray Games cut capers with Plymouth Rocks — feathers a-flyin', eyes bright with flecks of fire.

But *these* groans becoming squalls were different, like a mountain cat had seized Sophia's mama, and hit was a-tearing her apart!

Deep down, as simply as cloistered, isolated Highland children are ever aware, Sophia suffered through her mother's misery. Most Cumberland Plateau women-children have fathomed the importance of remaining silent. Wasn't it the same feeling that came when full-of-years Gypsy cow went off alone out on the ridge, searching and straining to drop another calf? Dull-eyed Sweet Dumpling to mare her foal?

Sophia likely knew something important was happening, and she wanted to help, but she knew she was better off taking a full barefooted stride back and letting nature be done with as nature saw fit. Some things are better off not meddled with. Eyes wide, wanting to see, then shut tight, she may have held fast to her faceless shuck doll with cornstalk legs. Likely Sophia just wanted a little sister, that was all—not too much to ask, wouldn't you think? But if it were bound to be a sorry-butted brother, she'd make sure he knew who was in charge! But then, she'd help him all a body could.

But, *why* a boy? Somebody to run roughshod over all creation? Somebody to gallivant around the cabin, lording it over the circling family?

No, Ma'am.

Honey, boys are more or less like rank bulls with open heifers in red clover pastures, if you want to know the sorry truth about it—no heading them off and sending them back down the holler.

And the rain crow *hoo-hoooed*!

Mick consoled Martha when her gasps were loudest, like she was shouting back to the thunder baby over Cedar Riffles, up there where God was moving his furniture around in Heaven. Mick kept water biling on the stove for Martha's close friend, Addie Burkhart, who arrived just in time to deliver the baby. Every mama needs such a lady person with long knowledge of what it takes to bring a new life into this sorry old world. When something goes wrong, they usually know what to do. Pray, if nothing else. Get down on their bony, popping knees and hold tight with their hands propped against their heads.

Martha had likely prepared midday dinner—today-killed red-tailed squirrel, fresh mustard greens to go with leftover buttered pone. Something like that. Everybody was happy on a well-tended stomach. Highland mothers knew that truth to be evident on the day of a birthing or the day of

5

a dying. Both were a kind of celebration. One without the other wouldn't be worth fiddlesticks.

Mick closed the two windows tight, as well as the only door to the cabin, to keep rain from a-coming in. As he waited patiently for the baby's head to appear he wondered if this second-born just might be a boy.

Mick might have beseeched, "Lord, Lord, Lord! A boy would be wondrous enough to make you want to whip your weight in wildcats. Might have myself a nip on it. Might feel more substantial by it."

After all, Mick needed a strong-willed son to circle 'round steep hillside land, turning new-ground sod with a bull-tongue plow, sowing seed, harvesting corn and Burley tobacco in thick and thin. With some birthin's you have your boy, if you're lucky. With some you have your girl, you just couldn't tell which one was going to pop out.

We need a boy!

Mitchell Stuart, who could neither read nor write but who was as bright as any college man concerning earth and sky, sun and rain, wished his son would not repeat the mistakes of Granddaddy—drinking, ridge-running, fathering nineteen children on Big *and* Little Sandys. He had a right to do it if he wanted to, but somewhere somebody might ought to draw a line. Like holding the reins on a chompin' horse—at some point you need to be thinkin' ahead toward a better way back to the barn.

Think on it, a new Stuart man-child might become a touch schoolhouse-educated! Might be a leader of some sort: whistle-tootin' engineer on the smoke-snortin' EK, the Eastern Kentucky railroad; maybe yardmaster on the through trains on the Chesapeake and Ohio line. Might become a teacher for all those wet-behind-the-ears boys and girls generally and otherwise not up to very much good. Superintendent of Greenup County schools? You just never could tell.

Mick studied Martha's face, where grit showed in the purse of her lips. She wasn't thinking about sons or daughters, or if they might grow up to become preachers or poets. Even her Baptist persuasion couldn't overrule the simple fact of the childbirthin' matter. Motherin' was as real as rain falling from the sky. There was no rain hat or umbrella or leak-proof shoes for motherin'. There were you and the Good Lord and His peculiar way of organizing life on this here Earth. The Good Lord just decided not to make most things easy. Some lives He meant to be long and some He meant to be short, but why He went out of His way and to all the trouble to lay down *pain* was a right smart hard thing to figure.

There were these nine-pound hammers in the birth canal, nearly unbearable pressure in arching hip bones, enough to make you lose whatever good common sense you had! Why, in the name of Heaven, would He do it that a-way? Seems like he could have come up with a better plan.

*Goldarn* it!

How come the woman had to do all the birthing work while the man stood around and popped his knuckles? If men had to have babies, wouldn't be airy.

Here was *pain* a-pulling through every nerve cell of Martha Stuart's stout body, all five feet eleven inches of her, head and shoulders over Pa, he being no more than pint-size, five-feet-seven, give or take. So small he could wiggle his way into narrow, low-ceiling mine spaces in search of coal slabs on nearby hills, he so pencil-thin he looked like last year's scarecrow on a slanted-up corn patch.

Martha, too, knew her way around a grubbing hoe. She loved the out-of-doors. Feeling dark, crumbling earth between her fingers and toes. Schooled only to the second grade, Martha was doing no more than her mother, Violet Anne Pennington Hilton, had done, when in the century past, Violet was birthing *five* children without airy complaint, then dying at the age of forty.

And the rain crow *hoo-hoo...hoooed!*

The gray, long-tailed, blinkin'-eyed birds knew what was coming.

Need not a-bother blatherin' to Highland women about what smarts. They might say, keep those distant thoughts to your outlander self. "Don't worry about the likes of us. We know what we can do, what we can't do, and what we don't want to do. Don't cross us! You hear?"

There it is!!!

"Oh, God!" Mick might have blurted out when for the first time he saw the baby, head to toe, shoulders to privates—

a BOY!

Thunder bummmmped, lightning flashed, splitting the American hickories, tallest trees atop W-Hollow hills. Hot air spoooo-ked surest-footed mules. Feeler hairs bristled, stiffened in their long pointy ears, tingled with a-feared sensations, driving brutes to kick like precious Jesus and Joseph—slightest human provocation was reason enough for whirl-around, knock 'em windin' retribution.

The birth-time wrought and finished, the bruising moment when a new bairn took his first breath, his first keek at his W-Hollow world, was enough to make the bagpipe moan and the fiddler strum! All Highlanders gloried when newborn babes opened Heaven-sent eyes to inherit first light!

You did good, Mick, Martha might have said, reaching deep to gratitude, stretching forward a little, rising as much as possible, better to see the baby boy passed to his daddy after Addie Burkhart had cut the bloody umbilical cord.

Oh, the Lord is good, when you believe in Him!

Now, if'n you don't mind, bring 'im here so I can hold 'im, she might have coaxed, warmth unlocked from a storehouse of gratefulness. Likely she didn't favor the baby with kisses but just smiled on him with relief. Martha and Mick didn't take to kissing, even their own kind.

But by and by she'd bring herself to say, this is *my* boy, and he'll make me proud one day, and when people see him walking down the streets of Riverton, they'll say, "There goes Martha Hilton Stuart's boy."

The story goes, Mick asked Martha what she would name the child in his altogether snug up to her breast. Would it be another Mitchell? *Little Mick?*

Oh, no. No, Sir!

And why not? I'd like to know.

He'll needs be dressed up better'n that. But, no now, wait. No Isaac...Moses...nary Solomon. Nary Peter...Matthew...nor John. Nay.

What, then?

"I'll name him Jesse," said Martha, "that's what hit'll be—Jesse Hilton Stuart."

Now, this is how it might have happened on that stormy August day in 1906 in a place called W-Hollow. Exact details are not available. On

Judgment Day the Good Lord may reward us for resorting to imagination to set the scene for the story to follow. Nowhere in the Ten Commandments does it say "Thou shalt not imagine."

Jesse Stuart was born with plenty of imagination, and he came by it honestly. He was ordained to raise a ruckus, but it would never be to hurt somebody deliberately. Jesse's mother and father were "salt of the Earth." What that means is, they were *good* people, and they'd give you their last potato in the hill, but don't try to take something without asking first.

Later in life Jesse would have the cheek to avow the year of his birth was 1907! As good a guess as any would be that he just wanted to make himself one year younger! Squeeze one more year out of living! One more year of writing, because he knew his time was running out. In the history of creation as Jesse, climbing the beanstalk, might laugh and say, the difference in his birth years wouldn't be worth a persimmon over a pawpaw or a pansy over a petunia!

# JESSE AND THE BEANSTALK

*All night it poured and the dawn came clear,*
*only to darken into gray again.*
*But the river—the river!*

John Fox Jr.
*The Little Shepherd of Kingdom Come*

*Wake!*

The coldest months were a test of willpower—days and nights were frightfully bitter. Martha understood that most winters would be difficult. In years to come, Jesse would remember deep snows and birds dying by the hundreds, rabbits becoming thin in their silent desperation.

But after each thaw, the ice gave way, and the river rolled on.

Jesse's taproot drew from the saturated earth.

He was the kind of beanstalk boy who would climb far beyond normal heights, one with nature, having amazing memory. Nothing escaped his attention. His seeing and his hearing were as clear and sharp as a knife-edged wind whispering past the Writing Tree, through Shinglemill Hollow, then out from the soul of W-Hollow.

Martha and Mick—persistent, bold as bloodroot—owned hardly anything but themselves, and even those mysteries, their immortal souls, were bound for glory as *giff-gaff* to God, Heaven's last and best, an Appalachian spiritual give and take.

'Til then, they had an old cast-iron stove to cook on and to bile their sassafras tea, firewood stacked by the only door, loose lumps of coal handy as needed, shotgun to kill wild meat, grubbin' hoe for plantin' taters, scrubbin' board for keepin' shirts and underwear reasonably clean, roof over their heads, family Bible 'neath the coal oil lamp.

Don't you see? What else would they need?

Pity?

Not a'tall.

In early-twentieth-century Appalachia, just to breathe was called tolerable survival. As was said of many mountain folk, "They weren't much, but they were all they got." Maybe God smiled down and said to little Jesse and the Stuart clan, you're all you've got, so take it and make the best of it, whatever *you* decide to do, and remember it's *all* mine, just as you are all mine and I am all yours. You'll find me in Cedar Riffles, and you'll find me in Little Sandy, and you'll find me in every child born of man and woman.

And that's why you may hear it in the wind—let's be taking care of this here young 'un, as W-Hollow mothers and fathers would say of each child born to them. Oh, there'd be stories of neglect and meanness, and outsiders would come to brand them as Hatfields and McCoys, Beverly Hillbillies, loose spokes in a wobbling *Kentucky Cycle*.

Mick and Martha drew down from their ancestors the strength they needed to keep on keeping on. The time was two decades before anything fancy like a Frontier Nursing Service, several counties to the south. Wouldn't be no Eastern college-educated chirping young ladies riding up W-Hollow a-wearing purty wide-hipped pants and saucy hats—no hell-bent, city-talking fussies taking charge like a body didn't know a blessed thing. Oh, down there in the highest Appalachian mountains, there'd be some Frontier ladies who'd have a speck or two of sense, many who'd give all they had. And, yes, there were the pioneering settlement schools, notably the Hindman Settlement School in Knott County, Kentucky. As Martha and Mick would remind you, Jesse wasn't born with jingle-jangles or store-bought slippers. He never attended much more than a one-room elementary school. He walked many miles, coming and going. From the very beginning he served notice that he'd not be bullyragged by anybody. But he was not completely self-absorbed, for there was an underlying sensitivity toward people and place. He walked the wooded miles each day with natural ease.

Jesse Stuart was a singular force of nature. As a juvenile with survival instinct, he battled water snakes in Little Sandy, shot and slung rabbits and squirrels over his shoulder and brought them home for his mama to cook. When challenged by thugs at school, Jesse returned the favor with the power of his fists, his own nine-pound hammers driving noses and jaws to earth like worn-out railroad spikes. Every day was a new day of surviving as best he knew how.

Jesse was well formed from the start, if later school-age pictures are any clue. At age six, to his mother, he must have seemed sound in every way, his early keenings in fine fettle, a powerfully pleasing token. But there was little chance for regular pediatric care, no systematic listening with stethoscope to monitor the rhythm of the beating inside his developing chest.

Jesse was started off right on mother's milk, chicken and dumplings, and cornbread soaked in butter. Martha made sure her children were well fed, Jesse remembering one feast ranging from spareribs and sweetmilk to roasted goose and gravy. He may have needed a more nutritional fare, which doctors in time would be certain to prescribe. He might have developed and maintained cleaner arteries leading to and from a genetically questionable heart, as modern electrocardiograms would have detected. But it could be argued that there were tradeoffs: in the beginning, Jesse's health was balanced with purer water and purer air, and his exercise came in long walks through the hills of W-Hollow. His pumping heart would just have to learn to keep up with his taut muscles and his long, loping stride. When he sat down for meals, it was a family occasion of good cheer and bonding, a summing up of the confidence, commitment, and consistency born anew in the character of Jesse Hilton Stuart. No matter how much he may have exaggerated the array of dishes on the table, it was the flavor of the sustaining fruits of the Earth that nurtured the seed and flowered the beanstalk.

Jesse was fated to explore every nook and cranny of his sliver of the world and one day to write it down so that millions of readers in many countries could understand and enjoy and hold it in their minds and their hearts. His was a fascination and a love for the Kentucky Highlands, its people, and its creatures.

Dogs!

A time-honored trait of the true Kentuckian is a human kinship with dogs. Jesse had many favorites, each sharing a special time and place in what he later joyfully called the Democratic World of Dogs. In such a society there was room for everybody.

Take your flea-infested hound dogs, yawning and stretching from dreams of one more blood-pumping chase. It was their nature, their mission, their special calling. These were neither lap dogs nor candidates for Westminster trophies. Just as Jesse would win no Pulitzer or Nobel Prize, W-Hollow dogs were not pampered but were appreciated and praised when veneration was earned—mainly they were left to their natural instincts, like bad-eyed Catahoula curs. If they were not honored with a ham bone, they'd still do what they believed they had to do.

You could pretty much tell when hunting dogs were happy—you could see it in their eyes and by the way their long tongues were bright red, drooling with delight, first and foremost when the moon was full! The hunt was not the next best thing to Gloryland—it *was* Gloryland!

Lean, curve-tailed, belly-tight foxhounds—Lightning, Thunderbolt, Shooting Star, Fleet, Black-Boy, Bad Eye, Molly, Big Jump, Jerry-B Boneyard—barooed across the waters with echoes like unchurched choral refrains. Stouthearted Walker hounds were uncaged, slapped on the butt, and sent forth to sing with rhythms of full-moon voice. That there was all it took to be sent out to make hog-nosed polecats pucker their anal glands.

Jerry-B Boneyard, baroooing for the membership of the great dog democracy, would tell you, if he could talk—Ladieees and Gennnts—Brer Fox will know real fast that what goes around comes around. He will, now! We Good Old Boy Dogs and Good Old Girl Dogs will give that sly devil a taste of how Brer Rabbit feels in that bite-down instant when there's not a blessed thing to do but bleat.

Young Jesse was also fascinated with the reptilian world and welcomed its membership according to kind. Black snakes glided across Highland paths to shelter in summer beneath spring-fed rock castles. In winter the leathery creatures, non-venomous and therefore relatively harmless, sought warmth under creaking cabin floors. Serpents had a right to hold out hope for a respected portion of the brotherhood and the sisterhood—no matter what the copperhead spewed or the preacher man Amened. The idea of associating the snake with the Devil was one of man's more durable tall tales.

Kentucky soil and water were Jesse's beginning and ending. There'd be no other spot on earth as anchoring as this place, where a superabundance of trees spread and pushed up their tops, reaching for Heaven. His sense of place was deep, with feeder roots widening, drawing up the moisture, the essence of Earth. His life was like a seed descending from a perennial plant, nestling deep in loamy soil compacted by millions of footprints of those who'd gone before, the sturdy stem pushing up to breathe the Highland air.

The waters of the Highlands of Kentucky were moving as they had for centuries, as they would in their relentless flow to the sea—eternally—to the oceans of collected passion. Without the phenomenon of the water cycle, Jesse and all God's people would frantically turn as dry and brittle as starving grasshoppers in a summer drought. This great water cycle would capture the spirit of Jesse Stuart in his boyhood years and become the infrastructure of his God-given talent for future writing—poetry and storytelling.

Jesse quickly learned from heritages descending from both sides of the family tree. From the time of Jesse's boyhood breaths—whirlwind cries of their own—he gathered unto himself from great-grandfather Raphy, grandfather Mitchell, and father Mitch. And, before them, there'd been the Stuarts of Ayrshire in the old country of big-hearted Bobby Burns. Don't discount the curious melding of love and hate in the eighteenth-century Scottish Highland House of Stewart, when Robert the Bruce, in the seventh generation after Robert de Bruis, stormed off as a Norman knight to accompany William the Conqueror's invasion of England in 1066—all were unwashed, unadorned, and few could read or write. All this was at the core of the stuff of which Jesse Stuart was made.

As soul brother Bobby would say:

> *Good Lord, what is man! For as simple he looks,*
> *Do but try to develop his hooks and his crooks,*
> *With his depths and his shallows, his good and his evil,*
> *All in all, he's a problem must puzzle the devil.*

Stuarts and Stewarts too had crossed the water from Scotland to Virginia—names spelled differently to match present satisfaction—six brothers including Raphy and his descending line, who understood heritage in dribs and drabs. Aye, 'twas Mick who'd waited patiently in the close-fitted log cabin during that frog-strangling thunderstorm for his Martha to deliver Jesse.

Hadn't the Hyltons, and later the Hiltons, also crossed the big pond to New England and Virginia? Weren't they, you might say, a cut or two above your everyday pioneer? They knew what several books were. Don't you know, they had a sense of destiny with a little touch of nobility thrown in for taste and trouble? They weren't a sorry bunch of rowdy hillbillies like them characters come later in Jesse's famous *Taps for Private Tussie* book—them freeloaders a-squattin' up and down God's creation!

The Hiltons lived in the time and spirit of Tom Paine, Ben Franklin, and Tom Jefferson. Stir with Scottish grandsires the likes of Bobby Burns and there now you had a passel of folks with vision, strength, and from-the-toes-up laughter with a glimmer of hope for the future.

Mick and Martha were not readers, and they would not know it was Ben Franklin who said: "Dost thou love life? Then do not squander time, for that's the stuff life is made of." They'd not know it was Tom Jefferson who said: "I steer my bark with Hope in the head, leaving Fear astern." Even though they did not read or have the money to buy books for their children, they could have understood Tom Paine's "My country is the world, and my religion is to do good."

Stuarts and Hiltons were blended—proud and stubborn people of earth, water, and whistling wind—and one of Jesse's earliest recollections was included in the "Author's Introduction" to a 1966 Signet Books reprinting of "Nest Egg" in *A Jesse Stuart Reader*:

> *When I look back over the years to the days when I was very young, I remember first of all going to the fields with my father. Even at six years old, I had chores to do to help him and I was proud of them. I carried drinking water for him, and I walked along behind him when he was plowing to uncover the corn that had been buried by dirt from the plow. When I got tired, I'd go to sleep under a shade tree.*

*Another early memory of my childhood is gathering eggs on our farm for the market in Greenup. Since we hardly ever had much cash money in those days, we had to use butter and eggs for barter in Greenup to get the things that we couldn't make or raise on the farm, things like salt, pepper, coffee, and sugar. Every Saturday my father and I would walk the 5 miles to Greenup; it seemed like a great journey to me. And it was all the more exciting to me because I had gathered the eggs we were carrying.*

"When Jesse was about seven years old, the Stuart family went to a revival at Plum Grove Church," described in a dissertation, *A Farmer Singing: The Life of Jesse Stuart*, written in 1981 by Baylor University professor Frank Leavell.

*Jesse and Sophia huddled on the back row night after night while five Baptist preachers relayed at the pulpit conjuring up and shouting down the Devil and calling sinners to the mourners' bench. ...Despite their dramatic conversion and their regular church attendance, Mick and Martha cared little for the frenzied revival meetings where the people cried and shouted and rolled on the floor....They did not shout their religion but lived it....In these early religious awakenings are the seeds of one of the most profound and prevalent themes in Stuart's writings: the mystic union between God, man, and nature.*

Professor Leavell relies on Jesse's autobiography *Beyond Dark Hills*, a good source from which to come to an appreciable understanding of Jesse Stuart's early spiritual life.

*When I became twelve years of age, the time that "my accountability" began, I dreaded to do what the hill preacher told the people they would have to do before they would get to Heaven, the place God kept for his people. The preacher said one would have to fall to one's knees at the altar, in the cornfield, in the apple orchard, in the woods—just any place, but on the knees to show humbleness. There underneath the heavens, cry out to God and say: "God, I've stolen sheep. God, I've loved my neighbor's wife. And God, I talked about Tessie Holbrook. God, I carried a pistol for*

*Wayne Wright. Won't you forgive me for these things, Lord, and many others? I've been a mean man. Make me a soldier of the Cross." God would say then, "You are saved, Young Man. Get up out of the dust and follow me. Take up the Cross and follow me." There would be a light upon the young man's face. He would be happy. Now I dreaded to do this. I knew I had to do it. The preacher was right. He knew, for many times he said he was the chosen one of God, gone out to preach God's word. He knew about God—maybe he had talked to God....When I got right with God, I would go out on the hilltop. I would put my face down against the wet oak leaves on the ground. I would get rid of the wheelbarrow load of sins I had done. I had broken Aunt Viola Hilton's eggs. I threw them against a slick beech tree to watch the yolk run down the bark. I had stolen Mr. Wheeler's sweet apples. I had called boys bad names. I would get rid of all this. But I must get out in a lonely place—away from everybody. I wanted to get down against the leaves.*

Jesse was coming to terms with his "kingdom within," a theme that would play in his mind throughout his life. He was not just a Methodist or a Baptist, any more than he'd have been just a Buddhist if he'd been born on a Tibetan mountaintop. He was Jesse Stuart, not entirely a world unto himself, yet a strong individual with a passion to be.

As for the Devil, Jesse wrote in the "God: And the Evening Sky" chapter of *Beyond Dark Hills:*

*God and the Devil were at war....The greatest fights the Devil and God had at Plum Grove were on Sunday nights at church and at the spring revivals. When the summer moon rode slowly up the sky over the summer hills and the evening was filled with insect sounds—the katydids and the jar flies buzzing—then there would be the frogs croaking along the streams and in the little swamps, the whippoorwills calling from the pastures around the church house— this was when the old women and the old men would come walking in to church. The women would wear shawls around their shoulders—black shawls used for church purposes. The men would come dressed in overalls and denim-jackets. Their faces were*

*colored by the wind and the sun to a brown leather tan. They were
hard men. They were strong men. They had worked in the tobacco
fields and the fields of tall corn. They had come to help God fight the
Devil. They came like they did in the days of old—a little Puritan
band.*

Stuarts—hunkered in pride and poverty—were distrustful of anybody
living close enough for neighbors' chickens to mix. Never mind that
crossbreeding would produce hybrid vigor. That was beside the point. For a
fact, when rough and ready Gray Game cocks started straddling Plymouth
Rock hens, worsening and reddening combs, flap-flapping feathers, mixing
yolks, then, to top it off, bringing strange chickens home to roost on
crowded hen house pine poles—well, by thunder, coal-mining, tenant-
farming Stuarts took it as a token from God Almighty—time to come alive!

"We have to move now. I can stand this place no longer," said Martha,
after the death of Jesse's baby brother, Herbert Lee. By one count, the
Stuart family moved eight times, Mick and Martha unceasingly on the
lookout for what seemed to be a better tenant-landlord arrangement. Jesse
later vowed that one day he would buy every acre his mother and father
and their children lived on as tenants, and he did just that. With that
utterance, a self-driven, self-motivated dream began to take shape. Whether
or not Jesse's heart could withstand the pressures accompanying his
ambition was another matter. As a child and throughout his life, he was
fearless and restless, determined as a woolly bear becoming a tiger moth.

Martha and Mick did not live to see their son's complete dream of
ownership of home and farm come true, but their spirits would know.
They'd be up in Heaven looking down with pride, urging Jesse to keep
working to be what he wanted to be.

His day would surely come.

When the tenant Stuart family relocated from Cedar Riffles to rent
another farm in W-Hollow, Jesse, eleven years old, helped to guide slow-
moving oxen Buck and Berry as they muscled the wagon in dead of winter.
Jesse was living from without and within his heritage. His being was
strengthening like a muscle that's built in the using of it—a heart beating
courageously because it feels the blood warming the arms and the legs.
Jesse's description comes from the "Destiny of Hills" chapter of his 1938

autobiography *Beyond Dark Hills*:

> *We moved from Cedar Riffles on a sled. It was a winter day when we moved. Our new destiny was a log house in W-Hollow ....It was from the new home my sister and I started to school. We walked two miles to and from the old log schoolhouse at Plum Grove....My sister* [Sophia] *became my boss.*

No one would be Jesse's boss for very long.

Jesse's touch, his feel for the goodness of life, was as true as a bumble-bee sting, potent as a polecat's last defense, sweet as pawpaw juice on a summer afternoon. Nothing short of a cornered bear could turn back the boy from W-Hollow.

# AX AND SPROUTING HOE

*If prices hold up I think I might maybe be ready*
*to pay on a place year after next.*
*I allow to have a place of my own.*
Elizabeth Madox Roberts
*The Time of Man*

*Work!*

The red-bellied woodpecker hammers the sides of the pine trees like a creature possessed, and the honeybee whirs from wild flower to wild flower in white clover pasture, relentless in extracting the essence of fragrance. The North American beaver gnaws its favorite alder trees to the ground, wrestling the wood to the water to build a home, safe and secure— no money directly involved unless a price be attached for later marketing profits. Were there no human economics, the woodpecker, honeybee, and beaver would go on doing what they've been doing for centuries.

Jesse said his first remembrance was the sound of wind over Cedar Riffles. He said it howled over the treetops and hovered down where the water streaked the stones. Highland lads have felt the need to draw closer to the cycling miracle. To remain apart from rivulets of water is as unnatural as cursing the rising sun or bemoaning the movement of darkening, rain-filled clouds.

In his awakening years, Jesse would often go to the headwaters of Little Sandy for reprieves from other members of the human family and in the years of maturation he'd come to know the satisfaction of standing straight and tall, hands on hips. Or he might quietly hunker down, drawing in his knees as a mainstay for contemplative support. It is possible he might drop prayerfully to his knees to give simple thanks for the movement of the life-giving stream.

There were thoughts too of hunger in the wail of the wind and the rippling of the water, a constant craving for food, edged by certain knowledge that without money it could not be bought. Unless it was grown, it could not be bartered. Therefore the topsoil must be turned and finely textured for the tobacco beds to be sown each spring. Corn must be planted in places where stumps were stubbornly rotting, and potatoes dug from their hillside entrenchment. Domestic animals must be fed, particularly in winter, and wild animals must in all seasons be harvested for food and hides.

Pride and joy?

Pride was not as sinful as many holy men proclaimed in a trusted Proverb passed down from generation to generation: — "Pride goeth before destruction, and an haughty spirit before a fall." But what of the joyful spirit in the mind to bring about positive outcomes before each sun went down? Surely there was a way out of poverty. Hear me! There's no pot of gold at the end of the rainbow, no guaranteed solutions across the river in the state of Ohio. Let Buckeyes scorn Briars like seventeen-year locusts, Jesse Stuart was one of those who quickly figured that prosperity would not fall from the sky — it would come, if it came at all, as the result of blood, sweat, and tears. And that would be right there on one's own piece of *owned* property.

Jesse motivated himself to succeed in the Highland game of survival. The notion came to him as naturally as Brer Bee bringing home the honey, Brer Beaver building his own enclosure. Brer Squirrel didn't have to be told to gather and store food for winter and the hardest of times. Call Jesse Stuart a Kentucky peckerwood and you might stir up a grievance.

Mountain men who chose neither to work nor to be curious in a widening world would think it an oddity that there was one critter in their midst who had such an unusual combination of determination and imagination. Some might not understand young Jesse's feeling of deep loneliness and impatient longing, as if he'd been pushed up from earth like a bursting double-butted oak acorn left to find its own height and foliage.

But there he was!

Jesse accepted God's challenge, captured it in the palm of his hand, and squeezed it, held onto it for dear life. And somehow he knew there was more to human survival than blossoming talent. There might be such a thing as good luck, but more likely in the years leading up to the Great Depression there was—

### Hard Luck

*I know he made cross-ties to earn his bread.*
*I know his crops burned in last summer's drouths,*
*And this is all he finds to buy the food*
*That goes to fill ten hungry children's mouths.*
*He gets eight cents to make a standard tie*
*Of hardwood tree—I think a man can make*
*Fifteen of these—a dollar twenty-cents per day—*
*Keeps his children from starving in a way.*
*Better to work on just a little pay.*
*It's all because the summer fields stayed dry,*
*Crops failed, and there was nothing left to do*
*But make cross-ties for men that pay so little;*
*Go home and eat corn-bread and play the fiddle.*
*They say the rich are having hard-luck too.*

*Sonnet 264*
*Man with a Bull-Tongue Plow*

Jesse, child of tenant farmers, knew the painful uncertainty of uprootedness, of not *owning* the dwelling place, not cradling the deed in folded arm across the chest, not filing the textured sheet of legal paper at the courthouse, forbearing long-delayed gratification of land*holding*.

Yes, by thunder, and by all favorable signs of the moon, the fundamental bonding of soil and human flesh was the knowing of the simple and powerful feeling of a body's *own* dirt between a body's own toes and caked up there on furrowed forehead by sweat beading down. It was all a part of the meaning and the makings of *work*.

Human perspiration was an element in the watery universe, each drop having brotherhood and sisterhood with the whole. Each man and woman, mostly water to begin with, was in perpetual flow as groundswells to

23

eventually sweep away anything choosing stubbornly to stand still. Highlanders knew it and learned to respect the "tide," meaning flash flood.

"Speakin' of rain."

"Holler'n rain!"

Then, "Tide's comin'!"

Jesse saw moving water as a way beyond dark hills, like one of his early heroes, Englishman John Masefield—

> *I must go down to the seas again to the vagrant gypsy life,*
> *To the gull's way and the whale's way where the*
> *wind's like a whetted knife;*
> *And all I ask is a merry yarn from a laughing fellow-rover,*
> *And quiet sleep and a sweet dream when the long trick's over.*
>
> *Sea Fever*

Masefield's "Sea Fever" would one day capture the imagination of Jesse Stuart. "Merry yarns from a laughing fellow-rover" would become part and parcel of Jesse's innate desire to become the best storyteller he knew how to be from the wildwood called W-Hollow. His voice and his style might be as rough as a cob in an outhouse on a cold winter's night, but Jesse's craft would emerge in time from formal education, peopled by teachers who recognized natural talent, crude though the shavings may have been at the beginning of the whittling.

Mick and Martha Stuart did not require schoolin' to understand the connection, this sacred binding of time and man and woman with watered Good Earth. Jesse inherited from them the abiding dream of "a place of my own." He knew it would be possible only with work, that it would have to include freedom to think, and that eventually, just possibly, it might include a life as a writer.

Jesse was twenty years old when Kentucky author Elizabeth Madox Roberts, whose character Ellen Chesser, in *The Time of Man*, found a way to persevere with the "wandering tenant-farmer."

The meaning of the single word "tenant," with its long history of inequality and demeaning deprivation, is a dubious notch up from "sharecropper," with its marginal advantage over "migrant worker." In either case, it means to be beholden to a landlord, often one living in detached, distant ease. To be a tenant farmer has historically meant to live with the fear of being "put out" in favor of new cannon fodder. Young couples married in the morass of the Great Depression too often appeared with hardly more than old, coughing pickup trucks with broken tailpipes and rust-riddled mufflers, one low-beam headlight, a hole in the floorboard, and, in later time, a collection of faded lottery tickets with numbers scratched away.

And the whining children.

Erskine Caldwell's *Tobacco Road* and the characterization of Jeeter Lester, exemplifying deep-South sharecropper poverty, ignorance, and licentious sexual behavior, would not become the core of Jesse Stuart's portrayals of the potential worth and dignity of man. Jeeter's distorted idea of work was not Jesse's. Most Stuarts placed a high value on work, which, along with even a smidgen of good luck, *might* elevate them to the higher ground of stewardship.

Sense of place, a notion and a passion with a self-generated commitment, has led many Highland families to private ownership. It lies at the heart of a people whose ancestors long ago were disenfranchised peasants. Serfdom in any form was insufferable. John Bunyan's man with the hoe, in *The Pilgrim's Progress*, written more than two hundred years before the birth of Jesse Stuart, heralded the coming of young, strong, Kentucky Highland men with gleaming bull-tongue plows.

Hands hardened.

Feet thick-soled.

Hearts over-burdened.

Mick and Martha took Jesse and his older sister to another piece of nearby crop-rented land and a house owned by Uncle Martin (Hankas) Hilton. Called the Hilton House, built about 1875, it was to become the birthplace of Jesse's brother Herbert Lee in 1909, sister Mary in 1912, and brother James in 1915, the year the Stuart family had to vacate and move to another tenant house, "The Chapman House," the home that would become Jesse's lifelong residence.

From 1918 to 1921 the Stuarts moved to a tenant house up the hill from the "Hilton House." Mick sharecropped and worked extra for fifty cents a day for Winfield Flaughtery, who owned most of W-Hollow. Jesse's brother

Martin Vernon was born in 1918 and the youngest of the Stuart children, sister Glennis, was born in 1921.

Jesse later bought "The Old Chapman House," which had been built in 1845 and occupied by many families over the years, and it would become his home of homes. He bought it in the late 1930s along with other tracts of adjacent land. The old structure, which had been used to house livestock and store hay, was fated to become a place for books, the permanent residence of Jesse Stuart the internationally acclaimed author.

Before Jesse and his siblings could write their names or any letter of the alphabet, they'd heard the soothing sound of their mother's voice, and the Appalachian folk melodies would lodge in Jesse's childhood mind, and they'd stay there on the shelves of his flashing memory like a riffled deck of battered playing cards. Jesse Stuart seldom forgot anything. He collected images and stored them like gnawing bones for the day when they might become useful in the telling of another story. His appetite for remembrances was insatiable. He was forever asking questions, things like "Who's your mama?" "Who's your daddy?" and sometimes the feisty "Whose daddy are you?" He was like a sponge soaking up every drop of water.

Spring would come, and warming times before the fireplace would shift outside. It was a simpler time, before "weather channels" and advice about "grabbing umbrellas when going out the door." If there was rain falling, it felt pleasant on the face, a chance to reach out and grab it with the tip of the tongue; if there was a tornado coming it could be sensed by the nature of the wind and the pale, yellowing character of the sky.

From the time he was six years old, Jesse's parents made him acquainted with the ax and the sprouting hoe—for there were trees to be felled, weeds to be chopped, warm dirt to be pulled up snug around tender, transplanted tobacco plants, copperhead snakes to feel sharp steel coming down on poisonous heads. Jesse worked in a fever when his father was away at jobs in the mine and on C&O right of way.

The kid who would one day wield the bull-tongue plow was breathing the first, intoxicating feeling of responsibility. He seized it the way a hound takes hold of a groundhog—by the scruff of the neck.

When Mick walked the long miles home from the mine and the railroad, he marveled at Jesse's strength growing like a beanstalk reaching for the sky. He was the boy his daddy had dreamed of having. Jesse was a workhoss! Jesse savored his daddy's words of praise in the "Opossums and Poetry" chapter of *Beyond Dark Hills*.

> *That boy of mine is tearing that place all to pieces. I'd put him against any man in the country. He's worked them mules down lean.*

Jesse's brother Herbert lived only four years—double pneumonia claimed him, his death scarring Jesse like a branding iron. At seven years old, Jesse's awareness, anguish bled on a new-honed blade of reason, became a hurt writhing in a Highland child's grief. He'd lost his closest and dearest friend.

In his autobiographical *Beyond Dark Hills*, in the chapter entitled "The Destiny of Hills," Jesse relived the dark day of Herbert's funeral.

> *I remember the songs they sang, some of the words the preacher said. I remember how cold my feet got standing in the mud and how the people cried. All of the others in the family cried but I did not. I cried when I went back home and he was gone.*

Mick and Martha kept moving from one piece of sharecropped land to another. Hear the voice of Jesse:

> *It was a winter day when we moved. Snow lay heavy on the ground and a yoke of oxen pulled the sled with everything we had on it....Rent was raised on my father. Twelve dollars in cash was too much to pay a month for the use of one-hundred acres of land and pasture for his cattle....Again we were ready to go....The same spring wagon that hauled my brother away took our furnitures on the road again....Our new place was the last log house in the head of W-Hollow. It was the most desolate place I have ever seen. Those were the darkest days I have ever seen.*
>
> *Beyond Dark Hills*

Hear the voice of Jesse's mother, Martha:

> *Well, I feel free in moving on now. Herbert is buried on land that belongs to my father....You know I just couldn't stand to move on and*

*leave his grave on property owned by other people....We don't own any land to bury him on, but I can rest tonight knowing that his body lies on my father's soil.*

*Beyond Dark Hills*

Hear the one-tracked voice of Jesse's father, Mick:

*Cattle are powerful things....Watch old Berry get down there and pull. "Lay over there, Buck, and quit that a-crowdin' Berry." That Buck is a lazy ox. I wish I had another one as good as Berry to match. I'd tear down hillsides with them.*

*Beyond Dark Hills*

Listen to Mick and Martha in unison, as remembered by Jesse in his *Beyond Dark Hills*:

*We'll have to clear cropping lands....We must start in a new place and clean it up for somebody else.*

When he was eleven years old Jesse learned what it meant to cultivate the stumpy soil. The mule's stride required the plowboy to stay in step, powerful muscles in the brute's legs and shoulders sending messages to human weaknesses, building up biceps, giving fists uncommon toughness, making the heart pound faster. The investment in plow and brute animals was taken more seriously and with greater care than weakling concern for human health. What John Deere invented in 1846, the steel moldboard plow—and how to pay for it—were reckoned to be more urgent even than the flow of blood through the chambers of the heart.

Once upon a time, before he became a teenager, on a cold April day, Jesse refused to walk in his father's footsteps through one of the last snows of the year. It was a kind of protest, a demonstration of individualism, and a passage of time.

What did you say?

He was doing what?

The son was making his own footsteps, and he was telling himself that the day would come when he would break free of his father's fate. The son was ahead of his time, and it was natural that he explore his own reality.

Jesse's solitary walks retraced ancient warrior pathways, where the new youth learned that persimmons were pleasant desserts when ripe and soft. Pawpaws were stubby bananas to be eaten at just the right moment before they blackened. Imported fruit was not "store-bought" because there was so little money. Every penny was golden and treasured. To be wasteful was to be wanton.

Remembrance of Jesse makes a mind and a spirit crave to reach down and connect to the head of the Cedar Riffles holler to reflect about how it was one hundred years ago when hungry men hallooed their hound dogs, women patiently stirred pots of rabbit and squirrel stew, and children grew silent when thunder babies cried in the region bemoaned as "impoverished" Appalachia.

Jesse was nine years old when T.S. Eliot published *Prufrock and Other Observations*. Ezra Pound was rising to new heights of poetic "reforms." The United States had entered World War I. In the Highlands of Kentucky, Jesse was unread, too young for the army, too isolated, too unsophisticated to have any notion of literary achievement.

Jesse's second brother, Martin Vernon, also contracted bronchial pneumonia, and he lived only a few days. The births of seven children and the deaths of two sons turned Martha from the freshness of youth to the weariness of middle age. The deaths of Herbert Lee and Martin Vernon blazed scars on Jesse's mind and contributed to his obsession with death, a theme repeated many times in his writing, beginning with "One Life" in *Harvest of Youth*.

> *One life*
> *Is a wisp of fog*
> *Between eternities...*
> *No second choice, for Death wipes the*
> *Slate clean.*

There was grieving for the loss of his two brothers, and Jesse was becoming a more weathered, resolute twelve-year-old Appalachian youth in a time of precarious need. Besides, he was on the leading edge of sexual maturity, the burdening, awkward age. The sap was soon to be rising, and the strong urge to procreate was about to become overpowering. Jesse was able to transmute his sexual drive.

He worked. And he worked. And he worked.

Jesse Stuart was to become a Highland Horatio Alger.

As for the "uneducated" Mick and Martha Stuart, they needed the extra hands, the alert eyes, the strong back, and the will to plant the seeds and harvest the crops. They were not disappointed. Their first-born son was kinsman to the critters, sly as Brer Fox, nimble and clever as Brer Squirrel, brother of Brer Rabbit chased by hounds running ahead of hunters with double-barreled shotguns cocked and cradled in crooks of arms.

The sensitive child was puzzled by the simple *awareness* of life. He was often fascinated about the prospect of not breathing, of taking the last breath, of becoming nothing more than compost breaking apart in Plum Grove Cemetery.

At times it was like a strange dream turning ghastly. Breathing in and breathing out alone was woe enough. This deepened Jesse's despair, his loneliness, and the accompanying fever to overcompensate. His heart was like a pump requiring constant priming. He began to live like a turbine fulfilling an incessant demand for converting Ohio Valley water into electric power. It was his passion. Others took it as ego-driven obsession.

Had Mick and Martha succeeded in creating a headstrong wight—big "I," little "you"—yearning to feast on fame and fortune as if it was his Greek god Duty? Future poet, short story writer, novelist, lecturer, school principal and superintendent, teacher, farmer—Jesse Stuart from the beginning, in 1906, was bigger than life, probably filling the Cedar Riffles cabin with squalls growing into shouts, talking back to the thunder baby.

"I'm here and I have taken my rightful place and you're going to have to move over yonder and put up with me," a twinge he may have felt by adolescence, time of genius rubbing its eyes and awakening. "I'm not your Highland Nobody. I'm going to *be* somebody. I don't know what I'm going to *be*, but I *have* to be *somebody!*"

Each early morning when a boy like Jesse went to the barn to begin a new day of work, the neatly stored harness was waiting for him beside the horses's stalls. The bridle came first, Jesse's right hand guiding the forehead piece up over the horse's ears, the left hand maneuvering the bit inside the willing mouth. Then the horse could be led from the stall to stand

and wait for the leather yolk to be pulled tight. Shoulder straps would be thrown up and over from the left side. Horses, like people, work better when there's more consistency and fewer surprises. After the harness is unreeled back over the rump, the horse's tail is relocated and nicely smoothed down.

Hitching a team to a wagon and driving the horses out to load up piles of yellow corn by the sides of the tented shocks is good for a young man's soul. Good for the horses too, because they enjoy the companionship felt in the reins, held confidently by a young man who knows what he's doing. Besides, part of each pile of golden corn will find its way into each stall's lick-cleaned trough, and nothing so much pleases a horse as two or three ears of corn, even if they're barely nubbins.

Corn is fundamental. Oats would be fancy.

Jesse Stuart was never fancy, and maybe that's the reason why he did not qualify for tea with the Queen. He was American from top to bottom, a Kentucky Highlander who could be as outrageous as he pleased. The main thing was an honest day's work for an honest day's pay—depending on how money was measured.

> *There came a frost and hit the corn. The blades turned white and began to fall. "Save that feed, Son. The cattle will need it this winter. You will have to miss school long enough to cut that knob piece of corn."*
>
> *"I'll cut it all on Saturday"' I said.*
>
> *That Saturday I dressed well to keep the blades from cutting my face and hands. I "railroaded" the corn from daylight until four o'clock that afternoon. I cut twelve hills square on a steep hillside. I tied one middle band around the shocks and two outward bands to make it stand well. My father would not believe that I had cut fifty-four shocks until he counted them. He opened his eyes wider when I went back that night and cut twenty-four by moonlight. "Go to the store and get anything you want. My credit is good and nothing I've got is too good for a boy that will work like you."*
>
> *The corn was out of danger now. The frost-bitten blades were safe for the cattle. It is a great thing to have a strong body, I have often*

*thought.*

These remembrances were gathered together in "Opossums and Poetry," and they are rooted there for all time. It's a good thing to turn to these pages in times of drought, when weather may seem vengeful.

The seasons in Kentucky are famous for their forgiveness—no cold being too cold too long, no heat being too hot too long. It was this that held Jesse in a rhythm that saved him from remorse and played a part in his creativity.

> *Autumn came again. The oak trees in northeast Kentucky were shedding their leaves. The flying leaves were of many colors. The crows began to fly in pilfering trains over the country. And wild geese went southward with many a honking cry. It was all beautiful back there and the best place in the world after all. The corn was getting ready to be cut now. The brown fields of heavy corn looked very pleasant. It was the victory of hard labor.*
>
> *Beyond Dark Hills*

But, Mick and Martha could not have forecast the strains unleashed by the passage of future years on the chambers of Jesse's heart—local politics, publishing world bottom-liners, lecture-circuit timekeepers, scholarly knickknackers, cultural critics, and charter pilot cloud-eaters. To these, add Jesse's bursts of bravado, his self-inventing compulsive nature, exploding in to one enormous, complex, and fatal addiction—writing, writing, writing!

A future cardiologist might have diagnosed Jesse as a very young, emerging Type A, and there'd be a heavy price to pay for it. Jesse's window of life on Earth was as fated as Brer Rabbit's in the briar patch— it could be fairly argued that he quickened the trembling death he so dearly dreaded.

Yet in the early time of his wrenching life, Jesse Stuart could look down into the waters of Cedar Riffles, and he could imagine himself to be on a drifting twig taking him far beyond his dark hills. He could see himself all the way to the Mississippi, out into the Gulf of Mexico, on across the ocean to his original Highland homeland.

# PROFESSOR HARD HAND

*So careless were many of the early teachers that one superintendent
recalled having visited a rural school where he listened
outside the door to the teacher quarreling with his students
because they bothered him while he was hulling black walnuts.*

Thomas D. Clark
*A History of Kentucky*

*Readin', writin', and 'rithmetic!*

His rendezvous with book-learning and the beginning of book-writing
began quickly during his first years in the tiny schoolhouse, where faces
were well-scrubbed and hind ends were regularly tanned. Jesse Stuart was
like a land turtle about to have a new, polished shell. He was going to lose
some of the muddy ooze of Little Sandy, but not too much. It was not his
nature to take on too many airs.

The year Jesse and Sophia first walked the long miles together to the
Plum Grove schoolhouse was the same year Alec Waugh wrote *The Loom
of Youth*, a novel about public-school life in England. The ideas expressed
in this controversial writing—supremacy of athletes, structured levels of
"littleness" of thought—whirled down like winged water maple seeds and
took stubborn root in many parts of the United States.

Teachers in the Highlands and the mountains of Kentucky did not think
of themselves as advocates for mediocrity. But students were seldom
expected to be "different." Exceptional behavior would likely attract
majority scorn. Jesse was fortunate in his early discovery of teachers who
cared and dared to dream that genius in their midst was possible.

At Plum Grove School, as many as fifty students were wedged inside the one-room firetrap, like stick-tights to britches legs. Jesse's early schoolteachers included Mr. Calvin Clarke, Miss Nora Riggs, Miss Elta Cooper, Miss Claris Brown, Mr. Everett Hilton, and a fictional put-together teacher, "Professor Iron Hand."

They taught everybody—first through eighth grades—an experience Jesse would all his life hold close to his heart. Impressions that would not wash away, they stuck to him good and strong, like the steely-eyed barn cat savoring milk foam on the outsides of the bucket. There was the warmth of the pot-bellied stove, where the delight of the boys was to keep the fire glowing until the iron legs knew what heat was all about. There was the essence of young human bodies bonded together with smells of blackboard and chalk, and there were pegs on which to hang tattered coats and caps and space for overshoes if a body was lucky enough to have them. Jesse's enthusiasm appears in "Destiny of Hills" chapter of *Beyond Dark Hills*.

> *I'll declare it was the finest place to me I'd ever been up to that time. It was a place where I saw a lot of people. Thirty or thirty-five people were a multitude for me to see together. And the things called words and people—there was something fascinating about both. Words are marvelous things. They are something which you can do anything with but take hold of with your hands. You can put them on paper and they mean something. I tried them out first by writing notes. I wrote one to a girl and was severely whipped for it. The girls sat on one side of the schoolhouse and the boys on the other, and I threw the note across to Mabel Jones.*

Jesse would cherish these mental images—they'd guide him like lighthouse lanterns toward three of his most important adult creations: an autobiographical trilogy—*Beyond Dark Hills*, *The Thread That Runs So True*, and *To Teach, To Love*. The theme is constant—being true to oneself, having a strong sense of place, and possessing a passion to share the fruits of learning.

In the isolated hills of Greenup County, in the first decade of the twentieth century, downriver from Ashland, there was not one mile of paved road and only a handful of one-room schools. That's right—not one mile of paved road and precious few schools of any kind. Well paid, well educated, professional teachers were virtually nonexistent. Preparation was earnest and well intended but meager if at all. Adequate pay was unheard of. Yet typically there was, as in the Stuart family, a powerful *desire* for learning, a dream of accomplishment.

When Jesse was only three years old, his father took him to see a schoolhouse, and it was there that Mick had said that since he hadn't received an education, couldn't read or write, he didn't want his children to miss out on it.

Because of Jesse's frequent fictive accounting of fact, it's likely he later imagined his father said this. It was a hint of the emerging Highland storyteller—using imagined speech to forward the movement of the narrative. Whether or not Mick actually said it is neither here nor there.

The day would come when Jesse would happily walk home from school and tell his father that there was something he, Jesse, could do that his father couldn't. It was not so much a case of boasting as it was a show of appreciation.

Jesse could write his name. And he could read books.

Rather than be mortified, Mick resolved to learn to write his own name if nothing else. Reading might take a mite longer. It was not a case of indifference or stupidity, far from it.

Jesse would later say, his father was his first teacher. Mick schooled Jesse in natural wonders, beginning with the elements of weather, the relationship of man to beast, and the guilt-free necessity of hunting and raising animals for slaughter. And he insisted on the need to be able, at least, to write one's own name, then to get all the education possible.

An eighteen-year-old high school graduate, Calvin Clarke, green as an early summer gourd, was Jesse's first formal schoolteacher. A spiny disciplinarian, Clarke frequently thumped Jesse and his classmates for fighting. It was the early Appalachian era of poorly financed and ill-equipped organized sports, which might have served at least minimally as structured outlets for explosive, youthful energy. It was an environment where fighting was as natural as a yard full of roosters and hens.

Over a period of two years, Mr. Clarke did manage to teach Jesse to find his way through the multiplication tables—one times one is one, eleven times eleven is something or other—but, more important, Martha and Mick's child discovered the glorious reality of books. Meaning no disrespect for the family Bible, which usually lay open by the kerosene lamp in a prominent place at home, these other books were like bread from Heaven too. They, like music, helped soothe the savage breast. Words were special creatures in the stream of knowledge leading to wisdom. Jesse Stuart's world beyond W-Hollow was opening wider. It began with reading his primer, savoring every word.

Nora Riggs was Jesse's next teacher at Plum Grove.

Miss Nora? She was a bonnie lass—as Bobby Burns would say:

> *To see her is to love her*
> *And love but her forever,*
> *For Nature made her what she is,*
> *And ne'er made anither!*
>
> *Bonnie Lesley*

Jesse swooned.

After only three months of enduring her admirers and encouraging them to reach higher, Miss Nora returned to her studies at Eastern Kentucky Teachers College. She didn't graduate but instead got married, the normal and noble thing for a Highland woman to do.

Miss Elta Cooper followed Nora Riggs at Plum Grove School, but she too soon married, and after Miss Cooper came Miss Claris Brown. She was eighteen years old, and she had another commonplace problem for female teachers—trouble disciplining her students. Jesse remembers the disgusting day when Miss Brown's students tricked her into drinking pee. It was a loathsome piece of business that should never have happened. Jesse's telling of it reveals his embarrassment.

Upon Miss Claris Brown's departure came a man, Everett Hilton, who knew how to wield the switch. Discipline was restored at least temporarily. Eventually Mr. Hilton became the head of Vocational Education for Kentucky, and other teachers would arrive to ring the one-room schoolhouse bell. But they needed to remember they were dealing with the rawest of material.

Jesse's father may have thought education was a necessity, but his practical mind and his survival instinct led him, when crops were failing, to remove his son from school. It was a common practice to keep students at home to help in difficult times. Who else would cut and house the tobacco? Cut and shock the corn? Plow another round of "new ground?" There might be a trace of awkwardness on a student's face, but all knew what they must do, and they did it. Regrettably, many students didn't return to school with the same enthusiasm, if they returned at all. They became "unschooled" and therefore were stigmatized.

Mick hired Jesse out for twenty-five cents a day. Mick and his horse, Fred, worked for two dollars a day, and Martha worked for twenty-five cents a day. Jesse began to think that he might not be able to go to high school.

When Jesse was thirteen years old, he walked four miles to the county seat, Greenup, and found a job paving streets. Instead of twenty-five cents a day, he was making thirty cents an hour. After ten hours, Jesse walked the four miles back home. One day, when the concrete mixer was parked in front of Greenup High School, Jesse saw well-dressed students laughing and talking, going through the open door, and he decided he wanted to be among them. So he quit his job and applied for admission. Sophia joined him there. Mary would follow, then James, and Glennis. No one would have placed bets on it, but all five of the Stuart children would eventually earn college degrees and become teachers.

Mick and Martha were rightfully proud.

When the 1922-23 Greenup High School freshman class picture was taken, Jesse sat in a window with two other boys. He had a well-scrubbed, carefully combed appearance, no outward sign of rebellion, but he was the only boy in the picture who was not wearing a coat and tie. There were six boys sitting in the foreground in a variety of assertive poses, while Jesse was as far back as anybody could be and still be in the picture. Looking at Jesse through a magnifying glass, from the vantage point of a new century, trying to fit together the pieces of a complicated puzzle, there seems no reason to think that the only boy without coat and tie would one day become Poet Laureate of Kentucky.

*I saw many boys wearing fine clothes I envied. I wanted a long red sweater like Burl Mavis wore and a necktie like the one I had seen Fred Mansfield wear. I wanted many things I could not get. When I ate my lunch that I brought wrapped in a newspaper, I always got away from the other boys. I went around by the old flour mills. I didn't want them to see biscuits with meat and mustard between, and the corn bread.*

*Beyond Dark Hills*

After the freshman year at Greenup, Jesse returned to the farm and worked, but high school had changed him. Jesse had asked his teacher, Miss Lykins, what was the oldest college in America—she said that would be Harvard. He said that was where he wanted to go.

*My sophomore year in Greenup High School was a happy time in my life. When I went back to Greenup, I felt just about the equal of Burl Mavis. "I would be better than Burl, I let myself think, if I only had some clothes." I had an idea—two of them. I could buy my own books, my sister's books and buy myself some clothes. I would ask my father's permission to make crossties to sell from the timber on the farm. I would hunt the fur-bearing animals in those surrounding hills with old Black-Boy. I could make money. I was too tall now to wear knee pants. And I was getting too old to wear them now.*

*Beyond Dark Hills*

Miss Lena Wells Lykins, who taught math, was one of the school-teachers most admired by Jesse. She would have a profound effect on him, and without her he might have remained a rank weed withered by W-Hollow sun. While Sophia was making A's in algebra, Jesse couldn't seem to grasp mathematics. One day he walked out of school and headed home. The next day, when he didn't return to the classroom, Miss Lykins walked all the way to W-Hollow to confront Jesse.

"Quit Greenup High School because you can't get a subject, huh?.... Jesse, are you going to be a quitter?"

Ma'am, she laid into that youngin' like a bumblebee on a bare butt. She zeroed in and zapped Jesse with: "You're not going through life like this!" Thoroughly disgusted, she walked back that night to Greenup, and a humble and chastened Jesse lit the way with a lantern. Miss Lena Wells

Lykins had gotten her student's attention. She became a lifelong friend and confidante, and when he became an adult, Jesse would write her a constant stream of letters.

Because of this teacher who cared about her pupils, Jesse Stuart returned to high school, and though he may not have realized it at the time, he was destined to become a model for others to follow. Mr. Horatio Alger would have pinned a medal on him and claimed him for his own—a Highland Luck and Pluck was coming into a fuller, richer understanding of the importance of hard work as a cornerstone for a taller structure. Alger, the master of the nineteenth-century rags-to-riches philosophy, lived again in Jesse Stuart, who, you could say, preserved the persistence of a W-Hollow land turtle in slow times, the quivering speed of Brer Rabbit in flush times.

In his sophomore year of high school, Jesse furiously hewed oak crossties and sold them wherever he could find a market. With fifty dollars earned, he went on a spending spree across the Ohio River, in Ironton. He bought new clothes and paid for schoolbooks for his sister and himself. He hunted possums and sold their meat and hides to make more money. Jesse was on fire and stayed that way most of his life.

It was the year he began to write poetry. He credited wind in the dead leaves and lonely sounds at night, but it was also because of another insightful teacher by the name of Harriett McFarland Hatton. Jesse thrived in her English class. She encouraged and inspired her students to write about what they knew best—based on personal observation of their own surroundings, expressed in the art of closing the gap between thought and written word. Jesse was at home with creatures of nature, and he began to write about them. He captured words on paper as quickly as possible, netting ideas and observations as if they were butterflies. He invariably carried pencil and paper salvaged from discarded tobacco wrappings. Some of Jesse's poems were impressed on the underside of poplar leaves. He wrote hurriedly and compulsively.

It was Mrs. Hatton who introduced Jesse to the Scottish poet Robert Burns, who became Jesse's main hero.

> *I would read his poetry every spare minute I had. I carried his*
> *poems wherever I went. I thought I had never heard words more*

*beautiful than those in "Flow Gently, Sweet Afton"....And my*
*prayer then was to write poetry that would endure like the poetry of*
*Robert Burns.*

*Beyond Dark Hills*

Mrs. Hatton's husband was superintendent of the Greenup Independent School System, and he also taught and made a lasting impression on Jesse, who credited Robert Hatton with instilling such values as ambition and a sense of purpose. Good teachers know that a kind word spoken to a struggling student means more than divine inspiration. A teacher might say, "You will become a writer" or "You will become our poet laureate," and that one remark will fuel the fire already kindled.

Midway through high school, Jesse engaged in what might be called his first manhood-proving excursion, akin to the heady, hormonal experience of most boys who've come to the time and place when their sap is rising and they're unsure whether they're boy or man. Jesse took a trip with his friend Tillman Cartwell all the way to the adjoining county, Carter, to a place in the area of caves called Horseshoe Bottom. What made Jesse's adventure different from most was that he also took Alfred Lord Tennyson with him and sat in the opening of one of the many caves to "read Tennyson for hours."

Jesse soaked it up:

*Sunset and evening star,*
*And one clear call for me!*
*And may there be no moaning of the bar*
*When I put out to sea...*

*Twilight and evening bell,*
*And after that the dark!*
*And may there be no sadness of farewell,*
*When I embark...*

*Crossing the Bar*

Stuart chickens blinked with the first glimmer of the rising sun, and the fierce-eyed Nest Egg rooster reared up full wattle on the branch of the old oak tree, glorifying the birth of each new W-Hollow day. Hens fluttered down from crowded limbs and swagging pine poles to cluck and scratch the ground for lazy grubs, then to lay speckled brown eggs in secret places.

Jesse was just sixteen years old when he wrote an English theme— "Nest Egg"—in his sophomore year of high school. Destined to become one of Jesse Stuart's best-known short stories, it was the forerunner of hundreds in his lifetime. The deathly battle of the screech owl and the rooster would be published and republished again and again, a good story coming from the land and the creatures living on it. The fable symbolizes birth by unavoidable chance, death coming in the most unforgiving way at the most unexpected hour. To read "Nest Egg" is to experience some of Jesse's richest creativity.

> *Nest Egg wasn't six months old when he started crowin'. Now he was much larger than his mother. He was tall and he had big legs and little straight spurs that looked like long locust thorns. His mother still ran with him and clucked to him, but he didn't pay his mother much attention. He would often stand lookin' at the spring sun and never bat his eyes. He had a mean-lookin' eye and a long crooked bill that looked like a chicken hawk's bill. He didn't look like his mother. Pa said that he was a cross between a Sebright and a black game. He had almost every variety of colors. I thought he was a mongrel rooster—a mixture of many breeds.*

Jesse was fascinated by the infinite possibilities of the mongrel, the underdog, runt of the litter, likely loser becoming a winner.

> *I stood over Nest Egg and cried.*
> *No ust to cry, Shan, Pa said. Nest Egg's dead. That owl fouled him. It flew into the chicken roost and lit on his back when he was asleep. It pecked his head until it finished 'im.*
> *But I haf to cry, I said, watching Pa take his bandanna from his pocket to wipe the tears from his eyes.*
>
> *A Jesse Stuart Reader*

With the passage of almost another century, not only young students but adults should be encouraged to read "Nest Egg" for its rich symbolism and literary naturalism. The first decades of the twenty-first century will be well paid if teachers use this classic short story as a way of bringing more students to a better functional understanding of what it means to write about their own surroundings. As in the case of Jesse Stuart, it could mean the beginning of an important career. Who knows? Maybe a *life*.

Jesse's junior year in high school was marked as much by a fight he had with a bully as by yearning to write like Lord Tennyson or Bobby Burns. It's a fact that Jesse was aggressive, and he'd not allow bullying to go unchallenged. This may have been one reason why he failed to develop what could be called the mental refinement necessary to become a universally recognized and accepted person of letters. Jesse was Jesse, and if that was good enough for family and friends, it was good enough for him.

Jesse became a temporary teacher while he was still a student in high school. In his third year he took a teachers' examination and received a second-class certificate. "Sixty-eight dollars a month beat making crossties and opossum hunting. It was easy-made money." In *To Teach, To Love*, Jesse describes how he introduced and administered the paddle to those he believed needed it, including a few girls for cursing and chewing tobacco behind the schoolhouse.

As a boy growing up to become a teacher and a writer, Jesse accepted discipline as an essential tool for learning. He would later write of the fictionalized "Professor Hard Hand," who took neither lip nor lapse from anybody. His specialty: the green willow switch, even the two-by-four if he believed it to be necessary.

But the young teacher learned something that began to take the place of "Hard Hand" paddling. Jesse later wrote about it in *The Thread That Runs So True*: the idea that teachers could and should inspire their pupils; the notion that a greater America would evolve; the importance of an educated citizenry; the responsibility of each individual to do her or his share.

Jesse's first full-time teaching job was at Cane Creek Elementary School in Greenup County ("Lonesome Valley" in *The Thread That Runs So True*) when he was eighteen years old. With its one room and thirty-five students, Jesse *was* the faculty. Later, when he was twenty-three, he was hired to teach and be principal at Warnock High School in Greenup County ("Winston

High School" in *The Thread That Runs So True*, the Appalachian teacher's manifesto, never out of print since it was first published by Scribners in 1949.)

Jesse didn't daintily dip his oar and gently dribble the water. He pulled up hip boots, rolled up his sleeves, and rowed his boat as if there were neither yesterdays nor tomorrows. There were only todays, and there was nothing he could or wished to do to change that reality.

Jesse dared to dream the big dream—going to Harvard—but he didn't know how to get there. He had neither the money nor a scholarship. He didn't have family or political connections. Yet that didn't keep him from dreaming, or from writing.

### Harvard or the Sea

*I have lived my youth in one unsettled state*
*And months of barren earth is life too much for me.*
*The glorious close will bring me Harvard or the sea.*
*Nine months earth-prisoned! How can I bear to wait?*
*Since I was twelve, I have been foot-free to the soil;*
*Pocketless a dime, I've rambled through many a town*
*When the winter moon and silver stars slanted down;*
*Bunked with toughs; did with them a tremendous toil;*
*Met pals, forgot; stopped and took my school life stay.*
*Now within Harvard's halls there is one life for me.*
*Another life is on waste waters' blue immensity*
*That will make me turn my back on home, forget the day*
*My feet were bound to earth. Then Great Seducer Sea,*
*Be last to pant and lick your wet lips over me.*

*Harvest of Youth*

It's well to remember that Jesse's life was nothing like those of some teenagers in the twenty-first century: no fast food hamburgers, no drugs to boost the ego and create artificial good feelings. In his early life, Jesse lived in a relatively primitive time and place, where there was no television, no electricity to turn it on if it had been available. He was all the richer for not having it dominate his life with a constant flow of bad news, bizarre behavior, display of body piercings, and merchandised sports mania. In his youth, there was no telephone in his home, and he didn't walk through the woods with a cell phone growing out of his ear. He had no "plastic" money. In fact, he had virtually no money at all. But the riches Jesse did have were the best of all—love of nature and the potential goodness of humanity. In this regard he was a wealthy young man.

Jesse began to talk to his mother about the idea of breaking free of W-Hollow, and she acknowledged that she too desired to leave to *be* somebody. At best, her relationship with Mick had been stretched to the outer limits of long suffering. Martha was one of the Appalachian women who worked as hard as boatloads of men and often was a blamed sight smarter. Mountain women like Martha smoked their pipes, birthed their babies, and raised their children to take what little they had and work as if there were no tomorrows. And when their babies died, the Marthas saw to it that the burials were properly attended to.

Jesse Stuart would probably argue that he didn't need to know that there was a Theodore Dreiser portraying life as he saw fit to tell it from the streets of New York City. Jesse would not compare his writing techniques with a Sinclair Lewis preparing for a career as anointed social critic in Minnesota. And, Jesse would not structure his life in the mold of Robert Penn Warren, the "deep South" Kentuckian, taking his stand with the "Fugitives" and the "Agrarians" at Vanderbilt.

Why shouldn't there be bull-tongued sonnets, stinging satire, sidesplitting stories written about sinning—drinking white lightning, birth and death, and mankind's growing closer with nature in the corner of Appalachia called Greenup County?

Years after he was barefoot and britches-legs-up, Jesse would write about himself in *Beyond Dark Hills*, and he would make it clear how proud he was to be descended from noble and sometimes ignoble mountaineers, all sleeping and waiting for him to join them.

# WINDOWPANES OF
# THE GREAT DEPRESSION

*I know one woman who could not tell you the month
in which her children were born,
but could always tell you if it was fodder-pulling time,
grubbing time, or cold weather.*

Verna Mae Slone
*What My Heart Wants to Tell*

*Whoa!*

Never mind that conditions were so bad, Mick plunged into debt. At the end of World War I, he bought his first farm in W-Hollow, about fifty acres for $300. James Stuart recalled that it took seventeen years to pay off the mortgage, the only farm Mick and Martha would ever own.

In 1921, Jesse and his grandfather Nathan Hilton built a pine log house in W-Hollow, and the Stuarts moved into it. Mick built a smokehouse and a log pen for fattening hogs. Jesse and his father understood later that the times were hard and the family was poor, but at the moment it was happening the family didn't think of it in fearful terms. Eventually, the roof and walls of the house would begin to sag and the structure would have to be replaced, a reminder of short-lived circumstance.

Jesse's high-school days were over and "work" was turning more toward the plague, if you wanted to know the unvarnished truth about it. Take the mean-kickin' mule—his sweat was rank, and his aim was dangerous.

The heat in the W-Hollow hayfield felt like the hinges of Hades. Human hands were drawn tight and were becoming bone-tired. Feet were blistered, and the summer sun beat down. Other times, the weather cooked up and unwound a corker. Made you want to kick up your own dern heels! Made you want to cut and run some, just enough to pleasure your appetite for something *different.*

In the roaring twenties, blowing on the doorway of the Great Depression, "the carnival" was an Appalachian youth's inexpensive dream—not a circus, not a county fair, no, several notches down—but affordable. And reachable, unless you were a hermit.

When advance carnival knackers circled a mountain river town, they practiced the stealth of scout birds of prey—sweet talk at the local drugstore, a little snip-snip, splash-splash at the barber shop, friendly inquiries and a handful of free-ride tickets dished out at the courthouse, joke or two at the jail, and it wasn't long before a raggle-taggle caravan arrived with temptations too great to resist for lonesome, hot-to-trot plowboys with a few coins rubbing in their overalls.

Jesse's descriptions bring back summer memories for the rest of us, and it's possible to open the carnival gate of our own minds. In there, on the shelves of distant memory, the sticky cotton candy still tickles the tip of the nose, the moon is paper, and the sky is cardboard as in the song about make believe. Remember? Arms would wrap around the yellow, silked waist of youth, a feeling to last as warm and promising as a feather pillow in old age. Gypsy voices floated on the air like gray, ghostly choruses, and all was magical. Hardly anything is intended to be real at a carnival, and that's the way it was, like the lyrics the golden throats would sing on "Make Believe Ballroom" on WLW Radio in Cincinnati before there was a blatant, mind-sucking idiot box known as television.

It was the age of a young Louis Armstrong and Joe "King" Oliver's band, heavyweight champion Jack Dempsey, and F. Scott Fitzgerald's *Tales of the Jazz Age.* Such a ripsnortin' time it was! But the first half of the 1920s was also the time of Benito Mussolini's March on Rome and Adolph Hitler's "Beer Hall Putsch."

Life *is* a cabaret, old chum!

"Come one, come all! Don't be shy, now! Bring your girlie in for the grrreatest show this side of Noo Yawk Ciddy. Step right up, lads and lassies, move smartly now, time's a-wastin'. You there, yessir, you with the

'I want some of this' written up and down and crosswise your face. You want it, we got it! Don't hang back. After today we move on down to Maysville-town. You're seeing it all before them and Cincinnati does."

Ladies and gents, let's just put it down as the sorriest pack of starved carnival dogs ever was rounded up for the animal shelter. There might have been Henrí, the flame-swallower from Pittsburgh with his rapeseed oil-covered throat and a mouthful of kerosene to light the torch, gurgle the flames, and spew out the fire. And there, in imagination, might be a George, dear soul, the knock'em down kewpie doll warhorse from Wheeling. You remember old George, don't you? He was the right man for the carnival: down on his luck, loser to the ladies, health eaten up by the constant cigarette dangling from the left side of his mouth, ashes growing so long they curved. Sure, you 'member ol' George.

And where are the others?

Why, there they are, don't you see?—Honey Pie, the spun sugarhouse vamp from Huntington, and Lucy the alligator-skin, yellow-eyed lady from Louisville. Don't forget Mose, the black, boiled-peanut impresario from Montgomery, Alabama, staying two states away from the Ku Klux Klan, along with strongman bell ringers, age-guessers, shell gamesters, high card galley whackers, and mangy pony ride cowboys. There likely was a gaggle of sorry powdered, lipsticked women, too, and a squeaky-freaky Ferris wheel and merry-go-round needing more grease than they ever got in a month of Sundays.

Jesse had a teenage girlfriend whose name was Maria Sheen. Sometimes, they'd slip off to visit and be awed by the sound of riverboats docking at Greenup, and they'd hear the squealing calliopes a-blowin' steam, the cocky calliope players a-grinnin' like cats in a new mown hay pasture. But the showboats tended to be a tad expensive, and the captain and his river rats were a notch or two on the uppity side.

Here's the thing.

The carnival passing through town was a poor boy's salvation. Jesse said goodbye for a while to Maria, and he headed down the shoreline with the carnival crowd. He was off to see the Wizard! It's unclear how far he went, or whether Jesse's "carnival time" was an autobiographical fictive elaboration. His brother James doubted he went very far. James valued

Jesse's presence on the farm and as a hunting companion in the woods. About all we get in *Beyond Dark Hills* is the following:

> *The street carnival was a fascinating place to me, the painted showmen, the dancing girls, the vagabond life and the old dull music of the merry-go-round—the whole thing was fascinating! The whole works was a merry-go-round. I made up my mind to get a job and follow it. I didn't tell Maria what my intentions were. I heard people say: "Damn cheap bunch following a fair, ain't they? Look at them women with painted lips after the greenhorn boys. They're taking the bait set for them too. Damn ornery people. They ought to all be shot." I didn't feel that way about them. I felt as if they were people getting a satisfaction out of living by going from town to town. Where a man settles to one place, his life would someday become empty, I thought. I would follow the merry-go-round.*

What all plowboys had not learned in the tobacco patch and the corn rows a-windin' 'round the hill, they'd soon learn from their new tent mates—lost souls the likes of Henrí the flame swallower, who later each day put aside his rapeseed oil and kerosene and dressed and painted up as Hank the Family Clown.

"Now let me tell you 'bout the wimmen with this here carnival," Hank might have said, unstoppering a bottle of Kentucky Cock, offering the greenhorn a swig. It was the decent, accommodating thing to do. Besides, most drinkers don't admire drinking alone.

"I don't drink."

"My God," moaned Hank. "And you call yoreself a *Kaintuck?* Here I am thinking I've stumbled upon the Good Lord's blessing," he might mournfully have declared, washing down the curse with three gulps, then wiping his mouth with his smelly, raggedy sleeve. "Listen here," he said, "You'll be a dern sight better off without the bottle, but a little nip with a roommate improves sleeping relationships remarkably, if I do say so myself."

Hank belched. The front tent flap fluttered.

"My pa warned me," said the greenhorn. "He told me drinking ran on his side of the tree, and he told me to lay off. Not to say we didn't brew some white lightnin' in case of snake bite, one thing and 'nother."

"What did yore pa tell you 'bout wimmen?"

"Not mech."

"What did yore ma tell you 'bout wimmen?"

"She said they oughter be treated right."

"Got a girlfriend?"

"Yep, I left her back in the direction of home."

"Well, let me tell you 'bout the gals with this here carnival," Hank could have opined, upstoppering again, gulping twice, warming to the task of social responsibility, not to mention manners. "These here fillies are out for one thing...."

"What's that?" said the novice, sap taking an unaccustomed upward turn.

"Money, Honey. I mean, money in the morning, money at high noon, heaps of money after the sun goes down. They were born with five-dollar bills hangin' out their mouths. Some of 'em move on to ten- and twenty-dollar bills."

Any greenhorn could see the carnival women laughing, flinging their arms up and toward the back of gawky male necks. These hungry and aging-before-their-time feline creatures liked to rub their tired, tightened up bosoms against the men's muscular, sunburned arms, and that generally led the way to a nearby automobile on the other side of a jungle of tall stink weeds.

"My boy," said Hank, "Don't let these carney cats claw their way into your pocketbook. They'll take ever'thing in it. Ever' nickel and ever' dime! They'll tell you how drop-dead wonderful you are, how big and strong you are, and ever' word that comes outen their mouths is loaded with enough canker to ruin you for good. Mind me now. Don't pay no never mind to their little sob stories, neither. They got enough heartache tales to take 'em 'round the world with Nellie Bly"—the "Bly" coming out on a quavery string of bubbling burps.

The H. "High Pockets" Jones crowd, owners and head carneys, steered tight rowboats, demanding total compliance with what they piously deemed "rules of the road," which they invented as they conned their way between ports of call. The first time "High Pockets" caught sight of a boy like Jesse, he'd be impressed with the youth's wide shoulders, big hands, beguiling behavior, desire to work—looking like a Buster Brown that could be shined.

The way Jesse remembered it, in the scant details he's left us, he was assigned to the Merry Mix-up, a mechanical shaking of bones and eyeballs. Jesse's job was to take up tickets, snap the riders into their chewing-gum-begrimed seats, and be dadblamed sure nobody got their money's worth. Any "High Pockets" worth his salt liked to say he favored pinching every penny 'til Abe ached and rubbed every nickel 'til Geronimo grinned. That sort of thing would be all right with Jesse, because he was tight-wadded too, like his Ma and Pa.

"Come one, come all, ride the Merry Mix-up! Fifteen cents is all it takes. C'mon now, give that girlie of yours a thrill. Step right up. Time's a-wastin'!" A voice like Jesse's, somewhere between squeaky and full-bodied, could squeal and bellow with newfound authority. He was enjoying himself immensely, feeling a surge of reborn get-up-and-go.

Things ran as smooth as deer gut on a doorknob, as they say, until the monotony of creaking machinery wore down youth's fretful enthusiasm. Sap surfaced in the middle of the night like kudzu in a snarling Doberman-guarded junkyard. Prostitutes in parked cars got the go-by because most boys like Jesse at least knew the difference between down-and-dirty sin and some playful fooling around. Pretty local girls would be in plentiful supply to make an eyeful, and their bewitching laughter easily and usually wound up getting the best of better judgment. As for Jesse's part, he remembered seeing to it that the freshest of the lovely bunch rode extra turns on the Merry Mix-Up and didn't pay for anything.

He looked the other way.

Jesse upped the bet, threw caution to the wind, and enlisted an accomplice to fake the taking of tickets. This little trick afforded him the opportunity to ride alongside the prettiest lassies on the face of God's good earth—that's what it amounted to, sakes alive.

Sittin' free!

Grabbin' for the stars!

Tasting the world to Hell and gone past piddlin' little old Cedar Riffles.

The oddling was ridin' high! Cuttin' didos in the grandest style, slyly draping one arm around the cuties' bare shoulders, waving the other hand to make a swell statement.

Didn't last long.

Old High Pockets was on to such games quicker than a carney could yell, "Hey, Rube!" This here would be dastardly trouble needing to be fixed. And it would be tended to like finding a snake sleeping at the foot of the bed—throw back the kivers and let the ax handle fall.

"All right, Mr. Briar, you've got one hour to gather up what belongs to you and be dadblamed gone from sight," High Pockets likely would have said.

"I want my money...I want what's rightfully mine," the accused would wail.

"You've already got *my* money," said High Pockets, and that was that.

Let's say this is the way it happened. We've taken what Jesse says he remembered, and we've stretched it a little here and there, the way he did when he invented stories. The business of tall-tale telling is a whole lot of fun! You know—going back in one's own memory and doing a little rerun with sweepings from the floor.

So imagine, Jesse goes to Hank, who at that moment is painting his face for the afternoon's work as the sad, sad clown—thick white lips, blackened face, red bilious nose, turned-up fedora concealing a brain burned by rapeseed oil and kerosene.

Jesse tells Hank he's sorry to be leaving him, if nobody else is in this godforsaken contraption called a carnival. And you know, Hank, you're all right in Jesse's book.

Hank stares at his turned up shoes and appears both pained and relieved. "You've got no business following the likes of us. You've got the look of a young man with promise—a future, I mean. You need to walk, run, or jump back the way you came, and *amount* to something. You hear me, boy? *Amount* to something."

Maybe a small piece of every living soul wants to swallow flames and pretend to be somebody else. Just about every boy and girl, standing on the cliff of becoming twenty years of age, wants to reconstruct their lives in a way the "old folks" don't know about. Youth smells change a-comin', and most Highlanders are no different.

Knowing when to say goodbye and doing it in a way to lessen hurt is a painful lesson to learn. Knowing just the right thing to say to a grand man like Henrí the Fire-Eater AKA Hank the Family Clown takes a special talent and a heart in the right place.

"Don't burn yourself up or down with flames," says Jesse as he heads home in the general direction of Riverton.

For Jesse, of course, the taste of carnival was not the Mardi Gras of New Orleans or the Carnival of Rio de Janeiro. But his experience whetted his appetite to see more of the world. For Jesse, the opening of "new worlds" would come with the opening of the door leading to rooms filled with words set down on paper to be shared with readers he'd never personally visit. Yet if he could do just that—extend his hand in friendship—he'd not be found hiding.

> *At night when the lights blinked for the carnival to close, I went out to my tent to sleep. Many nights I could not go to sleep. I would go to bed and then get up and write poetry. I was not mastering poetry but it was mastering me. I just couldn't help writing poetry, I thought now that only little soft men wrote poetry. I wrote poetry about the cornfields since I had left them. Before, when I was working there, they were ugly. But now they had become beautiful to me. They were in my blood, I could not forget them. I thought about my brother and sisters at home and what they were doing. I wondered what they were doing for somebody to plow since I had gone. I wondered if the weeds were taking the corn and the suckers were out long on the tobacco and if the worms had eaten holes in the broad leaves. I was not sorry I had left but I pitied them back there with all the work to do. I often thought of Maria Sheen. I wanted to write poetry to her and about her. She was more beautiful than the cornfields. I had a feeling for the cornfields the same as I had for Maria Sheen. I wrote...sonnets for her in the tent one night.*
>
> *Beyond Dark Hills*

Fresh from graduation from Greenup High School, Jesse was like many young people since the days of Rome and the Holy Land. He was in the mood for adventure. He was young at heart, sap still rising to overflowing, and there had to be a bucket and spigot to tap it somewhere, somehow. Before he left W-Hollow, he'd told his mother it was time for him to see the world beyond dark hills. He had decided that Pa's life—plow in spring, chop weeds in summer, dig coal in winter—added up to a sorry bad back, bruised fingers, aching head, and swollen feet to boot. Jesse told his brother James to unhitch old Fred from the gate and bring him to the barn. When he told his mother he was leaving, she smiled and told him to go. She knew it was the right thing for him to do.

Even Horatio Alger could appreciate that all work and no play would make Jesse Stuart a dull boy!

> *I left James unharnessing the horses. I went to the house. I went upstairs and put on my gray suit and gray felt hat. I got my suitcase and went down to say good-by to my mother. She was cutting the weeds from around her currant vines in the garden. She was forever working. Ma probably worked in her dreams. She could flat outwork every man in the family .*
>
> *"I'm leaving," I said.*
>
> *"Well, be a good boy and when you come back the key will be above the door where we always keep it. The door might be unlocked when you come back. I trust that you will take care of yourself. I think you will. You know I would not hold you here. But remember chickens come home to roost. I have told you often that I would like to get out and go and go and go."*
>
> *Beyond Dark Hills*

Martha Stuart would never know one thing about a tea party. She'd not eat in a fancy restaurant. She'd not fly in an airplane. She'd be herself, and that would have to do. As for Jesse, he was footloose and fancy free.

> *I was leaving the old home now, the house my hands had helped to build. Every stone in the chimney I helped to place, the logs, the weatherboarding, the roof and everything. I had cleared the land, set out fruit trees, and made fences. I had helped to put the farm in shape and now I was going on. Would I go on and help to clear*

*another farm as my people had done?*
*My life was made empty by the farm in the hills. I was through.*

Beyond Dark Hills

Actually, the farm filled Jesse's life, and he was anything but "through." He was having an old fashioned identity crisis, and his explanations were often inconsistent. He was a teenager needing to break clean away from his mother and father. Driven by a passion to become self-sufficient, adventure downriver became his path to Tomorrowland, and poetry became his harbor.

### I

*I hear the lapping of the Sandy water,*
*I hear it lapping—lapping night and day,*
*And I go down and sit beside this water*
*And throw in sticks and watch them float away.*
*Long years ago barefooted I walked there,*
*Unlocked the old johnboat and let it glide*
*Down the birch-shaded aisle of lapping water...*
*I had sweet Maria Sheen close by my side.*
*And how we mingled happy words and laughter!*
*The raincrow croaked for a downpour of rain,*
*The lizard roved the scaly bark for sun*
*While Maria Sheen sat closer by my side.*
*I do not know if water kissed the grain*
*And if that lizard found his patch of sun,*
*But I do know who said she'd be my bride.*

### II

*And when I hear the lapping, lapping water,*
*I think of her whom I still love so dearly.*
*It all comes back in music of the water*
*The childhood Love I know I'll marry surely.*
*Her skin is milkweed dark, her eyes sky-blue,*
*Her teeth are bloodroot white, her hair is black*
*As thick rainclouds...her lips are soft as new*

*Bark peeled from a slippery elm and her back*
*Is straight as a horseweed upon the shore.*
*Her legs are brown as the buff-colored corn.*
*As I hear water lapping on the shore,*
*And as I see the sun rise up this morn,*
*I think of her that I shall see once more,*
*The sweetest mountain girl I've ever known.*

*Beyond Dark Hills*

# NO PUSSYFOOTIN' AROUND

*If you ever wish to see me,*
*enter the forest of your own heart.*

James Lane Allen
*The Kentucky Warbler*

*We all go the same way home.*

After his brief time with the street carnival, Jesse's heart was barely on the brink of the world outside W-Hollow. Hank the Clown, Mr. High Pockets and his hookers, and the coveys of Saturday night pretties had helped to gloss over a few greenhorn warts. From the top of Jesse's tousled head of hair to the thick soles of his W-Hollow feet, he was just one big old country boy—frustrated and scarred because he could find precious little approval away from the plow.

His heart pumped, restlessly.

When he returned from the carnival caper in 1926, Jesse spotted a bunch of local young men headed in another direction—they were bound for Camp Knox, about two hundred miles away to the west. In 1918 the federal government had established the military site as a field artillery training range just south of Louisville. It was the time of supreme sacrifice for hundreds of Americans fighting in World War I—Belleau Wood, Verdun, Chateau-Thierry—in the "war to end all wars."

Jesse had spent a brief period in the Citizens Military Training Camp at Knox when he was still in high school, an acceptable way of making a few dollars, folded and creased perfectly inside a handy package of newfound self-sufficiency. In his youthful imagination maybe he wrongly thought the camp experience might lead to West Point—Jesse's hormonal combustion engine was going and blowing like steam from a pop-off valve.

Jesse had about as much business at Camp Knox as he did at West Point, where he fantasized that he might vanquish a few new worlds. Perhaps he imagined he'd be a hero returning one glorious day to Riverton, Kentucky, and there'd be a patriot's parade. Why, his mother would wave and shed a tear, and his father would hook his thumbs in his overalls and maybe crack a little smile. *Way to go, Jesse!* Even brother James would help hold back the crowds. Sisters Sophia, Mary, and baby sister Glennis would be waving flags.

Jesse was no soldier. Oh, he could have been if he had truly wanted to be, but to him in this early time of his life, saluting was about as absurd as blowing a kiss to a herd of buffalo. Bouncing a quarter on bedcovers was ludicrous, as well as potentially wasteful. Jesse was more interested in books than guns, words than bullets, and by the time of his twentieth birthday he was no longer eager to blast rabbits on the run from hiding places, or to drop fat squirrels from black walnut limbs. And his notion of bravery didn't include the art of driving a bayonet into the heart of another human being.

Jesse's humanitarianism preceded WW II, the Korean Conflict, the Vietnam War, the Gulf War, and the War in Iraq. Yet he was not a pacifist. He was a patriot in the best sense of the word. The innocence he felt during and immediately after World War I would mature after Pearl Harbor, when he would proudly wear the uniform of the United States Navy and do what he honestly believed was his duty to his country. Before that was to happen, though, Jesse had a heap of growing up to do.

This green-as-a-gourd young "soldier" from Greenup County was granted a weekend pass in 1926 to go up to Louisville, which was the most likely place to search for something to read. The Book of the Month Club was founded at that time, the same year William Faulkner published *A Soldier's Pay* and Ernest Hemingway published *The Sun Also Rises*. But Jesse was neither Benji nor Jake—he was Jesse, and he was more attracted to Robert Burns and Edgar Allan Poe and literary phantoms of the eighteenth and nineteenth centuries. With meager funds he managed to buy a few copies of each, and he brought them back to camp, where the military establishment's written word served only to explain weapons and military strategy.

Jesse cached his treasured books in the window at the end of his bunk, where he could see them and reach for them, day or night. Just to place his fingertips on the book covers was to have satisfaction. To read and reread "The Cotter's Saturday Night" and "The Raven" was sheer joy. But he was awarded demerits for the "disorder" of his allotted space, where everything was expected to be spit-and-polish without benefit of *auld nick-nackets* or *nevermores*. Burns and Poe had no business stirring up the mind of one of Uncle Sam's young soldiers.

Jesse didn't want just to read a Burns or Poe, he wanted to *be* a Burns or Poe, desperately, but the youth had not come to the time of confidence in himself. He needed models, something different from Faulkner or Hemingway. It was too early in Jesse's life for him to realize that the point of a bull-tongue plow slicing through and cleanly laying over God's soil was the beginning of all life, including writing. Well, he had a notion about what it meant. Let's say, the mental picture came in a golden frame of land, water, and sky—not just anywhere, but in the most special of places.

Jesse, who loved Kentucky land, lamented the destruction of homesteads in the construction of Camp Knox. Even the little community of Stithton was lost, as if a giant dam had been built, the water of Salt River creating, in Jesse's imagination, a new, unnatural impoundment. The rights of people were submerged in the urgency of building a giant military complex—Fort Knox—future home of the Third Army and Gen. George S. Patton, the patron saint of all American warriors. Later, in 1937, the U.S. Bullion Depository opened as if it were the national Nest Egg, and "Fort Knox" became the nation's eternal symbol of monetary power and "might makes right."

Twenty-year-old Jesse Stuart was not instant military material. First of all, he was anything but a follower. Barracks inspections bored him. Drill sergeants' obscenities struck him as hot and mean-spirited as bullyboys scrawling dirty words on outhouse walls at Plum Grove School. Drill grounds and marching in step were mindless things to do. When Jesse's left foot came down, searching for the cadence of the drillmaster's call, the right foot from W-Hollow was likely as not to be nowhere in the rhythm of the "left-right, left-right, left right...."

At this time, a whole lot of bonny music was playing inside Jesse's head, telling him it was time to return home again to Greenup County. The daughters of Zeus did not intend for Jesse Hilton Stuart to become a tank captain, foot soldier, or fighter pilot. Hadn't the influence of Bobby Burns and Edgar Allan Poe, Mrs. Harriett Hatton and Miss Lena Wells Lykins told him to gather up his growing collection of poems and find a college, *somewhere*? Shouldn't he be finding an audience for his God-given natural talent? Wasn't that the meaning of acceptance?

Jesse had hardly any money, and his high school grades were not impressive. He was haunted by the poverty of his family. He needed to remind himself constantly of his determination not to follow in the plodding footsteps of his long-suffering father—log cabin to coal mine to railroad, where men, like Mississippi gandy dancers, drove spikes and spent their best years realigning old track.

> *I worked hard with Dad in the fields that fall. We played hard together. But things to me were not what they once were. I dreamed of something beyond the hills. I wanted to go and go and go. I had to do something more.*
>
> *To Teach, To Love*

The day when Jesse announced that he wanted to go to college, his father said, flat out: "You can't go."

Jesse replied: "Dad, I'm going to amount to something."

The bull-tongue plowboy packed his bag and came upon his mother in the kitchen.

"Where you going, Jesse?"

"I'm leaving home."

"Why, I think it's wonderful, Jesse. Go ahead. Chickens come home to roost. You'll be back."

> *To Teach, To Love*

Twice she'd told him this, the first time when he went off to join the carnival, now again when he was leaving to look for a job in the days before his departure for college. Martha was a wise woman, and she knew her chickens well.

Jesse walked out of W-Hollow, still little more man than an itching boy, but he went looking for serious work. If he were ever to go to college, he needed money, pure and simple. It might not be much money, but even a little bit might open the necessary doors, might give him the leverage needed to nudge the world.

After the street carnival and the Camp Knox circuses, Jesse landed on his feet as a standby laborer at the steel mill in Ashland, where flames could not be stage-managed with rapeseed oil tomfoolery. At Armco, Jesse quickly worked his way up to become the man with a blacksmith's sledgehammer. He was the right man for the right job at the right time.

For months he worked, and on one occasion he narrowly escaped death. Another employee was assigned to a particularly dangerous air hammer and was killed. If Jesse had been on the job as scheduled, he would have died, and there would never have been a *Taps for Private Tussie* or a *Thread That Runs So True*. Life would have been over before it had barely begun.

The time at the steel mill was an endless string of Steinbeckian drinking and fighting, a world apart from what Carl Sandburg had described as "beautiful" in *Smoke and Steel*. Jesse, not known for pussyfootin' around, lashed out from the pits of the Armco fires:

> *Carl Sandburg, I've got a question to ask you: Have you jerked hot slabs of steel on a track with a long hook and licked salt like a cow to make you sweat? Have you singed your eyebrows with the heat of steel and the wisps of hair that fell over your forehead when you stooped down? Tell me, Carl Sandburg, have you? I am reading your books because I work in steel now. I know you have never worked in steel.*

> *Beyond Dark Hills*

Make room for a newcomer, Mr. Sandburg!

Jesse the man-child was emerging, elbowing his way onto the crowded stage of literature, and he would endure many pratfalls—he'd be rash and often insufferable. But he'd not drop character—wherever he went, he'd still be Jesse Stuart! People would know he was in their presence.

> *Since I am young I'll sow my seeds*

*In earth with passion burning white...*
*My bleeding hands the thorny weeds,*
*My lips a mad man's curse to night.*

*My flesh may thin until it reels,*
*The recompense for happy pain...*
*Wind hounds may chase and bite the heel*
*Of this young braggart sowing grain.*

*Harvest of Youth*

Jesse stared into the furnace heat and heard his inner voice whisper: Jesse, my son, you'd better never forget the importance of going to college. If you're going to make something of yourself, you're going to have to move beyond dark hills. The easy way is seldom if ever the best way. You're going to have to take charge of your own life even though Fate deals the hand and invariably holds the trump card. You could stay in this steel mill until you drop in your tracks, you could fall into the vat and it would hardly be mentioned in the local newspaper. Your breath could become smoke and hardly anybody would notice.

Jesse was proud of his steel mill experience, but he was prouder of the little engine purring inside his chest.

September 1926—another autumn of Prohibition, the Jazz Age, and "flaming youth." While Hemingway, Fitzgerald, and others of the "Lost Generation" were becoming famous, basking in their celebrity status, Jesse Stuart was hitchhiking west on U.S. 60 in the foggy direction of Morehead State Teachers College, then on to Kentucky Wesleyan College in Winchester. It didn't matter whether these schools wanted him or not (and apparently they didn't), he'd already shipped his trunk, stuffed with verse and manuscripts to Berea College, south of Lexington. He had abandoned the idea of going to Harvard, Vanderbilt, or the University of Virginia. But he was doggone sure going some place where he'd be welcomed and it didn't cost an arm and a leg to sign up for the first semester.

Jesse was leaving Greenup County with twenty-nine dollars and thirty cents in his pocket and two changes of clothes in a flimsy pasteboard suitcase. Some rides lasted only a few miles, so he slept in haystacks when they were handy and sometimes found shelter in barns and deserted churches. The harvest moon was bright, and he was a twenty-year-old youth driven by desire to *be somebody*. At this time in his life, he fully understood that *being* what he most wanted to be—a writer—wasn't likely to happen by staying in Greenup County.

His soul cried out for space.

Wanderlust whipped him on.

He headed south from Lexington on U.S. 25 through Richmond to Berea College, but was unable to persuade the admissions officer to take him in.

> *"Why is it you want to come to Berea College, Mr. Stuart?"*
>
> *"The first reason is, it is a place where a man can work his way when he doesn't have money and just has to pay a little when he does have money. The second reason is, it is a good school."*
>
> *"Mr. Stuart, do you place Berea College above all other schools?"*
>
> *"No, Sir, I do not. I put Harvard, Vanderbilt University and the University of Virginia above Berea College."*
>
> *"Well, Mr. Stuart, why don't you attend one of your favorite schools?"*
>
> *"I don't have the money. And I prefer Berea College to any of the small schools."*
>
> *"Well, Mr. Stuart, to make a long story short, we have one-hundred and five students on our waiting list, and we can't use you until next year and maybe not then. But I'll tell you a place where you can go. I have a very dear friend teaching there. He was at Berea for twenty years, and now he is president of Lincoln Memorial, at Harrogate, Tennessee. If you go there, you tell him I sent you....Make the best of life. I'm sorry we can't keep you here. Good-by."*
>
> *Beyond Dark Hills*

With his old paper suitcase scrunched on one end where he'd sat on it between hitchhiked miles, Jesse walked to the Berea train depot and waited for the southbound Louisville and Nashville passenger train #31, which at that moment was winding along Harts Fork, across Hays Fork of Silver

Creek, past Dead Horse Knob. The engine—a J-4 type steam powerhouse—was hard to get started, but veteran engineers like A.L. Stone and firemen like W.S. McCord, who more than likely hadn't been to college, knew how to manipulate their monster's momentum. They brought patience and experience to the task, knowing the Cincinnati-to-Corbin track as well as they knew their own backyards. The announcing whistle whined at the edge of Berea, and old #31 slowed to its stop at the red-brick depot near the Berea College campus.

Rituals were repeated at each station: engineers and conductors checking their twenty-three jeweled Hamiltons, firemen their supply of Appalachian black gold, baggage men transferring mailbags with official notices—bills to pay, and maybe some sweetheart letters for regional distribution.

A local boy named "Cotton" Isaacs loved to sit on one of the baggage carts, chin resting on his folded arms on the back brace, wishing he too could be headed south. Many's the time "Cotton" watched the L&N engines roll mightily in and out of the station.

The engineer squinted at his gold railroad watch to reassure himself that he was on time—10 p.m.—ready for the overnight run to the southern mountains and beyond. "Cotton" Isaacs was pained that he'd not be going too. But maybe someday, someday, his time would come.

The train's conductor withdrew his well-worn timepiece from his waistcoat, squint-eyed the time, and amused himself in thinking that arriving and departing passengers were like migrating birds—flapping into each other in feathered space. They were like the high-flying geese fleeing the northern winter, heading south for warmth and a better chance to survive.

Usually there was a flurry of new students arriving from all parts of the nation to find a new home at Berea College, established for the education of the poor. These were the fortunate ones. There were more applicants than there was room for admissions, and some of these didn't make the cutoff and were advised to keep moving, farther south to Harrogate, Tennessee, home of Lincoln Memorial University, chicken roost for the poorest of the poor.

Jesse was one of these migrating birds.

It's not clear whether he bought a ticket from the Berea depot ticket agent, Mr. Roebuck, because students quickly learned that some long-suffering conductors were generous with space in the smoking cars of the L&N trains. Hard-pressed to be sure who was ticketed and who was hiding, conductors like R.C. Ogden were past masters at sizing up gangling youths in desperate need of a free ride and spare crumbs from the dining car tables.

"All a'booorrrd!!!"

The train left the Berea depot on time, 10:30 p.m., and headed south through the gathering darkness, through Sinks, Livingston, East Bernstadt, London, and on to the mainline juncture depot in Corbin.

Jesse was hungry. But good gosh a-mighty, he was happy! His stomach growled with the hurt of poverty, but his mind blurred with a greater ache and the excitement of wanting to *know*.

At Corbin, it was necessary for Jesse to leave the main line and hitch a ride on the local train. He probably barely managed to sleep as another engineer and fireman drove the train southeast out of Corbin toward Barbourville, Four Mile, and Pineville, then on a straight plunge to Middlesboro and Cumberland Gap, where Kentucky, Tennessee, and Virginia commingle in thick early morning mist.

Clouds envelop the pinnacle at 1,640 feet, then drift downward to the valley, where Walker, Boone, Findlay, and the other Long Hunters passed through with their cur dogs sniffin' the way. Much like Jesse, they were searching through the forests of their hearts, exploring for a better life. Like Jesse they were fed up with playing it safe.

So it was with Jesse in that late summer of 1926. Sweaty hands on a bull-tongue plow might have been enough for his unschooled daddy, but it was not nearly enough for the son. An inner voice had told him to stop in the furrow long enough to think, to write, to think, to write, then to sit down and etch the ideas on big old poplar leaves and scraps of throw-away tobacco paper, later one day to see the bits and pieces come together in *Man with a Bull-Tongue Plow*, *Taps for Private Tussie*, and *The Thread That Runs So True*.

Here's the thing about Jesse Stuart: he wanted a chance to prove himself. His was no grand illusion. He had an innate desire to become a good, popular writer. What made him different? He had soul. And it was his heart that carried him far, breathing new life into the words of James Lane Allen in his enduring *Kentucky Warbler*: "If you ever wish to see me, enter the forest of your own heart."

Just turned twenty years of age, Jesse was about to reach a crucial time—a new turning point, the first year in college, where the library shelves would be more promising, teachers more challenging, course work more demanding. Even so, he was virtually penniless with no way to go but up. He was not discouraged. He was like the steam locomotive crossing over the mountain—he knew the only way for him to succeed was to be positive and never to turn back. He'd learned that lesson from Miss Lena Wells Lykins when she walked from Greenup to W-Hollow and laid it on the line: was he a quitter or a self-starter? No way was he going to be a quitter. Yessir, and he'd show the officers at Camp Knox, the foremen at Armco Steel, the admissions officer at Berea, and Jesse's daddy too—he was going to *be* somebody.

After sunrise in that late summer of 1926, the engine of the local L&N labored up the rising grade in the train tunnel built in 1889, where steam and smoke sucked air like a suffocating sponge. The crossing over was a heavy burden, but the breathing was easier on the descending grade to the blackened aperture on the Tennessee side. A new foothold was about to signal a fresh start for Jesse Hilton Stuart.

Behind him lay Riverton on the Ohio and W-Hollow on Cedar Riffles, while one more mile ahead stretched the thousand-acre Lincoln Memorial University campus, inspired by another Kentuckian, who once said: "It is indispensable to have a habit of observation and reflection," meaning this for the poor as well as the wealthy, particularly Appalachian poor.

Jesse was in no mood for defeat. He was taking the bull by the horns, and nobody was going to stand in his way. There was a bounce in his step when Jesse bounded down from the train at Harrogate on the edge of Lincoln Memorial University on yon side of Poor Valley Ridge in eastern Tennessee. The air was cool, drenched with Indian summer fog, and Jesse breathed deeply.

The ancient trees were showing the first hints of pale green becoming soft yellow, and the young man from W-Hollow was free to discover a new plowshare.

> *Morning came and I got off at Harrogate. There wasn't any depot at Harrogate. It was a wide-open country place.*
>
> *"Where is Lincoln Memorial?" a girl asked me.*
>
> *"I don't know. I'm hunting for Lincoln Memorial too."*
>
> *"Right this way. This way. Bring your baggage and get in for Lincoln Memorial."*
>
> *A freckle-face boy drove a ton Ford truck. We all piled in. The girls, two of them, rode in the front seat, and the boys stood up in the truck bed. It was only one mile to Lincoln. We were soon there.*
>
> *"Say, Jim...where is the place anyway?"*
>
> *"Lincoln is hidden in the grass. You'll soon find her when we get all this grass cut and all that mountain of corn you see over there in the valley cut. We've got forty acres of hay to rake and God knows how many potatoes to dig. We've got to build some new henhouses over on the chicken farm, paint the dairy barn and lay three miles of water pipes. You'll find out where Lincoln Memorial is when we get all this done."*
>
> *Beyond Dark Hills*

Lincoln Memorial University was a haven for a Kentucky briar like Jesse Stuart. Established in 1897, LMU was the fulfillment of Abraham Lincoln's 1863 dream that there should be "something for those people who have been shut out from the world all these years." Abe and Jesse had in common the candlelit darkness of one-room log birthplaces—neither youth would forget how he'd begun, both isolated in their beginnings from most of the world. There were other likenesses shared by the president and the poet that would become the heart and soul of LMU: emphasis on character more than "A's" in academic standing.

In 1926, Lincoln Memorial was as rough and tumble as Jesse himself. Hormones and egos drove the students, while the administration was struggling for its own survival and identity. As former LMU president Dr. Robert Kincaid later described it, these were

> *days of crisis, of struggle, of bitterness, of upheaval, and of re-alignment. A young poet was smashing the barriers of poverty and*

*restriction and...a young college was going through growing pains of development.*

Jesse enrolled as a freshman for the 1926-1927 school year at LMU. Elsewhere Sean O'Casey was writing *The Plough and the Stars* and Louis Bromfield was winning a Pulitzer for *Early Autumn*. Later, in his *Pleasant Valley* and *Malabar Farm*, written in carefully hedge-rowed, agriculturally prosperous north-central Ohio, Bromfield often spoke disparagingly of Kentucky migrants streaming northward from stone-broke Appalachian hillside farms.

Jesse had a different vision.

He had made the most fundamental of decisions: he would not work for "the other fellow," no, he'd be working for himself. He dreamed of owning as fine a farm as any north of the Ohio River, imagined being the equal of any agrarian who just happened to live in more prosperous Ohio.

Jesse wrote work-driven words in *The Land Beyond the River*, published almost a half century later. Throughout his life, the work ethic came as naturally as the sun rising above Poor Valley Ridge on that autumn morning of 1926 when he crossed over into Tennessee.

This, then, was the youth from W-Hollow as he reached the head of the long LMU admissions line and was asked if he could pay all his expenses. The answer was an obvious one: No, he could not pay all, but he could pay ten dollars for the first quarter. He proposed that he would work for one half of a day and go to school during the other half. The admissions officer looked at the boy from W-Hollow and tried again. Couldn't he get at least a little money from home? No, he couldn't, because there wasn't any to be gotten.

What kind of work could Jesse do?

He replied that he had worked on the family farm. He had worked in a steel mill. He had dug ditches, carried water, and helped to pave streets. He had taught school.

Jesse was admitted to his first year of college.

Lincoln Memorial University, the fulfillment of Abraham Lincoln's dream, was to see the consummation of Jesse's passion to become a writer. He began composing poems—hundreds of them springing to life like mountain mushrooms, as if Jesse were possessed, the hand hardly able to keep up with the threadlike thoughts spiraling forth.

Jesse stayed for the summer session in 1927 and continued to write poems. Within two years he had written more than five hundred, not counting those he lost or gave away to friends.

He worked his way through his freshman year at Lincoln Memorial washing pots and pans for breakfast, dinner, and supper at Norton Hall dining room. He cut corn, raked hay, and built fences. There were days when he seized bricks and hoisted them up to bricklayers, toiled with a chalked-faced stone crusher gang, and pushed his foot down on a shovel to help set out trees. He worked on a crew to lay a waterline all the way from Cudjo's Cave at Cumberland Gap to the campus at Lincoln Memorial. If there was work to be done, Jesse Stuart did it. His physical energy was amazing, mysteriously mixed with the curious compulsion to write poems as sensitive as they were spirited.

His new sense of place and purpose was unselfish.

Most of what we know about Jesse Stuart at Lincoln Memorial University is what he has told us in the "Beware: Books Hurt the Flesh" chapter of his 1938 autobiography, *Beyond Dark Hills*, and chapter three of his 1970 book, *To Teach, To Love*. In trying to understand Jesse the man, there's a world of contextual difference between the LMU of the year 1926 and that of 2005. In Jesse's day there was raw, fundamental student behavior, and he gave as good as he got. A notable example is Jesse's description of a mock-heroic battle in the hay field involving a classmate known for his "fits," an Animal House character who bellowed like a bull, barked like a pack of dogs, and was known by spittle flying from his mouth. Jesse cured the "disease." He felled the "attacker" with a broadside swipe of his pitchfork.

Jesse reveled in telling stories about manners in the dining hall, stories that may have been true, making allowance for freshman embellishment. He said he almost starved his first two months at Lincoln Memorial. He quickly learned to take leftover bread from the dining room table and stuff it into his pockets. He'd learned this lesson from the squirrels in W-Hollow.

By the end of the first quarter, Jesse says, he "stood fourth on the honor roll," but it's hard to tell exactly what that really meant. There probably were instances of grade inflation, then as now, and Jesse has made no secret about the fact that he would write papers for other students in exchange for help with algebra. He seldom missed opportunities to breathe new life into his original work. Several times he recycled the "Nest Egg" short story, first written as a theme in Mrs. Hatton's English class when he was a sixteen-year-old high school student in Greenup County.

The legends of schoolhouse shenanigans and blatant cheating will come as no surprise to seasoned teachers, those who've been known to buff up their own vitas with promises of "Work in Progress" and "All But Dissertation."

> *"Say, Professor Woodward, I have a better idea," Jesse said.*
> *"When you give me this A minus, it will go on my record as A if ever a transcript of my grades goes out. Why don't you let me get you two twenty-five-cent cigars and you give me a standing-up A without any trimmings!"*
> *"A smart young man....it's a fine idea."*
> *"When do you want these cigars?"*
> *"As soon as you can get them!*
>
> *To Teach, To Love*

Jesse got around to writing his mother to tell her where he was, and she wrote back to him telling him of her conversation with a W-Hollow preacher, who feared the worst:

> *"Write and make that boy of yourn come home. That college will send him right to hell. He was a right pert boy before he left here. Get him back. Just write and tell 'em you'll git the law after 'em. Hoss that boy right back here. This world don't need no eddicated people. What this world needs is more people with salvation."*
>
> *Beyond Dark Hills*

This quotation is an example of Jesse's propensity for weaving ideas through speech manufactured and dressed up for the occasion. The technique is a prevailing one throughout his career as a writer, pleasing his fans, driving his critics up walls of disbelief. Another Jesse Stuart invention: changing names as if he were playing games. Classmate Don

West became classmate "Ron East." West, who went on to publish eight poetry collections including the highly successful *Clods of Southern Earth* (1946), remained one of Jesse's closest friends at LMU. Later in life they fiercely disagreed about politics and Christianity.

When Christmas rolled around that first year at LMU, Jesse came down with a bad case of homesickness. He borrowed one dollar from "Ron East," which was all he said he had, and Jesse then hitchhiked north in the direction of W-Hollow. There were many stories along the way, and later Jesse would tell them, first in *Beyond Dark Hills* and again in *To Teach, To Love*. This saving and savoring, this rounding up and reusing of every spoken and written word, accounts in part for the huge number of Jesse Stuart books. He understood the importance and advantage of not throwing away anything.

After hitchhiking from Harrogate, Tennessee, to Lexington, Kentucky, Jesse spent sixty-seven cents of his one dollar bill to buy a train ticket east to Winchester. At that point he planned to stay in the toilet and not come out until the train reached Ashland. The conductor found him there and threatened to throw him off the train.

*"I'll kick your damn tail. I'll stop the train; I'll throw you off—you scum of creation!"* Jesse remembers the conductor saying.

So much for compassionate conductors.

Another youthful passenger interceded in Jesse's behalf, scraped together three dollars and sixty-four cents, which was the amount the conductor demanded, to which Jesse added his last thirty-three cents.

So Jesse rode the train on to Ashland. But now he had no money at all. Not one cent. It was Christmas Eve, and he had to hitchhike twenty miles back to Greenup County.

> *Hie away to Greenup,*
> *Hie away to prayer;*
> *Hie away to Greenup,*
> *I shall soon be there.*
>
> *Beyond Dark Hills*

From Ashland, on that Christmas morning, Jesse hitchhiked and walked to W-Hollow, where he was reunited with his mother and father. She was standing in the kitchen, looking out the window, and Mick was close by, thinking aloud how much his heart yearned for his prodigal son, who arrived home just in time for Christmas dinner. Martha had hoped he'd be there, and she was ready for him: spareribs and roasted goose, cherries and wild grape jelly.

But first Jesse walked with his father, and they talked.

> *We missed you a powerful lot last summer. God only knows what a time we had without you. I plowed at night when I come in from work on the railroad. I worked in the moonlight. I worked by lantern light.*
>
> *Beyond Dark Hills*

Jesse admonished his father about his buying fifty acres of land, but Mick stood his ground. He said he not only *needed* the land, he *loved* it. This was the main idea to be handed down from one generation to the next, but Jesse could see the toll it was taking on his father as he was slowly and surely shoveling his way into his grave. Jesse could not then foresee that he too would one day do the same thing, yet within that toiling would come a greater purpose in life, however much sweat it might involve.

Mick told his son that he wanted him to finish college and come back and run for Greenup County School Superintendent. Mick said he'd rather Jesse do that than anything else. He implored his son, asking him if he'd want such a distinction. For Jesse to become superintendent of schools was Mick's idea of honest-to-God achievement, but Jesse said he wasn't sure what he'd do. He said he really didn't know *what* he wanted, which would have pleased Lincoln Memorial University and its founder who was driven to explore all possibilities.

The gap between Jesse and his father had not closed. Mick was too proud to plead. Jesse was too incomplete to give a consoling answer.

There was nobility in the simple act of "work," a bonding of Jesse and Mick with Highlanders like Elipha ("Life") Jay Preston, coal-miner father of Linda Scott DeRosier of Johnson County, Kentucky:

> *He was proud of being a hard worker. He was not proud of the status of his job, he was proud of being a hard worker, and frankly*

*talent ain't worth a damn if you don't put some gut work behind it....I
have real trouble with people who think they're too good to work.
And there's something about getting up every morning and going
forward and working....He worked harder than anybody else. He
was very proud of never having a day in a rocking chair because
when they had layoffs at the mines he'd leave there and go
someplace else and he'd lay in his application wherever he could
find work.*

*Interview*

Horatio Alger had said pretty much the same thing in his *Tattered Tom*
series in the nineteenth-century days before "work" lost much of its
worthiness and acceptability.

Mick and Jesse understood work, and they'd shared the joy that comes
to the hunter. Now father and son were coming to a major fork in the
road—Robert Frost's "The Road Not Taken."

*Two roads diverged in a wood, and I—
I took the one less traveled by,
And that has made all the difference.*

Jesse hunted with his father that winter of 1926, but the strong smell of
blue-smoke, ear-cracking gunfire was not the same as it used to be. Jesse's
aim could not match his father's, and the old pleasure of drawing down on
an animal, squeezing the trigger, seeing the dog fetch the fallen game—all
that had blurred. Jesse was no longer interested in the kill. Books and work
and Lincoln Memorial changed his mind and heart. He was a different and,
probably, a better Jesse. He understood that he had been happy at home in
W-Hollow until he went away to college. He knew that he was uninformed
and unschooled when compared to others his age, and he desperately
wanted to change that reality.

After eight days of his mother's home cooking—plenty of fried
chicken, dumplings, and generous helpings drawn from the thirty gallons
of peaches she'd canned—Jesse said it was time for him to return to LMU.
Again, he had no money, so Martha gave him seven dollars of her "egg
money" and Mick added five dollars he'd squirreled away from his work at
the mines and on the railroad tracks.

Jesse hitchhiked back to Lincoln Memorial.

During Jesse's 1927-1928 sophomore year at LMU, Sinclair Lewis published *Elmer Gantry* and Thornton Wilder published *The Bridge of San Luis Rey*. Lewis would become the first American to win the Nobel Prize for Literature, and Wilder would eventually win three Pulitzer Prizes. Lewis and Wilder were graduates of Yale. Jesse Stuart would graduate from Lincoln Memorial and would continue to write the unvarnished plowboy lines that would become the 703 sonnets in his 1934 book *Man with a Bull-Tongue Plow*. He would win neither Nobel nor Pulitzer Prize, but one day Jesse Stuart would become Poet Laureate of Kentucky. (Not until 1975 was he nominated for a Pulitzer Prize, for his forty-sixth book, *The World of Jesse Stuart*.)

Jesse registered for the second quarter at LMU—and he was now sixty dollars in debt. He didn't have a suit of clothes and everything he wore had patches on it. His elbows were coming through the cloth and there was a shine on the seat of his pants. He bet a fellow student that he could cut fifty shocks of corn in ten hours and if he couldn't he'd forfeit his only overcoat. If he had succeeded he would have won a new pair of shoes. He narrowly lost the bet and the overcoat was no longer his.

With spring came a hellacious fight involving upperclassmen and lowerclassmen; Jesse's rampaging description of it stretches the limits of believability. At best, it predates the comedian Jerry Clower's "Knock 'im out, John" and "Marcel and His Talking Chainsaw " fables, which also involved a tree and a Mississippi roadhouse door, but Jesse uses a different cast of Tennessee characters. Jesse's tall tale is a forerunner of his many short stories—"Split Cherry Tree," "Old Op and the Devil," and "Sunday Afternoon Hanging." He had fun in the telling of them, and he didn't lose his relentless drive to experiment, to learn, and, most important of all, to write.

Just when Jesse needed candid, forthright encouragement, he got it from his favorite teacher at Lincoln Memorial University. Of all his teachers at LMU, the one who mattered most to him was Harry Harrison Kroll, the head of the English Department. He urged Jesse to write more poetry, fewer short stories. In fact, Professor Kroll told Jesse he was too "scatterbrained" to write short stories. Though Jesse didn't stop revering his mentor, he ignored his opinion and went on to write approximately 450 short stories—unpolished gemstones like "Uncle Fonse Laughed," "Death Has Two Good Eyes," and "Hot-Collared Mule."

A published author himself, Kroll encouraged his young aspiring writers to concentrate on places and characters of whom the students had personal knowledge. While other more traditional teachers were taking the Elizabethan and Victorian high roads, Professor Kroll labored deep in the ditch of the here and now. He, like Stuart, was a sharecropper's son who wrote about the rural southern poor.

Mr. Kroll told Jesse and his classmates that if they had even a little talent they could become writers; the main thing was to *work* at it. Then as now, it was the way a farmer greets each new sunrise, a painter grips each new brush.

Jesse's complete admiration for Professor Kroll came with the publication of the professor's novel, *The Mountainy Singer*, but the book was taken to be "just plain sexy" and was one of the factors leading to his dismissal from LMU. In the summer of 1967, when Kroll died, a piece of Jesse died. He was at home in W-Hollow, and from there he wrote a tearful letter to Roland Carter, who had gone on to become a teacher at the University of Chattanooga:

> *We know now why we've not heard from Mr. Kroll. It's tragic news, our teacher is gone. He went this morning....I feel so, so, deeply about his death—and his valiant try—his great comeback when nearly eighty. He battled to the end.*

In his sophomore year at Lincoln Memorial, Jesse worked daily in the kitchen, drying pots, pans, and knives, forks, and spoons. The job paid for his room and board. It also assured him of plenty to eat.

Again, he had a confrontation with a student supervisor—there was a fight in the kitchen, and Jesse's account of it is frightening. The fight had begun after the supervisor "fired" Jesse, but Jesse had refused to leave the premises until he was told *why* he was being fired. The opponent hit Jesse across the chest with the flat side of a bread knife. Jesse hit the supervisor with every ounce of strength he could gather in one well-aimed fist. Dishes scattered everywhere, and the fight was over—Jesse survived the attack. There was nothing timid about Mick and Martha's baby boy.

Jesse called his sophomore year his "golden year." In order to see his poems in print, he decided he'd have to become editor of the student newspaper. After repeated attempts, he finally succeeded, and there very quickly on the front page appeared his first published poem! About the same time, his poetry was being accepted by small magazines. Jesse's struggle for recognition had gathered a good head of steam and had rounded the bend toward an obsession. He went after popular acceptance the way he cut corn and killed snakes in W-Hollow. One thing that propelled him was Alger's *Sink or Swim* signpost: "work, work, work, and work some more."

If Jesse's sophomore year was tough, he believed it paled in comparison with his junior year. His workstations included the dining hall, the post office, and the student newspaper office. He also had a heavy load of classes. But he persevered and graduated in 1929. He would become one of Lincoln Memorial University's most famous alumni.

After three years and two summers of work and study, Jesse finished with a Bachelor of Arts degree, the first of his father's people to earn a college diploma. He had hoped to earn every penny and to leave the university not owing it any money. But in the end Jesse owed $100.50. It was the year William Faulkner published *The Sound and the Fury*, first of the Yoknapatawpha series.

Jesse said his goodbyes, packed his suitcase, and began another hitchhike back to his own Yoknapatawpha—Greenup County, Kentucky.

He had gone to LMU for the very reasons that Abraham Lincoln founded it: to open the door to those Appalachian youth who couldn't afford to go anyplace else. *Work* was the master key. It was neither shunned nor stigmatized.

Jesse Stuart was on his way to making his mother and father very proud.

And the son would savor some of the sweetness for himself.

# ECONOMIC DESPAIR IN AMERICA

*1927 was a poor year and 1928 worse.*
*In 1929 the situation was quite bad indeed.*

Harry M. Caudill
*Night Comes to the Cumberlands*

*Welcome home, Jesse!*

After he graduated from Lincoln Memorial University, Jesse came back to Greenup County. It was the end of the summer of 1929, two months before "Black Friday" and the beginning of the Great Depression. Investors would not be jumping out of windows in W-Hollow; bread lines would not form there. Life in the Highlands of Kentucky was based essentially where it always had been—on family, the Bible, and the sheer determination to survive.

Martha was helping to scratch out a living in W-Hollow, Mick was working on the farm, in the coal mine, and on the railroad, and Jesse was coming to terms with his ties to the land, his prospective career as a teacher, and the inner voice urging him to write. He was unsure of himself, deeply troubled by a world colliding—economic despair in America, militaristic madness rolling along the hedgerows of Europe.

Jesse took a gentle, meandering walk with his mother, and they talked about her vegetable garden—her sweet corn with john beans and white half-runner beans spiraling up the stalks. She saved many kinds of seeds, counted each one, and kept them ready for planting at the best time of the moon. Accumulated wisdom was handed down, along with favorite family recipes, to distant generations. There'd be no charge for it, and "thanks" were not expected: Plant when the sign's in the bowels—you get nothing.

Plant when the sign's in the heart—nothing. The twin signs are the real time—that's the arms.

As for flower gardens, that would have been looked upon as another piece of foolishness, and there were perpetually plenty of wildflowers to savor in their seasons—Cumberland Rosemary and white-haired goldenrod—and the evergreen mountain laurel. Martha didn't have the "convenience" of quick-grown baby's breath and greenhouse hanging baskets—she accepted what nature bestowed. Besides, she had no automobile to drive to a shopping mall, if there'd been one.

As for Jesse, he was just glad to be home again.

And he'd rejoice in the knowledge of another Highland spring.

At his parents' urging, Jesse went to see the Greenup County superintendent of schools, who had expressed keen interest in this brand-spanking new college graduate, this "phenom," as they were called in Jesse's favorite professional sport, baseball. He wasn't going to be an Earle Combs, knocking line drives through the pitcher's mound, but he might have the right stuff to deal with old schoolhouse problems—attendance, discipline, and compliance with educational requirements. He might even bring, on the off chance, honest-to-God *knowledge* to the classroom.

The legend and the heritage of Jesse Stuart the teacher became deep-seated in Greenup County and, over the years, his recognition would widen far beyond Cedar Riffles. His cause would become a worldwide crusade for improved classrooms, teaching methods, and individual attention for all those to whom he'd laid down the challenge to open up their minds to learning. Individuality was the key to Jesse's teaching philosophy. He didn't think much of lumping human beings on a raft of meaningless numbers, averaging them, and taking the lazy way to shore. He spent as much time as possible with each boy and girl, some who'd have to be classified as men and women.

Jesse was hired to teach English, Latin, history, plane geometry, and algebra, even though he tried to tell the superintendent he didn't know enough about algebra to teach it. The superintendent needed a teacher and was in no mood to take "No" for an answer. Jesse found a way to do it—read, then learn—read, then think—think, then write—and write, write,

write—a game to be played! He would become an inspiration to many future educators who felt the urge to teach, daring to guide the thread of young minds through the eye of the needle—the stitching of a new quilt of knowledge.

During the summers of 1930 and 1931, Jesse did graduate work at George Peabody College for Teachers in Nashville, where the art and strategies of teaching were highest priority. He took courses in teaching, agriculture, and English literature. These were the fruitful years of Robert Frost's *Collected Poems* and Pearl Buck's *The Good Earth*, and Jesse decided that he'd not be afraid to stand up and be counted in the company of their growing reputations. He had a broadening vision that comes with the dropping of a pebble on the surface of a pool of water. He'd done that many times as a boy, long before he read about it in a book.

Teaching in the daytime, writing at night, Jesse was searching a variety of paths—Carl Sandburg's *Good Morning, America*, Walt Whitman's *Leaves of Grass*, Emily Dickinson's *The Single Hound*—poetry of the English language that touches hearts and minds in a New World beyond the Old World of Bobby Burns.

While in Nashville, he looked longingly toward the center of another literary phenomenon, a celebrated group of writers across the street from Peabody—at Vanderbilt University. They were the Agrarians, who rallied around John Crowe Ransom, the poet and critic who had attracted Kentuckians Allen Tate and Robert Penn Warren. The careers of Tate and Warren predated Jesse Stuart's; in time, they'd hover over him like dubious ghosts from a dimming, distant past.

When Jesse was walking miles to a one-room school in Greenup County, Allen Tate was attending Cross School for Boys in Louisville. Jesse worked his way through Lincoln Memorial University after Tate attended Georgetown University preparatory school in Washington, D.C. Tate was ready for Vanderbilt when he enrolled there in 1918—Jesse was woefully behind when he first appeared in Nashville twelve years later.

Robert Penn Warren was one year older than Jesse Stuart. While Jesse was struggling with algebra and quitting school to work for twenty-five cents a day, "Red" Warren was graduating *summa cum laude* from Vanderbilt. While Jesse was hanging on by blackboard fingernails, Warren was studying at Yale and was a Rhodes Scholar. When Warren returned to Vanderbilt to teach, Jesse Stuart was pulling up his scruffy bootstraps. When Jesse Stuart made up his mind about something, it would take a mighty force to turn him around.

That same year, 1930, witnessed the publication of Jesse's first book. From his earliest poems he selected the ones to appear in a vanity press book, *Harvest of Youth.*

> *If one swift-breathed yesterday I could recall*
> *Time would be springtime in sunny Tennessee*
> *When eerie birds sing in the boughs to solace me,*
> *And clouds blow westward over Lincoln Memorial—*
> *To see a sickle moon caught in a windy tree,*
> *To walk old roads curved into tree-lined faces,*
> *Live now as I did then and feel at least as free.*

Initially he hadn't understood the deadfalls of a vanity press. No one had warned him that it might be considered suspect. He probably decided he had a long way to go to be accepted as a poet and writer, and he had a mighty short time to get there. He was at all times in a hurry to move ahead, his heart racing to keep pace with his flailing arms and sprinting feet in his own little dust devil.

"Vanity press" typically means that some publishers will print any book the author is willing to pay for. But it's more complicated than that. Too often a vanity publisher offers false encouragement and conspires to persuade the author that he or she is "great," no matter how bad the author's writing may be. Caution takes a holiday. Egos are bruised. A vanity press sometimes calculates press runs so that up-front money benefits the publisher, all too often leaving the unsuspecting writer saddled with problems and expenses of distribution, promotion, and marketing. A vanity press is not the same as self- or independent-publishing, which is an alternative to circumvent the usual layers of agents, editors, publishers, bureaucrats, and wily entrepreneurs.

Jesse quickly realized that *Harvest of Youth*, dedicated to his favorite professor at Lincoln Memorial, Harry Harrison Kroll, was a conspicuous failure. He had borrowed one hundred dollars to have it published, and he received only fifty copies. He destroyed most of these. *Harvest of Youth* included sincere but fumbling verses he'd written in high school and during his undergraduate years at LMU. Jesse's vanity-book misadventure became a major embarrassment. He'd somehow finagled the modest financing of the earnest misadventure, but when the book arrived, even the production was substandard. He knew he'd made a bad mistake, and he made haste to correct it. He tried to destroy as many copies as possible, and he deeply regretted the incident. It made him feel like a cheat, like rigging rides on the Merry Mix-up, and he didn't need anybody to tell him how foolish he'd been. Today, original copies of *Harvest of Youth* are the dream of every Jesse Stuart collector. These rare heirlooms (only two or three in existence) easily command prices of approximately $10,000—each.

Jesse's counsel:

> *If I have any advice to give a writer—young or old, but inexperienced, I would tell him not to let his vanity get away with him or the Vanity Publisher to get away with his pocketbook....I have hundreds of poems and sonnets in my possession now that I have written and kept—and hundreds have been destroyed—and I say to you that never will one of these be published if I have to pay for publication. I'll never give a book to the public again if I have to pay one cent to have it published. This is my honest confession to you.*

Jesse's warning appeared in *Honest Confession of a Literary Sin*, published in 1977. If there was a fault, it lay on the doorstep of the vanity press. His creative heart was beating with promise for the future.

Jesse challenged his students to enter competitive academic contests, and they enthusiastically responded by riding on mules to town to win their share of the prizes. Jesse's reward was to be asked to become principal of Greenup High School—only four years after he'd been a student there himself. As for a salary, he would make less money than some of his teachers.

Ethel McBrayer had been one of Jesse's students, one who grew up to become a teacher, then principal of Greenup Independent High School, and later principal of Greenup Elementary School.

Ethel McBrayer's picture of the man with the bull-tongue plow is framed with the sureness of a shy but steady Highland woman in her own twilight time—generous, yet with a balanced sense of justice; wise, but with a knowing twinkle in her eye.

"Jesse Stuart couldn't be quiet. He fidgeted. He was very compulsive, gung-ho about life—couldn't be calm and couldn't slow down....Stuarts were very aggressive people."

Richard Prince was in Jesse's second grade class at Cane Creek School: "Jesse had control over older boys. If there was trouble...he had to do a thumping sometimes."

Vernon Plummer went to McKell High school when Jesse was principal:

> *He was a character, a regular guy. You had to have a written report for an absence. I took him one, and he laughed and said "Are you sure you weren't squirrel hunting?" One time on the bus, a boy hit me in the eye with a paper wad. When I got to school my eye was all red and swollen. Jesse got all excited. He wanted to know what was wrong. He said, "Why didn't you hit him with your fist?" I guess he thought you ought to settle things that way, I guess. Most principals didn't talk like that. He was a real man.*
>
> *Once he had a fight with a boy who got smart with him. It was right there in the principal's office. In later years I saw him occasionally. He had a great memory. He knew people's names. I visited him after about ten years, and he knew my name. I have about thirty of his books. He was great on education, pushed the idea for everybody to get a good education. Everybody liked him.*
>
> *"How would you sum him up?"*
>
> *"He was a good teacher and a good man—a great man."*
>
> *Interview*

After a brief but respectable passage of time on the job in the principal's office, Jesse asked for a raise—from $1,000 a year to $1,200 a year, an increase of a little more than fifty cents a day, if you counted every day in the year. Jesse had not yet learned that to ask for a raise is often the kiss of death, or at least an excuse for bringing in another "phenom."

The superintendent fired him. The year was 1931.

Jesse hossed to the barn at W-Hollow, lathering with another hurt, looking for friendly hay in his trough, all the while driven by the goddesses to be a writer of Highland poems. There'd be earth and sky stories, tall tales, maybe a dozen or more about his people, the good and the bad, the lovely and the ugly. In his mid-twenties, Jesse wasn't sure whether he wanted to be farmer, teacher, school administrator, or writer—or all four.

He needed money.

More than that, he chomped for respect.

As much as his heart would bear, he'd sweated with his father on the hardscrabble farm. He'd had his "carnival" fling. He'd blacksmithed in the steel mill. He'd worked his way through college. He'd taught in a one-room school. He'd been school principal when he was only a few years older than his students, and he'd been summarily fired—but he'd written and published hundreds of poems. Still, all this didn't add up to the lasting acceptance he'd dreamed of having. He felt trapped in the "dark hills" of eastern Kentucky.

There must be an answer, but what could he do?

In the depths of the Great Depression, with millions unemployed and "down-and-outers" forming long lines outside New York City soup kitchens, Jesse borrowed $250 from a Greenup, Kentucky, bank, gave $50 to his brother James so that he could attend Berea College, and gave his mother $50 to spend however she chose. With the remaining $150 Jesse gladly cleaned out his desk in the principal's office at Greenup High School and said goodbye to "Uncle" Rank Larks, an old man with the good sense to take a special interest in talented youth.

> *Jesse, it's a plum shame that you are leavin' here. You know I hate to see you go worse than if you was one of my boys. I've knowed your Ma since she was a little girl wearin' ribbons on her hair. They ain't no better woman than your Ma. They ain't no better man than your Pap. Your Pa's the hardest-workin' man in this county. He grumbles a lot, but he's a good man. You know I hate to see you go.*
>
> *Beyond Dark Hills*

Twenty-five-year-old Jesse caught the bus and headed southwest.

Instinctively he understood the importance of being in the company of other writers, even if their work was more polished and celebrated. So he bundled up his bruised passion born of Bobby Burns, along with the $150, all he had, and headed back to Nashville, where he tromped across 21st Street to hallowed Vanderbilt University.

Jesse was going to be there or know the reason why. He was going to check out Robert Penn Warren, Donald Davidson, John Crowe Ransom, Allen Tate, and the other "Fugitives" widely known as the "Agrarians," who in 1930 published *I'll Take My Stand: The South and the Agrarian Tradition*.

Literary critic Daniel J. Boorstin has said, "All students of American life should read it [*I'll Take My Stand*], the better to know what they are not, and to wonder what they might have been."

Jesse had probably heard about the reactionary book while at Peabody, where he felt the nearby excitement of southern fountainhead ideas like Warren's "The Briar Patch"—*The chief problem for all alike* [black and white] *is the restoration of society at large to a balance and security which the industrial régime is far from promising to achieve.*

For Jesse, this confederacy of agrarians would eventually lead to his condemnation of the strip mine industry's removal of Kentucky mountaintops and their woolly promises of restoration and repopulation. As Wendell Berry has persuasively argued, people will not choose to return to devastated land—loveliness and nature are not so easily manufactured.

Jesse probably read Donald Davidson's "A Mirror for Artists"—

*The despised hinterland, which is rather carefree about the matter, somehow manages to beget the great majority of American artists. True, they often migrate to New York, at considerable risk to their growth; they as often move away again, to Europe or some treasured local retreat.*

Jesse's treasured local retreat would be Cedar Riffles in a valley of the Cumberland Plateau, and it would be the same kind and wise Donald Davidson who would encourage Jesse to return there and write there.

Jesse's poems by now numbered in the thousands, his short stories in the hundreds.

Jesse rolled up his sleeves, took a deep breath, sized up the code, learned the passwords, and enrolled at Vanderbilt (1931-1932), where he'd be as out of place as if he'd gone to Harvard or Oxford. The mismatch wouldn't be entirely Jesse's fault. He was a victim of intellectual elitism overlaying his own poverty-laced self-inventions. Jesse was, after all, a briar with more poems than pennies in his pockets, more raw energy than a Cumberland River turbine. His fluttering verse was sometimes strung together like migrant birds looking for a warm, friendly gourd.

He gambled by thinking a published work (*Harvest of Youth*) in hand might be a key to opening combination-locked academic doors at Vanderbilt. He was as wrong as he was headstrong.

Dr. Edwin Mims, professor of English at Vanderbilt, had Jesse in one of his classes and advised him that graduate study at Vanderbilt was probably over his head, which was the understatement of a lifetime. One assignment was for the students to write an autobiographical term paper not to exceed eighteen typewritten pages.

In eleven days and nights, Jesse wrote a 322-page manuscript and submitted it to Professor Mims, who was a portrait of Vanderbilt academe — arched eyebrows and a cultivated, high-handed demeanor. He barely tolerated the young man from the Plum Grove hills of Greenup County, Kentucky.

"You write all of this for me to read. Stuart, you aggravate me—you are not passing my work and then you go and write all of this." Jesse remembered Dr. Mims's words as if they'd been daggered into his brain. The student had done his best. He was not like the typical student who did only what was required and not one whit more.

About one week later Jesse passed Dr. Mims's door. The grim professor looked up and waved his cane as if to demonstrate his power as a graduate school duelist. Jesse stopped and entered the office, but he was in no mood to be skewered. Professor and student glared at each other.

> *He never spoke—he just looked at me. His eyes pierced me and finally I let my gaze pierce him. I looked hard at him. He looked hard at me. If he was going to start a row with me, I thought I would not stand it any longer.*
>
> *Beyond Dark Hills*

Dr. Mims finally spoke:

*I have been teaching school for forty years, and I have never read anything so crudely written and yet beautiful, tremendous, and powerful as that term paper you have written.*

Beyond Dark Hills

Jesse remembered that Dr. Mims's smile was "a hard smile."

Jesse felt the pinch of curious praise: "So crudely written and so beautiful and it needs punctuation." Nevertheless, that term paper was later published, in 1938, as *Beyond Dark Hills*, and is essential to a fuller, richer understanding of Jesse Stuart.

"Do you really like it?" Jesse asked, leery that it might be some kind of professorial joke.

"I took it home and let the family read it. It is a great piece of work—I can't go out with you to lunch today but I am paying for your lunch—here, take this dollar and eat on me today." Jesse was hungry for food as well as praise.

Jesse's other classes at Vanderbilt included Victorian Literature under Dr. Mims, "The Novel" under Robert Penn Warren, American Literature with John Donald Wade, and Elizabethan Poetry under Donald Davidson. Jesse's grades failed to meet graduate school expectations.

Jesse would recall his first semester at Vanderbilt as the hardest time he'd ever had in school. His poor grades were due in large part to the fact that he didn't study. He didn't have time to study—he was forced to work in order to live.

A dishwasher at LMU, Jesse became a janitor at Vanderbilt, where he managed to get by on one meal a day. He sacrificed his health to walk the same hallways as Robert Penn Warren and John Crowe Ransom, both Rhodes scholars, and John Donald Wade. "Red" Warren would one day win three Pulitzer prizes and become the nation's first Poet Laureate. Allen Tate received a classical education in southern private schools and eventually taught at Oxford. John Donald Wade earned degrees in English from Harvard and Columbia.

Jesse's favorite Fugitive teacher was Donald Davidson, for it was he who advised Jesse to "go home" and to write about what he knew best. It was probably the best advice Jesse Stuart ever received. Davidson was a Fugitive's fugitive. His works included "Why the Modern South Has a

Great Literature," "The Tall Men," and *Lee in the Mountains, and Other Poems*. He did not compromise, not even his defense of racial segregation. He lived in a past from which, for him, there was no reason to escape.

During the years 1931-1932, Jesse's master's degree thesis was to be a critical study of Kentucky writer John Fox Jr., author of *The Little Shepherd of Kingdom Come* (1903) and *The Trail of the Lonesome Pine* (1908). Neither the thesis nor the master's degree was to be.

On February 19, 1932, a fire burned down Vanderbilt University's Wesley Hall.

Jesse was one of the students living on the fourth floor, where the flames started on that Friday afternoon—the first alarm sounding at 4:45. Jesse looked out from a window, saw the firemen's streams of water, and escaped the building where about seventy-five students and five families lived, including Professor Davidson. All escaped without injury, but for Jesse it was a huge personal loss.

Jesse remembered in *Beyond Dark Hills*:

> *I ran back upstairs and the smoke came in and blinded me. The building burned all night. The next morning only the brick walls stood, with smoke oozing from the pile of ruins. I lost the job where I had been able to eke out eleven meals per week, enough rations to keep strength in my body. I lost all the clothes but the suit I had on my back, and the crotch split in the pants where I was trying to save a few of my books from the burning building. I lost all I had, but the greatest loss was not the few old clothes I had—I lost my thesis, and the term paper I had rewritten for the fifth time, fifty sonnets, part of a novel and several poems.*

Wesley Hall, built in 1880, housed the university's School of Divinity, with its rare collections in the Tigert and Boland libraries. The university's loss was estimated to be approximately $400,000, but Jesse's loss was incalculable.

For Jesse Stuart, the roller coaster ride had innocently begun on Cedar Riffles, had risen to Lincoln Memorial, but the crash at the bottom came the day Wesley Hall was reduced to ashes.

His grades, too, were in shambles, and his graduate studies had come to a halt. He would not be going ahead toward a master's degree, much less a Ph.D. He had been victorious at Lincoln Memorial University but was temporarily defeated at Vanderbilt University. Later in life he remembered, in a November 29, 1967, letter to his former Lincoln Memorial University classmate Roland "Nick" Carter, that he *"left Vanderbilt a very despondent, depressed man."*

He wrote to his high school friend Naomi Deane Norris, back in Greenup, and he told her that neither advanced degrees nor substantial wealth was as important to him as the simple act of being himself—his truest self.

Naomi Deane's eyes had often met Jesse's at Greenup High School. He was different from most of the other boys.

In the Spring 1972 issue of *The Peabody Reflector*, Jesse recounted his early relationship with Naomi Deane during their high school days and later when she was a teacher and he was superintendent:

> *In my young manhood when I was looking for a wife, I wanted to marry a young woman who was a school teacher....I wanted a wife who loved a home. I wanted a home-builder....*
>
> *While she was in college and I was in college, we who had dates with others, still remained "conscious" of each other. Neither one was serious enough now to think of marriage.*
>
> *When I came back from Vanderbilt University and Peabody College, where I had done graduate work....I was the youngest County School Superintendent ever to qualify and serve in one of Kentucky's 120 counties....Each school session I was required by Kentucky law to visit every school under my jurisdiction at least one time. I had 82 "one- and two-room" schools, a high school and two junior highs to visit.*
>
> *The cleanest and most decorated school among the 85 I visited was a one-room school, Lower Laurel, where Miss Naomi Deane Norris was teacher. When I visited this school I found a very pretty young woman, with whom I had had dates; besides having the most*

*decorated and prettiest classroom I had visited she was one of the very best teachers in the Greenup County School System....She had used wild autumn flowers and leaves, flora and fauna, native to this area, to decorate her school....I stayed longer at her school and I complimented her before her students for having such a beautiful room....Miss Naomi Norris had done all of this—and there was a Greenup County School Board's ban on the superintendent dating his teachers or teachers dating teachers or students.*

*When I left the Greenup County Superintendency to become principal of McKell High School, where I would have opportunity to teach and to come in closer contact with students, Miss Naomi Norris got a position in her hometown, Greenup, Kentucky, at the Greenup Elementary School. While she was here living at her home, I had a few dates with her. But I was not in those days very welcome at her home, for when I was Greenup County Superintendent, I had had many lawsuits trying to get justice for our county school system.*

Jesse and Naomi Deane were attracted to each other and their friendship would flower in the fullness of time. Teaching brightened their garden path as assuredly as jonquils bloom in April. Jesse turned a negative at Vanderbilt into a positive at W-Hollow, where he and Naomi passed through the needle's eye.

# LETTER FROM
# A PUBLISHING HOUSE

*There is no country but the heart.*

Robert Penn Warren
*Flood*

*Know Jesse's heart!*

Jesse's heart was a-pumpin' like Old Silas Woodberry's milldam at Put-Off Ford on Little Sandy River. Why, Jesse must'a thought he was dadblamed indestructible. Didn't he 'member any of the stories told about Old Silas? How he tempted the Lord God Almighty? How the old milldam could only last just so long? Didn't a flash flood sweep the milldam away, and in that terrible moment shouldn't a lesson have been learned?

Jesse's brother James has left an invaluable account of the year 1932, when Jesse became the youngest school superintendent in the Commonwealth of Kentucky. He was only twenty-six years old. James remembered that the summer of 1932 was "hot and wet."

> *Jesse was back from a year of graduate school, and I was home from my first year of college....We started farming that year as soon as we returned home. Pa had already planted the corn. Jesse plowed the corn on the steep hills, and I chopped the weeds and sprouts with a long-handled shop hoe. Pa had a good summer's work of farming and fencing laid out for us. Times were hard, but we were not as unlucky as some people. We grew our own food. We ate what we raised. Even if prosperity wasn't with us in the summer of 1932,*

*Jesse and I had one of the best summers we ever had in our lives.*
*James Stuart's unpublished manuscript*
*Courtesy Jesse Stuart Foundation*

Once the point of a plow rims a steep slope, and after the rains come and wash away the topsoil, it is virtually impossible to return the land to its original condition. Mitchell Stuart understood the problem and resolved it.

> *"My father taught me the art of conservation. He used to rant and rave about how our neighbors treated their most valuable possession, land....He taught me never to let a ditch start in one of my fields. If one did start, he knew how to stop it, though he didn't know how to measure how much topsoil sent down that ditch. He said, 'While you try to measure, I can have it stopped.' And it was true. He plowed with the contour of the slopes long before our modern conservationists began to write essays advising it. He wouldn't let us draw a plow downhill. His fields were never hurt by erosion...He told me to let trees and wild flowers grow, keep forest fires away, work to prevent erosion, and wait for the timber to build a new topsoil."*
>
> *God's Oddling*

Meantime, Jesse and his brother James couldn't wait for their hormones to simmer down, as James remembered in that heaving time:

> *As soon as we came home that spring, we decided that we were tired of college. We wanted to swim in Little Sandy and the Ohio rivers. We wanted to take in all the square dances and hunt squirrels and ground hogs. We wanted to run over the hills again. When it rained and made the ground too wet to plow and hoe, we built fences. Our bodies took the hot summer sun in only a pair of cut-off overalls. Barbed wire and briars cut our legs, but we didn't mind this, since the freedom to live was ours. No one ever called us down except Mom.*
>
> *Unpublished manuscript*

Sometimes, a body gets "jo-fired"—"all-fired," a regular "hell on wheels!" Well, that was Jesse during this time in his life. Pa took one look at his rambunctious boys and told them that as soon as they got more of

**J**esse's parents, Mitchell ("Mick") and Martha Hilton (Hylton) Stuart. "Men must not be faint-hearted and women must endure hardships along with the men," said their eldest son, who turned work into words.

**E**ver mindful of his heritage, Jesse Stuart stands beside the one-room log cabin where he was born in 1906. "The spot is a lonely one," Jesse wrote in *Beyond Dark Hills.*

**S**even children were born to Mitchell and Martha Stuart. *(L. to R.)* Glennis, James, Mary, Jesse, Sophia, Martha, and Mitchell. Two more siblings, Herbert Lee and Martin Vernon, did not survive childhood. "How the tears would drop from Mom's eyes," Jesse recalled.

Jesse began writing poetry when he was a sophomore in high school. "I feasted on the poetry of Robert Burns." A spiritual return to Scotland became Jesse's youthful obsession, a land as inspiring as W-Hollow, Kentucky. Jesse made the connection and soared.

Courtesy Forrest C. Pogue Special Collections Library, Murray State University.

Jesse, Oscar Sammons, Thurman Darby, and James D. McCoy *(L. to R.)* appearing serious and purposeful in a Greenup High school senior picture. "We only know men born are men to die," Jesse would write in *Harvest of Youth*. Sammons and Darby would become two of Jesse's pallbearers in 1984.

Courtesy Carnegie-Vincent Library, University Archives and Special Collections, Lincoln Memorial University, Harrogate, TN

Jesse and future poet Don West (far right) were close friends and classmates at Lincoln Memorial University in Harrogate, Tennessee. Jesse graduated in three years and two summers. Jesse and Don were graduate students together at Vanderbilt University.

Jesse vowed he'd give Naomi Deane a home where they'd be beholden only to themselves— "Chapman House" in the heart of W-Hollow—"...a home filled with loving memories," said Deane— a place to anchor roots.


Courtesy Forrest C. Pogue Special Collections Library, Murray State University.

Courtesy Jesse Stuart Foundation

Courtesy Carnegie-Vincent Library, University Archives and Special Collections, Lincoln Memorial University, Harrogate, TN

Born into poverty in Greenup County, Kentucky, Jesse cultivated the image of a sweating, young, and powerful agrarian (*Man with a Bull-Tongue Plow* [1934]), who grew to become a resourceful, highly successful, internationally-known author of thousands of poems, hundreds of short stories, and more than sixty book titles. He was remembered by many at his alma mater, Lincoln Memorial University, as an original "hunk."

Jesse informed the Guggenheim Foundation that there was no reason to "pussyfoot about the truth," he wanted one of its treasured fellowships to study for a year in Bobby Burns country. He got it! July 9, 1937, Jesse boarded the *Samaria* in New York harbor and was soon outbound to Scotland. "Just a table-land of water before us and a star in the distance meeting the water. A fine trip."

In 1939, Jesse married Naomi Deane Norris. He served in the U.S. Navy in World War II. Their daughter, Jessica Jane, was born in 1942.

Ma's cornbread and biscuits, they'd "build muscles again and get rid of the light bread bloat."

The beanstalk boys decided that they'd grown considerably bigger than their britches. According to James they slept in the yard with "a quilt under us and a bed sheet over us." By day they swam in Little Sandy and by night they ran the ridges. There was little time left for sleep. When it rained on them at night they ran to their parents' house "as wet as dogs."

The boys grew tired of trying to slip past Pa in the house, and Pa was worn out with waking up thinking a regiment of foxes was in with the chickens.

> *Boys, I've made up my mind. This sleeping out, like a bunch of mules or hunting dogs, has got to stop. From now on, you will sleep in the house.*
>
> *Unpublished manuscript*

The ridgerunners had a better idea. They'd build a bunkhouse.

The pillbox building still stands today, but Jesse's old portable typewriter sits silently on the table where he began to write as if there were no tomorrow.

Grandpa Hilton, who was eighty-four years old, was living with the Stuarts, and he insisted on helping with the building of the bunkhouse, which would sit on top of a new cellar. James marveled at the old man's determination:

> *Lots of times, Grandpa would try as many as twenty rocks in one place before he found the right rock that suited him. It had to be done right or he wouldn't let it be done at all. Jesse continued to work on the farm. He kept his pockets filled with poems he had written on scraps of paper. That summer, he wrote three or four hundred poems.*
>
> *Unpublished manuscript*

James knew Jesse as a dependable brother. James could count on Jesse to do the right thing at the right time.

> *Five years later, Jesse gave me $200.00, which he had been paid for poems, to build another room. I built the second room for $185.00. I tried to give him the $15.00 left and he told me to keep it.*

*He said that anyone who could manage money like I did deserved
the leftover.*

*During the seven years that Jesse and I lived in the Bunkhouse, he
published three books, fifty short stories and over one hundred
poems....Thirty years after the first room was built, Jesse wrote a
short story titled "The House That James Built" and sold it for
enough money to repay him for all the money he spent building the
bunkhouse.*

*Unpublished manuscript*

Two Highland bachelor brothers building together was a key corner-log
in the unfinished business of their lives. The bunkhouse would also become
a temporary honeymoon cabin when wedding bells took a notion to strike.
That time was several years away.

Jesse Stuart's writings in the early decade of the thirties were simple,
recognizable, and understandable, beginning with *Man with a Bull-Tongue
Plow*, published by E.P. Dutton Co. of New York in 1934.

*This Land Is Mine*

*My land is fair for any eyes to see—*
*Now look, my friends—look to the east and west!*
*You see the purple hills far in the west—*
*Hills lined with pine and gum and black-oak tree—*
*Now to the east you see the fertile valley!*
*This land is mine, I sing of it to you—*
*My land beneath the skies of white and blue.*
*This land is mine, for I am part of it.*
*I am the land, for it is part of me—*
*We are akin and thus our kinship be!*
*It would make me a brother to the tree!*
*And far as eyes can see this land is mine.*
*Not for one foot of it I have a deed—*
*To own this land I do not need a deed—*
*They all belong to me—gum, oak, and pine.*

*Sonnet 7*
*Man with a Bull-Tongue Plow*

*Could I believe it? A letter from a publishing house. It says:
"Have you got any more poems like the ones you have in the autumn
issues of the* Virginia Quarterly *and the* Mercury?" "Yes," I write
and say, "I have seven-hundred and three in that batch." An answer:
"Send them to us if no one else has spoken for them."*

*Lord, no one had spoken for them. Certainly I would send them. I
packed them up and sent them away. A letter came with a contract. It
said: "This is a great book of poems. It is like a big river with
tributaries of life entering in. It is like a symphony of wind."*

With a winning title and 703 sonnets, Jesse Stuart instantly became a
popular national literary figure.That same year, 1934, William Saroyan
wrote *The Daring Young Man on the Flying Trapeze.* The description fit
Jesse like a buck rabbit hide skinned and stretched tight on a curing board.
He began assembling *Head o' W-Hollow,* his first collection of short
stories, including "300 Acres of Elbow Room," irreverent "Uncle Jeff,"
and slaphappy "Governor of Kentucky."

July 22, 1936. The first of a lifetime of letters to his teacher Lena Wells
Lykins and her husband, William Augustus Voiers, in Vanceburg, Kentucky.

*Dear Lena Wells and Gus:*

*I am off to school again.* [Jesse's third summer of teacher training]
*Came July 16th and entered George Peabody College for Teachers.
There were a couple of courses I wanted and I find myself taking a
full load. It's fun to be a student again. My brother Jim is here with
me. We room together at a Fraternity House. Last night we went to a
vaudeville at the Princess Theatre here in Nashville—saw a girl do
the hula-hula dance in her grass skirt—a real dark-skinned man—
either Spanish or Mexican played the guitar beautifully. Jim and I
just applauded and applauded when the girl did the dance. Women
sat around us sour as dough.*

*Again the many faces—the strange faces that throng the street,
new faces to learn—thousands of them—books to read—new life, the
ecstasy, the love of living, the dance, the joy, the pain—the
happiness and the slow but sure slipping away of it all for each
individual born into the world. I must move about more, know more*

*people—live more, study, read more—have a good time crossing the stage—never will get the opportunity to cross it again. Capture a portion, or portions of it for the pages of books. I am happily enrolled here as a student...so good night, and goodluck to both of you. I'll be seeing you in the latter part of August or September.*

*Sincerely, Jesse Stuart*

September 16, 1936. A letter to his Peabody College teacher, Alfred Leland Crabb, one of the most successful historical novelists in Tennessee literary history:

*...Autumn is coming on and there is poetry in the moods of autumn—her leaves flying to the earth and the wind blowing. I wish sometimes I had the time to write and write and write. Yet, I'm lost without school work and the endless flowing river of youth to that far-off sea of destiny.*

Jesse's description of the devastating 1937 Ohio River flood is included in a letter to Dr. Crabb, dated February 9 of that year. It's an example of Jesse's ability to capture the human moment and shape it into a story, his deep respect for the power and beauty of nature, and his vision of an unimpeachable moral authority for soil and water conservation. He's returning home from a speaking engagement in Tennessee:

*Had a good house and had excellent reception. Went to bed at twelve o'clock and got up at two-thirty—slept right through Nashville and woke up in Bowling Green, Kentucky. Was pretty well tired out. Got to South Portsmouth, Kentucky at eight o'clock and had to walk four miles and carry a heavy suitcase through a blinding rain storm. I walked it in less than forty minutes and was wet with rain and sweat mixed. I got home before they got in bed. Never made me sick. Got up the next morning feeling like a two-year-old. But the rising water! We are afraid of Old Man River here. He threatens—growls—barks and often cools down. But this time he kept on coming.*

*Tuesday morning we were wading water across the slough in front of King's house....Wednesday morning we had to cross in high-boots and Thursday by boat. The last busses that left McKell High School that Thursday had to cross over—plow through eight inches of water two places on the highways. Friday no school—certainly not for the highways were covered. We still didn't think it would reach the 1913 mark of 67' 10". But the river kept coming and Saturday it was up the steps* [of] *this house. Sunday it was in—we had to barge the cattle and the horses out—the hogs—ten big brood sows—about thirty chickens drowned—and we rowed boats through the maple tops—some sixty and seventy feet high to McKell School building where we lived for nine days I believe. I kept no account of time. It was a question of food. We joined other families in the schoolhouse. Water was everyway and not a drop to drink—ah, a little of good water in the furnace boiler pumped before the flood.*

*There has never been anything like it here. I brought coal oil from a tank. We had an oil stove. Once I crossed sixty feet of water with four drunk hyenas. Didn't know they were drunk until I was in the boat with them and out over the deep water. I was scared and still am when I think of it. They got into a row over the oars. I made it safely. One fell in the river going back but they pulled him to safety with a boat half filled with water. Garter snakes climbed to the tops of the trees. I caught a dozen—put them in all my pockets and saved them. You know I love a snake—it is such primitive form of life. At Greenup, Kentucky—I believe the hardest hit town along the river for it's just not there anymore—areoplanes dropped food to the people. Negroes and whites lived in homes together and ate together. For the first time ever in the history of our family—we had to take Red Cross coffee and sugar. Otherwise we had supplies for six months in advance my mother told me when I finally got home. There wasn't a store in Greenup left—we the people of the hill country had to get supplies from the Red Cross too. I slept on a cafeteria table amid the snores and guttural sounds—enjoyed my bed above the raging waters—no radio—no newspaper—nothing— seventeen days and no mail going or coming—lost the track of time. When the waters went down—away went county roads, fills, hillsides, railroad fills—our mail is routed through Ohio now—and we don't know when we can start school. I went finally—went around through the back of the county—Sandy was backed up for twenty-two miles or more and Tygart sixteen or more—walked about seven miles after I'd gone far as I could in a car. My home looked so good to me. Up among the hills and the pines away from the flood. Mom was so uneasy—no communications at all. I started the old job at home. Fed fourteen or fifteen head of cattle—two mules—seven hogs—got stove wood and water—did the work at the house and wrote a story or two.*

*Always, Jesse Stuart*

*P.S. The only cure for these floods is to put the trees back on the hills. No dams can hold such a river as we had. It fixed the dams. Man cannot tamper with nature too much. The Master has devised a great Universe and we have done too damned much meddling.*

Jesse's voice from the bunkhouse in W-Hollow was being heard across the moats protecting the literary castles. Lincoln Memorial University and Vanderbilt University had had contrasting hands in shaping the emerging genius of Jesse Stuart, but the elements that mattered most lay in his Highland heart. Robert Penn Warren would say it perfectly in his novel *Flood*: "There is no country but the heart."

Jesse's heart was working furiously to assure his destiny, his rightful place in the literature of Kentucky.

*Sir:*

*I am a farmer singing at the plow*
*And as I take my time to plow along*
*A steep Kentucky hill, I sing my song—*
*A one-horse farmer singing at the plow!....*
*I do not sing the songs you love to hear;*
*My basket songs are woven from the words*
*Of corn and crickets, trees and men and birds.*
*I sing the strains I know and love to sing.*
*And I can sing my lays like singing corn,*
*And flute them like a fluting gray corn-bird;*
*And I can pipe them like a hunter's horn—*
*All of my life these are the songs I've heard.*

> *And these crude strains no critic can call art,*
> *Yours very respectively, Jesse Stuart.*
>
> *Sonnet 1*
> *Man with a Bull-Tongue Plow*

In this sonnet can be seen one of Jesse's main characteristics — unadorned, blunt, rustic directness. It must have captured the attention and imagination of the John Simon Guggenheim Foundation's fellowship selection committee when, two years after the publication of *Man with a Bull-Tongue Plow*, Jesse's proposal arrived on their table in New York City.

*Dear Guggenheim Foundation:*

> *This is the first time I have ever asked for a scholarship of any sort....All of my life I have done things myself and made my own way....Now, I am going to Scotland if I have to work my way over on a cattle boat....Scotland holds some things for me that I want. My people are Scotch—the Stuarts—and we have been in the mountains of Kentucky and Virginia a long time....At the present I have thirty-five hundred unpublished poems. I don't know how many unpublished stories and manuscripts I have—but six or seven manuscripts. I want to do better work and not more of it. That is why I want to leave school teaching of a winter and farming during the summer. I want to get away—go to Scotland where I can get the background for a long novel I intend to do....Listen, if I get the scholarship I'll work....What I want is time, and I want this time in Scotland. I am hell-bent on going to Scotland to do it....I know this letter is jumbled up and I've said things I shouldn't have said in this application. But they are true. There is no need to pussyfoot about the truth. I say again, I'll try not to make a failure if I get the scholarship.*

He got the scholarship!

In late March of 1937, the Guggenheim selection committee informed the thirty-year-old "hillbilly" from Greenup County, Kentucky, that he would receive one of its sixty-one treasured fellowships. Jesse was beside himself with joy. He couldn't have been happier if he had received a personally signed copy of Bobby Burns's "Tam o' Shanter."

On July 9, 1937, Jesse boarded the ship *Samaria* in New York harbor, and he was soon outbound to Scotland. It would be difficult to overestimate the importance of this part of Jesse Stuart's career—not Vanderbilt, not Lincoln Memorial University, not even cool, clear Cedar Riffles could equal the immediate and lasting impact of the Guggenheim Fellowship in 1938—the year Pearl Buck won the Nobel Prize for Literature, the year Thomas Wolfe died at the age of thirty-eight, the same year Jesse Stuart's rising star was outbound on a wave of widening renown.

Jesse's "ship had come in," as the old-time landlocked were often heard to say. The expression was taken to mean huge treasure, relief from paying off mortgages, and freedom from eating cold fixings. For Jesse it meant $2,000, a storehouse of heritage, and a new opportunity to connect with the homeland of his hero, Bobby. It also meant new pressures on a beating heart that may have been flawed since birth.

Nine days after leaving America, the *Samaria* anchored in the river Clyde. Jesse cleared customs and immigration at Greenock, then boarded the train for Glasgow. He was a thirty-one-year-old tramp abroad with the irreverence of a Mark Twain. Jesse was eager to make the most of what the industrialist patrons-of-the-arts family of John Simon Guggenheim had bequeathed first to Aaron Copland in 1925, and twelve years later to Jesse Stuart.

He kept up his correspondence with Naomi Deane Norris, the teacher, who clearly by now was staking a claim to his heart.

> *Dear Dean* [Jesse's spelling was frequently inconsistent]: *Am in the Atlantic going from New York to Boston, Mass. Then to Scotland, Ireland, and England. The people on board are English, Irish, Scotch....Just a table-land of water before us and a star in the distance meeting the water. A fine trip.*
>
> *Good luck, Jesse Stuart*

> *Have drifted from north of Scotland down to Edinburgh where I expect to stay the winter. Had a good trip over. Scotland is one of the prettiest countries I've ever seen. I wish you could see the rivers, white stone houses, green fields, snow-capped hills, heather and the sheep.*
>
> *Always, Jesse Stuart*

Jesse treasured his mentors, those who challenged him and with whom he was able to establish a permanent relationship. Professor Alfred Leland Crabb at Peabody Teachers College became one of his most trusted friends.

*Sept. 4th, 1937*

*Dr. Crabb*
*Peabody College*
*Nashville, Tenn.*

*Dear Dr. Crabb:*

*I have just completed a tour of England, Wales and Scotland. I have covered about fifteen hundred miles on this tour. I'm getting a little tired out and all my shirts are dirty—eleven of them and the twelfth on my back is getting very dirty. Tomorrow I get back to my little room in Edinburgh.*

*It would take so long to tell you all I've seen on this trip—London, Canterbury, Oxford, Chester, England...Rhyl, Wales—then Windermere, England, the district of the lake poets—then back to Scotland again in the Burns Country. There is too much to be said about the Burns country. I'll perhaps say it in a different way when I can get out of this terrible emotion and write sanely. But all of my life I've wanted to see the Burns country. Now I've seen it. I'm within a few minutes walk of the old Kirkyard* [churchyard] *that holds his immortal dust!*

*How is our dear old America—the great expanse of land with skies drifting above—a land with good coffee and good cigars—with women who know how to dress! I have a time to hold myself down and keep the steam from escaping. Good old Kentucky and Tennessee. When I get back to America after first seeing the Kentucky hills, I'm packing my suitcases and coming to Nashville. I'm going to ride a big steel train over a long haul—hear the moan of the whistle fly over the empty land—see the dark trees etched against the winter sky if it is winter then...if it is summer I shall see the great green hills and see the flash of automobile lights on the highways—ah, old America is my home and if I do have to say it (and unashamed too) I'm an American product—just as much*

*American as the Indian maze* [maize] *corn that grows from her earth. I may have (do have) Scotch blood in my veins but damned if I can understand the highland Scotch. I like them for they are a sturdy and wonderful group of people but they don't speak English or I don't one. It is an evident fact there's a break someplace in the language. And as for the Scottish lasses that's my secret! ----!*

*I'll see you in America when the roses bloom again—maybe when the leaves start tumbling down again...at least I'll see you and make you unload the weight of humanity from your back.*

*Always, Jesse Stuart*

On September 10, 1937, Jesse wrote home to Naomi from 8 Viewforth Gardens, Edinburgh:

*Dear Dean Norris:*

*Tonight I'm sitting before my fire and writing this letter. A fire is man's best friend here now. My face is chapped red after coming back from south England, Wales and the west coast of Scotland. Edinburgh winters are hard they say. At least when the mists have cleared away, from my windows I can see the sea. Mountains extend up from the sea. Among these mountains where thousands of sheep feed, I've heard the bagpipes play. I can hear a bagpipe most anytime.*

*I'm sending you a couple of pictures. One is a picture of Robert Burns' statue inside his monument. It is the angel Death with a shelter for him. He has one hand on the plow, cap in other hand and he turns and faces the inevitable—either the morning or nothingness. The other is of myself in my new tailored plus-fours. My fire is burning a little low but the red glow of the embers is very pretty in this semi-dark little room.*

*Goodnight, Jesse Stuart*

*September 27, 1937*
*Dear Deane:*

*I think you are a mighty prompt person to send a box of cigars so soon. Thanks with all my heart despite the fact they charged me $5.43 duty on them at the customs. Did you ever hear of such*

*thing!...When it was delivered one man certainly heard some
swearing from an American and these words included: 'I don't mind
so much being held-up at the point of gun and robbed at night, but
being robbed in broad open daylight by the British Government is
ridiculous!'*

*In two more weeks I go to Denmark—I don't know where from
there. I'd be gone now but my book* [Beyond Dark Hills] *has me tied
down and the second installment of my Guggenheim money isn't
ready until October 10th. I'm very close on money now. However,
today I managed to see the Russian Ballet at the King's Cinema.
I have two pictures in my room. Yours and Bobbie Burns's—both on
the mantle. You don't mind to be beside the greatest poet that
Scotland has ever produced do you—a scoundrel in his day (some
thought and still think) but lives on through the years. My goodnight
kiss to you so far away—to you so reserved, so tall and handsome
and wonderful.*

*Always, Jesse Stuart*

In a letter to his boyhood friend and high school senior classmate back
in Greenup County, Judge Oscar Sammons, Jesse hinted that he was having
what might be called one last holiday fling:

*"There's a little Dane waiting down in London for Poppie
Christmastime! But afraid she'll have to shed her tears and wait.
She speaks English slightly—yet Poppie and she manage to convey
their thoughts to one another—at least they did crossing the North
Sea to her native Denmark!....Mum is the word on all transgressions
of the flesh and spirit."*

*November 4, 1937*
*Dear Deane:*

*I'm tired out—tired—tired—tired. Ten foreign countries on this trip.
Believe me I'm tired Deane. I have seen a lot....Back to my little room,
my fire, my Victrola. My fire right now is a dandy! Oh yes—have just
done a story you'd rack your ribs laughing at. It's called Sweet
Heaven. Think I'll send it to* Esquire.

*Goodnight, Jesse Stuart*

*November 14, 1937*
*Dear Deane:*

*If we were in England's geographic position we'd be in war in less than a month. The Americans would start one. I don't think they'd ever back-track or give in after they once said a thing. I feel for these poor people here—peace loving people—but steadily the ammunitions plants hum and millions of gas masks are being turned out—anti-aircraft guns are being mounted on tops of the houses. This city was frightfully bombed in the last war—and right in this section where I am—from my window I can see the sea. These people can see no future like we can in America. You know—another crop of men—and almost sure another war—But Great Britain will be prepared next time. She'll not be caught napping like in 1914. That's why they're staying out long as possible....Deane, this trip has been wonderful. It's been grand for me. All told I've been in eleven foreign countries and fourteen American states since last June....Goodnight to you Deane—I'd like to send you a picture of my little fireplace and room. I eat, sleep and work in this room. It is my home. When I'm away I get homesick to come back to it.*

*Always, Jesse Stuart*

*December 1, 1937*

*Deane, you asked me once when I was coming home. "I don't know," is my answer and when I do come home I'm off to California and South America if I have any money....This trip has changed me some. It has made me love my hills and people more. I'll have a time getting adjusted to that swift pace when I come home and getting filled up on steak and smoking good American cigars. I never felt better in my life—I weigh 207 pounds and you should see the color in my face.*

*December 10, 1937*

*I hope you will forgive this hazy letter. I'm a sick man. Keep this under your bonnet. I don't want it to get home. All this week I've been housed in. My face looks like it's been beaten. Dark circles are under my eyes. It's the old enemy—a terrible cold—which scares me to death ever since that T.B. test took on me 2+—the highest of*

*anybody at McKell except a couple of my students—one dead now—
the other was flat of her back for a rest cure. She was beautiful and
looked healthy—looked to be the strongest girl in school and was
voted the prettiest....So I'll close. My thought is inconsistent. My
head is going around in whirls. Just eat a piece of steak for me. I
can't ask you to smoke a cigar since you don't like the smoke of the
luscious weed!*

*Always, Jesse Stuart*

*P.S. Highways are blocked here and the snow still falling.*

While Jesse was writing regularly to Naomi Deane, he was honest
enough not to be carelessly using the word "love." His sowing of wild oats
was discreet, but he revealed in a letter to his steadfast friend Oscar
Sammons that he was "deeply interested" in a woman in Scotland.

*Jan. 10th 1938*
*8-Viewforth Gardens*
*Edinburgh, Scotland*

*Dear Oscar:*

*Let me tell you and this is straight. You may have a gallery of my
girls' pictures. But you don't have one's picture. You please hold this,
but I'm deeply interested in a Scottish girl. She is the only child. She
lives on a farm in Dunbar, Scotland. Her father is a Scottish Army
captain—has been—he's retired now. They have a big farm and a
thousand head of sheep. She is in the university here in Edinburgh.
Yes, her work is that of medicine. She's delivered plenty of babies,
not of her own but other women's. I'm deeply interested. She's very
pretty—large—blue-eyed—hair about the color of Deane's. She's 25.
Brother, she's physically attractive too. She climbs these mountains
right by my side. She can walk down most men. Her name is Hope.
Now this is not bull. This is straight. Please don't turn this loose. I
shall warn Deane if I go ahead. If not, she'll never know it.
Charlotte, you remember her, I think is pretty well engaged. She
wrote me that anyway. I think as much of her as any girl in
America—-the other one there you'd be surprised and you perhaps
will never know. But I shall marry and that shortly before the best of*

*my years slip by. Some energetic woman could appreciate what I
have been and what I am still. Why fiddle with the wind?...Scotland
may eventually be my home....I've had one grand time in Scotland. So
much I hate to leave.*

In a letter dated March 19, 1938, to Lena Wells Voiers:

*Yes I need a wife. But always something happens. These women
over here appreciate their men more than the American women. You
see men are scarce here. I'm sending you pictures of my Danish girl.
I think one hell of a lot of [her].... She lives in Copenhagen,
Denmark and the North Sea is not too wide for me to cross and see
her. When she was in London I went down twice to see her in one
month. 400 miles down there (distances one month 1600 miles to see
a girl). She is the type of woman of whom you speak and she is a
woman, husky, sensible and definitely appeals to me. I like big
women and when I marry, it is better I marry this type. The
American male seems to want a neat doll type of woman. Not so for
me when I marry. I want a big, strong, healthy woman. I've gone
only with two small women....You can see that [the Danish woman]
is a better model than the angel above her in Queen Victoria's statue
in front of Buckingham Palace in London. The one of her alone was
taken in St. James Park in London. She would really make a wife.
You should see her in person. Men usually look at her twice. As it is
many admire me, but few would have me. I'm not worried a great
deal about it but I tell you honestly and frankly I do think a lot of
this Danish girl. She speaks fairly good English, and German,
Swedish, and Norwegian as well. She likes the old man too and
plenty. If another girl looks at me she wants to break her up and
dash her in a mudhole. She's instinctively jealous and hates doll-
types of women.*

Curiously, Jesse seems to have wearied quickly of extended study of
Robert Burns and the Scottish "homeland." Beyond the British Isles and
Ireland, he stretched his itinerary and managed to visit twenty-five
European countries—Albania, Austria, Belgium, Bulgaria, Czechoslovakia,
Denmark, East Prussia, Estonia, Finland, France, Germany, Greece,

Hungary, Italy, Latvia, Lithuania, Luxembourg, Macedonia, Netherlands, Norway, Poland, Sweden, Switzerland, Turkey, and Yugoslavia—not part of the original proposal to the Guggenheim Foundation.

Jesse used his rail pass to his best advantage. He wrote travelogue newspaper columns for the folks back home in Greenup County, but he was deeply troubled by the rise of fascism and the German government's persecution of Jews. Jesse expressed his profound concern for the United States.

Possibly the most telling photograph of Jesse during the entire excursion is one taken of him posing in the doorway of Bobby Burns's birthplace. Jesse had somehow come upon the resources to buy, borrow, or rent plus fours (at least for purposes of the picture), argyle sweater and socks, wool suit, white shirt, and nicely knotted tie. Hands thrust into his pockets, smile impishly beaming on his face, Jesse completely fills the doorway. The costuming, as puzzling as it is almost painfully comical, speaks to Jesse's sense of humor.

After Jesse's return to the United States aboard the *Conte di Savoia*, he found he had lost the teaching job that had been promised to him upon his return. The new Greenup superintendent of schools refused to honor Jesse's leave of absence for the Guggenheim. Temporarily he crossed the Ohio River, to Portsmouth High School, to teach remedial English there.

One of Jesse's students at Portsmouth, Robert Lee Tucker, remembered in the January 1964 issue of *The Education Forum*—

> *Jesse Stuart could walk into a classroom and sense, in a literal way, where the shyest flowers were waiting for the light. In and out among the desks he prowled, snatching up our writings. Nothing in the class was sacred except Truth....Stuart believed, we quickly discovered, that complete and perfect self-expression was more to be desired than rubies and pearls. He believed with Twain that the difference between the right word and the almost right word was the difference between the lightning and the lightning bug.*

Jesse also accepted briefly the editorship of a small GOP newspaper, the *Greenup County Citizen*, which had carried his "With Jesse Stuart

Abroad" column after *The Greenup News* cancelled his "Fragments from Nothing" column. It also had given Jesse an outlet for descriptions and reflections about his European travels. Jesse's undying allegiance to the Republican Party — strong and heady as a hungry bull elephant in search of a juicy Democrat donkey — was a neat fit and coup for the *Greenup County Citizen.*

In his first editorial, Jesse described Congressman Joe Bates, a Democrat, as being "as alien as Cyclop's eye to native-born Greenup Countians...a man with a backbone like a jelly-fish." If Jesse had stopped there, he might have saved himself a whole lot of headache. But he had just returned from his tour of Europe, where Hitler was conquering the continent, and Jesse unleashed a vitriolic attack on Congressman Bates:

> *Down with this little Dictator who has not the speech delivery of a cold-eyed Hitler, nor the physical tempo of a Mussolini, nor (not quite yet) the 95 percent of the vote of the people like Dictator Stalin of Russia.*

Jesse's laying-it-on-thick editorial led to a bloody incident the following morning that made national news. The November 7, 1938, issue of *Time* magazine reported: "Stuart was having a milk-shake in Leslie's Drugstore" in Greenup when a local constable walked up, berated him for the editorial he'd written, and then, according to Jesse, proceeded to hit him over the head three times with a blackjack.

Jesse grappled on the floor with the constable, and spectators had to separate the two men. Bleeding profusely, Jesse was taken to the hospital in Ironton, Ohio. In his second editorial, Jesse wrote:

> *The blood I shed from the three wounds was more than a quart....For every drop I shed—yes, for every red, sticky drop—I shall write 10,000 words in ink exposing this "gang" work in Greenup County.*

The cover of *Time* carried a picture of swashbuckling André Malraux and the cutline "Out of bloody legends, golden legends come." The story about Malraux, the French novelist and adventurer, appeared in the book section just above the account of Jesse and his bloody blackjacking. The publicity and the growing popularity of the young man from W-Hollow could not have been more happily assisted. The pictures showing the dark frowns of Malraux and Stuart were publishing houses' wildest dreams come true.

Bloodied, but suddenly golden, the man from W-Hollow was a legend that had taken wing. He soared. It may even have caused a few at Vanderbilt to sit up and take notice. The previous month, Jesse's *Beyond Dark Hills* had been published, an edited version of the term paper he'd written as a graduate student at Vanderbilt. He had not gotten the piece of parchment that said "Master's Degree;" he had not won the favor of the "Agrarians" on the other side of 21st Street in Nashville, but he had been to Scotland on a Guggenheim Fellowship, and he had made up his mind to come home to the Highlands of Kentucky.

> *I know I do not need a Ph.D.*
> *To throw the fodder over to the cows*
> *And to interpret wind in the pine tree*
> *And to sit by and watch the cattle browse.*
> *Degrees are things to have on parlor walls,*
> *This written scroll that shows what one can do.*
> *Degrees would make good bedding for cow stalls;*
> *They surely would be enriched fertilizer.*
> *Oh, it is strange how people run a bluff*
> *And put themselves above the things they are.*
> *Some look upon unlettered men with scoff,*
> *These chosen intellectuals striving for*
> *To drop ten pole-beans down a craw-dad hole*
> *And give to charity—God bless their souls!*
>
> *Sonnet 690*
> *Man with a Bull-Tongue Plow*

Jesse's country was his heart and his heart was his country.

He soon left the classrooms and their politically driven administrative offices, left the minimally paying small-town journalism employment, and returned to W-Hollow to farm and to write. At the same time, he embarked upon a career of public speaking. Jesse's passion as writer, lecturer, and farmer had begun. But even though he would invest all his energy, his life was still incomplete—he needed a helpmeet.

# NAOMI DEANE NORRIS

*A man can't go his own free way all his days.*
*Comes a day when he has to divide himself up*
*and give part of his time and his ways to somebody else,*
*and to things that count for two people*
*and maybe more.*

Janice Holt Giles
*The Kentuckians*

*Love and Kisses!*

So many hellos, so many goodbyes, so many promises, so many dreams—Jesse Stuart was like a man seated at a banquet table—fork in one hand, knife in the other—life on a plate in the middle.

When Jesse returned from his Guggenheim excursion, he was an unmarried thirty-one-year-old. In no uncertain terms, his mother told him that it was time for him to begin a home of his own. He'd had his share of female friendships and flirtations, practicing well the age-old art of kissing and not telling, but there was no evidence that he was either playboy or wanton womanizer. In any event, the encounters with the ladies from Scotland and Denmark faded with the sunsets over Land's End.

A handsome man with national and international acclaim, Jesse knew his mother was right, and he set out to do something about it.

Her name was Naomi Deane Norris, eldest daughter of Emmett and Gladys Spence Norris. Jesse and Naomi had known each other since they were teenagers, they had corresponded when he was away at Lincoln Memorial and Vanderbilt and in Scotland, but now it was time for matters of the heart to take a more serious beat.

Naomi Deane was born April 16, 1908. She spent her childhood in the area of the Crane and Lost Creek tributaries of Little Sandy River near the Greenup-Carter County line, down where the Eastern Kentucky Railroad tunnels used to hum at Hopewell and Hunnewell but now sleep silently in obscurity. After her family moved to Greenup, Naomi first met Jesse in high school. She graduated in 1928 while he was at Lincoln Memorial. In the summers she studied for her teacher's degree at Morehead State College, and winters she taught school in Greenup County. In 1938 she earned her degree, fulfilling her promise to herself that she'd not marry until she had graduated from college.

As for Jesse, he now had no regular paycheck and possessed only the debatable distinction of returning with a gaggle of sheep bells from his Guggenheim adventure—one of those all-bishop's-crook and no-sheep situations. Adding insult to injury, some unidentified muse told him to borrow $3,800 to buy three hundred acres of "rough land" and two hundred sheep. It would be hard to say which was the worse part of it—the land or the sheep.

The adventure added up to two hundred burr-infested fleeces to shear, the possibility of four hundred lambs to try to save on the coldest nights of the year, approximately six hundred filthy hind ends to "tag," and eight hundred feet to trim for foot rot. Then there were the castrations and coping with the blood-thirsty dogs that love to kill for the sport of it. The muse hadn't warned Jesse that sheep stay awake at night thinking up new ways to die.

Naomi's startled reaction made plenty of good sense: "Why, Jesse, do you mean you're going to quit teaching? You have trained yourself for that profession. You have always said that teaching is the greatest profession in the world."

"That's right," said the wounded wight from W-Hollow.

*It is the greatest profession in the world. But look how it's treated me. Six years ago when I was superintendent of the county schools we talked about getting married, but we couldn't because we weren't making enough money. Since then I've been principal of a high school for four years and taught in one of the best schools in Ohio, and still even with your salary teaching second grade we haven't made enough money together to get married. I've quit teaching and gone into the sheep business. I haven't left the teaching profession; it's left me.*

*Mr. Gallion's School*

On July 19, 1939, Jesse "the shepherd" wrote to his friend Virgil Leon Sturgill, a high school teacher and fellow poet: "I'm buying wire, making fence and having sprouts cut: therefore, I need money. I'm sending out stories and they are not catching just right." Jesse's first novel, *Trees of Heaven*, needed realism.

There's a staged picture of Jesse standing on an ancient boulder, hand-feeding salt to a sorry collection of sheep, but there's no record of how they got to market, or how much money ever actually changed hands. He may have lost a bundle, and the bankers may have nervously chortled all the way to the "maa-maa" pen. This was one of those woe-is-me, wool-gathering times for Jesse. He'd been blackjacked for writing a bad-tempered newspaper editorial, and there were some Greenup Countians who resented what they believed was his gross stereotyping of people they personally knew in his autobiography *Beyond Dark Hills*.

Jesse wrote to Dr. Crabb on November 14, 1938:

*Things are looking better up here. Yesterday I was in Greenup—went unarmed—laughed and talked with old friends. The Congressman I fought was elected. Why not when the district of 20 counties has a Democratic majority of 16,000 votes? Yet, our school board was elected—only two members run this time—three in 1940. Our men were elected by excellent majorities.*

*My fight now is to sell a story or to sell two stories. A year in Europe put me behind. I'm just trying to build back and get on my feet again. I've got some awful rotten, ragged stories on the road and I have a few crack stories out.*

*I must close this letter. I want to take a walk through the woods. The rain has fallen and water is dripping from the bare branches of the oaks and I love to watch it.*

*Sincerely, Jesse Stuart*

113

Some might have figured that Jesse had become a "mite teched," but he was just moon-eyed about Naomi Deane Norris.

In the autumn of 1938, Jesse and Naomi began their serious courting, and one year later they were secretly married in Ashland at 12:25 a.m., October 14, 1939, which was a Saturday. The vows were exchanged as soon as possible after midnight because the newlyweds didn't want to press their luck by exchanging vows on Friday the thirteenth. Reason for the abruptness of Jesse and Naomi's decision to marry is unclear.

On their first day of marriage (they kept their secret for a month or more), Naomi returned home to her unsuspecting parents, and Jesse went back to a solitary room in Greenup. By this time he had written four major books in four different genres—

> *Next morning I was back writing on my* Trees of Heaven [Jesse's first novel] *which I finished October 22nd. In 75 days I had written 143,000 words. We continued dating at Naomi's home for I was hard pressed on this book. When I finished, I borrowed $100, rode tourist class sitting up all night on my way to New York....*

> The Peabody Reflector
> Spring, 1972

Take a seat on the *George Washington*...

"All a'booorrrd!"...The conductor making one last wipe of the hand rails, as Jesse would describe it, "So the ladies wouldn't soil their white gloves"...wave goodbye to Naomi standing on the platform at the depot in Ashland...light up a cigar in the smoking car...might just have brogans touched up with a quickie shine so as to flip a coin in the air to be caught by a grinning face...talk with the sheep buyers for the eastern market, telling them what they already knew—that there's nothing quite as fine as the Southdown ram/western ewe cross...the theatergoers taking their seats on plush, velvety upholstery in the Imperial Salon cars...breakfast in the diner with the table perfectly linen-clothed—tomato juice, coffee, whole wheat toast, two eggs over light, bacon, jam and biscuits.

Politicians push back, clear their throats and count their votes...the noisy, smarmy Judeo-Christian microcosm of America...feeling and seeing from the observation car the miles roll by through the West Virginia night, the Virginia sunrise and early morning fog...Washington D.C.—far beyond dark hills—the horn of old #21 sounding "like a cow bawling at milking time"...on up the eastern seaboard to Grand Central Station in New York City!

> *On the following morning after my arrival in New York City, I called Elliott Beach McRae* [president] *at E.P. Dutton and told him what I had brought to town. He told me to bring the manuscript over to the house. I walked over to E.P. Dutton and Company. I gave the* Trees of Heaven *to Louise Townsend Nichols....On the third day my phone rang* [at the YMCA].
> *"You've done it, you've done it," Miss Nichols said. "I think Mr. McRae wants to speak to you."*
> *"Come over to the publishing house," he said. "We've got a contract and a forward waiting for you."*

The advance money was a check for $250.

> *Money was not plentiful in 1939. But money had great value in 1939. And I paced that afternoon and got the afternoon train for Washington, D.C. I was at home next morning at eleven.*
>
> The Peabody Reflector
> Spring, 1972

Jesse was big, boisterous, and beset with a desire to write, no matter the consequences. He was as tough as a terrapin's shell—but underneath he was tender and caring.

And that's what Naomi Deane saw in him. She believed in him, and she was ready to dedicate her life to him. For that reason the book you're now reading is dedicated to her.

Jesse Stuart's marriage to Naomi Deane Norris helped him make an important turn toward improved behavior. He loved her with a passion that was explosive, yet sweet with unwavering loyalty. Once he decided to marry, there'd be no other romance. Her devotion to him was total. The time had come for absolute seriousness of purpose. Events were moving quickly, and young lovers were caught in a cataclysmic tide of romance and realism.

November 1939: storm clouds of war were moving closer to America. Germany occupied Bohemia and Moravia, Japan occupied Hainan, and Italy invaded Albania. For Jesse, the changing of the warring decades would be a time of earnest struggle for a young writer trying to reach an audience. He and Naomi cherished their secret marriage. She lived at home while Jesse continued to live in a rented room in Greenup. On November 16, 1939, Naomi finally told her parents of her marriage. They were simply outraged. Jesse would have to prove himself, and eventually he would, but for now he was a Stuart, and Naomi's marriage to one of "them" was a union the Norrises could hardly bear, apparently a case of cross-family distrust and prejudices, real or imagined. Naomi asked permission for Jesse to move temporarily into the Norris home. Naomi's father reluctantly agreed. The arrangement was awkward and tense. As soon as possible, the newlyweds were eager to move into the temporary "bunkhouse" at W-Hollow.

They looked again at the structure that would become their permanent home. Built in 1845 with yellow poplar logs and located at the mouth of Shinglemill Hollow it was called the "Old Chapman House." Many families, including the Stuarts, had lived there, but by the time of Jesse and Naomi's marriage it had become more barn than house. It sat forlornly waiting to be restored. That would take more time, increased speaker's fees, and anticipated book royalties.

James Stuart later remembered:

> *Cattle had been kept in the rear part and hay in the front and upstairs; the dog trot and log kitchen had been torn away. Jesse said he guessed he would tear the old house down. Naomi said, "No, Jesse, this is going to be our home."*
>
> *Unpublished manuscript*

Between 1940 and 1980, Jesse and Naomi added on to the house five times. The creek out to Shinglemill Hollow got in the way, so they built over top of it. Today, the water can be heard gurgling underneath the house.

*Dec. 4, 1939*
*Dear Roland:*
 *From Hiwassee College you wrote one of the finest letters you ever did in your life....You wrote Naomi Deane and me*

*congratulating us on our marriage....You asked me if we'd live on a*
*farm where my springs would feed me. You bet we have.*

As Jesse and Naomi were preparing to establish their permanent residence at W-Hollow, a letter arrived from Professor Crabb:

*I am glad you are going to live in W-Hollow, or thereabouts. If you*
*moved away your particular genius would likely wither. It requires*
*W-Hollow in which most appropriately to flower. There couldn't be*
*any blooms in New York City. Stay there and walk in the old paths.*
*Spend more and more time in describing the beauty of the people*
*and the place, and more and more time realizing that the ugliness of*
*the people and the place is necessary to accent the beauty.*

Through correspondence, Jesse and Naomi stayed in abiding touch with Professor and Mrs. Crabb.

The decade of the forties was the beginning of Jesse Stuart's nationwide lecture tours from New York City to California, while in the same period he was publishing *Trees of Heaven* (1940), writing a collection of short stories, *Men of the Mountains* (1941), and the hugely popular *Taps for Private Tussie* (1943).

*Taps* is the satiric story of welfare recipients in the mountains, a tale larded with raucous shenanigans and a relentless account of human orneriness. While many readers have relished the humor as a darker kind of *Beverly Hillbillies*, the underlying motivation for the parody was scorn of governmental social programs, primarily those of Roosevelt's New Deal.

Sales of *Taps for Private Tussie* possibly topped one-million copies and it was a Book-of-the-Month Club selection in 1943. Illustrations by Thomas Hart Benton in that edition were an additional factor in the book's remarkable success. It received the Thomas Jefferson Southern Award for the best Southern book of that year. Metro-Goldwyn-Mayer paid $50,000 for screen rights for *Taps*, but it's not clear how much of the money went to Jesse. It was never made into a movie perhaps because of pressure from the Pentagon, which claimed that such a mis-identification of a serviceman, as portrayed by Jesse, could not have happened.

*Taps for Private Tussie* led to rumors that Jesse and Naomi had become very wealthy, and that was partially true. They used the money to travel and to invest in more W-Hollow acres.

Wherever he roamed Jesse constantly worked on his manuscripts, sometimes several books at the same time—*Album of Destiny* and *Mongrel Mettle* (1944), *Foretaste of Glory* and *Tales from the Plum Grove Hills* (1946).

Jesse regarded *Album of Destiny* as one of his best volumes of verse, but this poetry, which had been praised by Robert Penn Warren and others, was not nearly as popular as *Taps for Private Tussie*. Jesse wanted to be remembered as a poet, but his fame at this time resulted from the short stories and novels that produced laughter.

Jesse was a compulsive letter writer, writing thousands in the span of a single year. Many of them were to Naomi while he was away on lecture tours. The decade of the '40s was a time when telephones were a luxury for the few.

*Sunday*
*Feb. 25th 1940*
*Twenty-Third Street*
*Young Men's Christian Association*
*215 West 23rd Street*
*New York, N.Y.*

*To My Darling:*
   *....Nearly froze to death on the sleeper before I got to Pittsburgh.*
   *Gave my talk there—saw the folks and sold 14 or 15 books. Had to bring all that load on to New York with me—twenty-two or twenty three books. But this is the way of things, one never knows. Grove City, just a few miles from Slippery Rock wants me for a talk this summer. I asked $100 for the talk. If they give it, you and I go there this summer and we're coming back to Slippery Rock for a visit. You'll like this group. They are about our age, clean, healthy, normal human beings—*
   *Left Slippery Rock day before yesterday and got to New York yesterday morning. Visited Dutton's yesterday—Honey the book* [Trees of Heaven] *will be beautiful. It tells on the jacket—down at the end—in a brief sentence about our marriage. The pictures*

[Woodi] *Ishmael has done are wonderful. I'm going to be able to get part of the originals for us.*

*Last night Woodie, Gwyn* [Woodi's wife] *and I saw Edgar Lee Masters. He cussed and laughed a lot.*

*Honey this morning I've done two columns for Russell Times—eleven pages each—my hand is a little sore. Last night I dreamed of you—how I'm a part of you and you a part of me mentally, physically and spiritually. I'm so in love with you. I wonder about you every minute and think about you. How complete this trip would be if you were with me. Remember, I'm not going to make much unless something else happens. I can't tell yet for I've not seen anyone.*

*I don't speak at Town Hall thank goodness for the woman I was to pinch-hit for has returned. If I had talked I wouldn't have gotten paid for it. It would not have been broadcast either—But Tuesday night I speak at Columbia University. I dread it.*

*In a few minutes I'm going to Ishmael's apartment to eat with them. Tonight I visit Masters again—tomorrow, Colliers, Harpers and Annie Laura* [Williams, Jesse's movie agent].

*Deane, I love, love, love, you. I am lonely without you, so lonely— I long for you—I love you more than anything in this world. All my love to you.*

*Always Your Stuart*

In 1940 Edgar Lee Masters wrote a letter to Jesse, the mountain man he'd first met in New York, praising him after reading "New Ground" in *American Prefaces*:

*Genius is a bend in the creek where bright water has gathered, and which mirrors the trees, the sky, and the bank. It just does that because it is there and the scenery is there. Talent is a fine mirror with a silver frame, with the name of the owner engraved on the back.*

Masters, who died ten years after writing this letter, is best known as the author of the satirical *Spoon River Anthology* of 1915. Masters's admiration for Jesse Stuart when he was only thirty-four years old was like a wise old man carefully laying another honey locust log on a young man's fire already ablaze on the W-Hollow hearth.

Jesse's frequent trips to see his New York publisher, Dutton, led to the decision that there was a promising future for him on the lecture circuit. It's unclear whose idea it was first or who made the initial contact, but the William B. Feakins company accepted Jesse, and he quickly became a popular choice for colleges, universities, teachers' groups, book clubs, and civic organizations.

> *Feb. 26th 1940*
> *Twenty-Third Street*
> *Young Men's Christian Association*
> *215 West 23rd Street*
> *New York, N.Y.*

*Dear Deane:*

*I was never so surprised in my life today when Mr. Feakins asked me if I were ready to go to California. I have a talk there March 5th and soon as this Columbia talk is over, I shall go from here to Chicago—stop there for one day to visit* Esquire *magazine's staff— then on to California.*

*You know I didn't take enough clothes. I never dreamed of such— but I'll be home before April—long before April and that will give us the spring time there together. I'm pleased in a way to get the job over with. I just hate it that I didn't bring enough clothes.*

*Now for something else. My book* [Trees of Heaven] *has one fine chance selling to the movies. Keep this under your hat Honey (The one with the Blue Birds for luck.) I saw Annie Laurie today. She sold two books to movie companies last week. I eat with Annie Laurie and Mrs. Bowers* [Florence, one of Jesse's editors at Dutton] *tomorrow. The drawings Woodie Ishmael did are tops. I saw the illustrations today in the proofs. They are ready for the printer now and we'll get advanced copies of* Trees of Heaven *toward the last of next month. There are 340 pages in this novel. Deane it's going to make a swell looking book.*

*Mrs. Bowers told me tonight that a Paramount picture man was* *eating with us tomorrow and she said that was a good sign. She said it looked good to her. Annie Laurie is asking $25,000.00 for movie rights—and will not come down less than $20,000.00. Gee, Honey, can it happen? What if it does—look what it will mean! If it doesn't don't be too badly disappointed for I've done and am still doing my best.*

*Honey, stay sweet—don't forget me. Sleep on my side of the bed—I love you—I love, love, love you! You never leave my mind. My loyalty to you always—*

*Sincerely with love, Stuart*

Jesse's undying love affair with the railroad mesmerized him, gave him a sense of the power of the Twentieth Century Limited, caused him to smile about the time he hid in the toilet to try to evade the Chesapeake & Ohio conductor. Now Jesse was somebody, becoming somebody, heading westward across a new, exhilarating landscape.

*Feb. 29th 1940*

*My Deane:*

*I'm writing you this one before I get the train for Chicago. I'm taking a day coach—must be on it for 16 hours. In Chicago, I'll get a sleeper to California.*

*It is said that the newness of marriage wears off for both in six months or so. I don't believe it. For me it wears on. There is not a minute (unless it is when I'm giving a talk) I don't think of you, Deane. You know, I love you more than anyone in the world and I need you. I wish to God your Curley head was on my shoulder. It will always be your pillow. You know this is a trip I have to make— and I'm making it and getting through with the job.*

*Deane this means we'll spend April together in Kentucky—it is the month when I want to get in Kentucky. Lord what April this year will mean to me—I'll have my wife—my Deane—and April in Kentucky!*

Jesse uppy-jumps (one of his colloquialisms, meaning "lickety-split") whenever an idea occurs, and the letters home to Naomi often turn abruptly from love to publishing-world business—

*Deane,* Collier's *has lost the story "The Last Roundup." Get the*

*carbon copy out of the stack (you know where I keep them) and have*
*Blanch* [Cales, local stenographer] *type two more copies. Send a*
*copy (not the carbon) to*

> Colliers Magazine
> *250 Park Ave.*
> *New York City*

At times, Jesse's tone becomes direct and demanding:

*You check this story before it goes, put my name and address on a*
*return envelope, you know how I send them. I'm revising another*
*story on the train (Love Is Where You Find It) and I'll send it direct*
*to Blanch to type. You get it—hold one copy and send the others.*
*Send this story to the same place (to* Collier's*). Wilkerson* [a
Collier's acquisition editor] *asked for its return. He is holding* Ma's
Man, *the story I wrote in four hours—when you was so sick you*
*couldn't lift your curly head so very well. If it sells, Honey, it means*
*$500 for four hours work. Don't mention anything about it or about*
Trees of Heaven *either. Let them sell, if they sell and be surprises.*

*You and I may be able to get out on the hill in April. It depends on*
*the roads. Anyway, this will be my last trip without you. Hell, I'm*
*staying away from you. I'm taking you along with me unless it's in*
*the case of emergency. I'm happy with you—every minute is good*
*with you. I'll be back to you about March 20th—in about three*
*weeks—maybe a few days over if more talks develop.*

*It's good to hear your parents liked the cover for* Trees of Heaven.
*Honey, I must go. It's train time. My love, love, love, to you.*

> *Always, Jesse Stuart*

*P.S. I love you. I love you.*

Each mile, each letter to Naomi is bursting with newfound excitement—
Jesse Stuart is a one-man army of enthusiasm. He's thirty-four years old,
whirling across the continent with the bravado of that long ago day when the
Union Pacific met the Central Pacific at Promontory Point.

*March 2, 1940*
*My Darling:*
*I'm on the Pacific Limited—we'll get into California Tuesday*

*morning or Monday evening—I hope it is Monday at six for I'm
tired of riding.*

Jesse is watching his pennies, conserving every coin for the day he
might return to hard times. The Great Depression had left its scar, and it
would be a reminder that carefulness was a virtue:

*I'm riding on tourist rates to cut expenses and I'm not allowed
back in the observation car where I can hear a radio. I got back
there today and was chased out—not only that but escorted to my
seat in the tourist car by a cranky old white-moustached
conductor—the Devil!*

Jesse's mind is not only possessed by writing and selling his stories, his
thoughts are never far away from his beloved W-Hollow farmland and the
hunkered-down father he left behind. As for Naomi Deane—

*And you for God's sake—I want to hear from you and hear often. I
shall be writing often as I can to you. I dream of you, feel for
you....It is a terrible feeling to know that you are not with me. This is
my last trip without you. I have to make this trip or be a ruined man
and I'm getting it over with. It will open more engagements I hope—
and we both go!*

Jesse's obsession with self-marketing is as merciless as when he was
killing water moccasins along Cedar Riffles.

*Am sending you a story that I'm revising. You have Blanch to type
it and you check over it—send it to* Collier's. *"Love Is Where You
Have Found it." It is a silly* Collier's *story—nothing to it. But if sells
it sells and we can use the money.*

*Now to break a little good news to you, I sold three stories on my
trip to Chicago to Arnold Gingrich, Editor of* Esquire. *I have the
checks in my pocket. One "When The Hen Crows," the other two not
definitely decided yet, (train is rocking awful now). I think the other
two will be "The People's Choice" and either "Ox" or "Knot Holes
in the Planks." Gee but it's great to get six hundred dollars isn't it!
We'll make it, Deane. Be sure to keep this strictly to yourself about
the sale of these stories!*

*Honey, now don't forget on about March 14th probably later—look into my story stack—find "Bud" and if it's in a messy condition—have Blanch to type it—and you send it to...Esquire.*

*Be sure to send enclosed self-addressed envelope. You know the way I fix them. I believe he's going to take this story too! Hold it until he selects three from the stories he now holds—so he won't take "Bud" in for one of the three he paid me for. I'll be selling him four if he takes "Bud" on top of the stories he's already bought. I strengthened my relationships with him. I'm going to try to sell him these stories this year. Why not? We need furniture, we need many things.*

*Deane, Honey, you will have to work with me now—I see prospective story sales. I believe we've got a good chance to make a little money this year. Don't be disappointed if we don't.*

*Always. I love you, Stuart*

Jesse misses his Appalachian home and quickly feels the pinch of having to be concerned with such earthly matters as clean shirts, shoes needing repair, and trousers begging for creases.

*March 4, 1940*
*My dear Deane:*

*We are still crossing Nevada....This country is what I'd call a wasteland—just treeless mountains and hard rocks looking at you from sides.*

*I am getting so tired of riding and very very tired of this journey... I need to take some medicine for I haven't had any exercise since we started and I'm all out of commission.*

*I have to have rubber heels put on my shoes soon as I reach Sacramento and I have to have my clothes pressed. You know I didn't take many with me, and about all the shirts I brought with me are colored shirts. But I'll get along, someway. I've worn this old dark suit to preserve the other two.*

Jesse's arrival in California is not as desperate as the Joad family's in *Grapes of Wrath*, but the plowboy's fingernail hold on the handles of celebrity status creates its share of stress.

On the stationery of Hotel Senator, 12th and L Streets, Sacramento, California—

*March 4, 1940*
*My Darling Wife:*

*Have just arrived in Sacramento, California—have just taken a hot bath and have eaten a bite of supper. Today we crossed the Sierra, Nevada, mountains and there was from six to ten feet of snow. In lots of places it looked as if we were going through a tunnel. Then we came off the mountains into Sacramento Valley—palm trees were growing in peoples' yards—the grass was green—apple orchards in bloom and weather warm as it is in early May in Kentucky.*

*....I want to find out about the crowd I'm to speak before—then I want to be on my toes. In this hot weather one is bound to lose a lot of pep—cold weather keeps me perked-up and hot weather makes me lazy. My stomach is out of order and I hope all can be adjusted by tomorrow so I can be on my toes. I'm really glad that I'm off that train! It's been the most tiresome ride I've ever taken despite all the country I saw. It's a long bleak streak from here back to New York City—well over 3,000 miles.*

Jesse knows the ancient rule—a performer is no better than the last time on stage. The only way to increase speaking fees is to build a widening reputation for pleasing an audience. It appears he is more motivated to succeed as an entertaining monologist than to work quietly in solitude.

*While I'm here I'm doing my best so I'll be called back here to speak sometime at higher rates for my talks. I only wish that you were with me—then this trip would be complete. We'd have to have more money than I have—I'm staying at this hotel until after my speech tomorrow then I'm sneaking out to a cheaper place—the Y.M.C.A. and wait until my next talk—also must have my laundry done as I have but two more clean shirts.*
*I'm out of ink, will send this letter and write you again tomorrow.*
*Always, Stuart*

*I'll write as long as the ink lasts. Tell me how you feel—what are you doing, tell me if you miss me—tell me something—I want to hear from you—I love you—I love y....*

Jesse's audiences are typically female and there's an impression that he communicates a strong physical chemistry that causes the fair sex to respond with unadorned delight. At the same time, Jesse's message of education reform strikes a chord with teachers on professional levels from secondary schools to universities.

*March 6, 1940*

*To My Deane:*

*...Yesterday, many women came forward and said the talk was the best that had been given here this year. The Tuesday Club is composed of about six or seven hundred women—ages from 40 to 70, nearly all are college graduates. It is one of the most intelligent audiences I've spoken to yet.*

*Yesterday I moved from the swank Senator Hotel. The cheapest room cost me $3 per night—and I only stayed one night. The Y.M.C.A. here isn't so hot. All I have in my room is a cot and dresser—not even a desk to write on. But I get this room for fifty cents a night. I buy my meals where I please—and food is terribly dear out here. Much costlier than in New York—and I weigh 195 pounds now....*

*If plans work successfully I may go down to the University of California for a talk. I'll know in a few days.*

*Now for more news. Duttons plan to publish my* Tales from the Plum Grove Hills *this autumn, and they want me to have this short story collection ready by May.* [It wasn't released until 1946] *How about my getting it ready soon as I come home and soon as your school is out, let's take it to New York together. Let's go to New York and spend a couple of weeks. Will that suit you?*

*Also Doubleday-Doran another book company asked me to write a book for them—this one, to be done aside from my contract at Duttons. But Honey, I'm not going to write it. It takes time to write a book (this one is not a novel) and while I'd be doing it—I could write a novel.*

Jesse longs for the day that he and Naomi will have their permanent residence at W-Hollow.

> ....*just we two—so we can work, plan, and build together—so we can go places together. I sure as hell hate to be away from you. I've longed for you and pined for you since I left that snowy cold night. Deane, I love you more than anyone on earth—and I'll love you more the longer I live with you. I can trust you; I can depend on you. You are built of better clay. You belong to me. When anyone, I don't care who it is, crosses you and tries to hurt you, my blood boils. With you as my wife, I can go places. Look what has happened since I've married you. I didn't have any reserve in stories. I had a novel* [Trees of Heaven] *not quite finished—yet, I'd started the book when I knew I was going to marry you. Yes, Deane, I knew it—now the novel is ready for publication—is ready to be released—and I've sold 7 stories:* "Hell's Acre," "Archie th' Oddlin," "Bird Neck," "Braska Come Through," "When the Hen Crows," "The People's Choice" *and I don't know the other one* Esquire *took. I've sold $1100 worth of stories....Honey, you know this is good money to make in* [such a] *short space of time. I have many more good prospects too....*
>
> *Last night I thought of you—this morning I thought of you—today, I think of you—because you are not with me. I am so lonely without you. I think about you each night and day—you have most of my thoughts since I left Kentucky—you in my arms for just even one kiss. Oh, Deanie life is great with you! It is a new wonderful life.*
>
> *Always your, Stuart*

*P.S. another page to this letter.*
<u>Please tear up</u>

> *I've lived the hours over with you since I've been away—you with your head on my shoulder—your curly hair touching my arm—and then you turn to me and I to you in the night.*

At times Jesse seemed unsure whether he wanted to write all the time or join a college faculty. He likely feared his bachelor's degree was not enough and his shattered graduate school experience at Vanderbilt would come back to haunt him when search committees began to probe, asking challenging academic questions.

> *March 8th 1940*
> *Y.M.C.A.*
> *Sacramento, Cal.*

*My dear Naomi Deane:*

> *I leave here and go to Berkeley to the University of California. I got this talk myself—though I won't make so much out of it. I ask for the "gate receipts" or $50—it's a gamble and I prefer to take "the gate"—yet, most of all, it is what I want—a contact with the university. If they should ever ask me to come here for the summer and teach—well, we're coming—I can tell you that. You'd say so too after you once see California.*

The earth tones of W-Hollow and the sounds of Cedar Riffles were dull and muted when contrasted with the vistas of the California coastline, the agricultural riches of the San Joaquin Valley, and the city of guile called Hollywood.

> *Deane there is more laughter, beauty, vice, flowers, white-stone buildings, automobiles, places of amusement, bums, cut-throats and panhandlers here than any state in the union—more poverty—more riches—more artificial life. It is a world to itself—people have freer minds yet there're more nuts, more crank religions than anywhere I know.*
>
> *Last night I was down in the gym where there was a bowling match here at the "Y"—There was only one woman there—one of the bowlers' wives—and she sat beside her husband and drank a Coca Cola. It made me want to be with you—almost a sudden terror seized me and I got so lonely I had to leave. I thought and thought about you.*

Then just as quickly thoughts turned back to Jesse's mission:

> *I wonder what happened to the stories that were sent to the* Atlantic Monthly, Harpers, *and* Household *magazines. If they have been returned, tear each envelope open and check the comment— also put on the cards in the files the day they were returned. I know*

*there couldn't be such good luck that <u>one</u> of them sold.*

*You'll be getting an advanced copy of* Trees of Heaven *pretty soon. You'll see it before I will. Gee we have so much before us this summer—through western Pennsylvania (or back that way) as we go to New York—two books, a song, 4 poems in* Harpers *for April, 4 in* Esq. *In Feb. and one in* American Mer[cury].—*besides the stories in magazines and the one in the text book and my personal sketch making* Who's Who in America *and* Twentieth Century Writers—*all this year! If ever I speak again, you're going along—and we'll laugh together—don't be discouraged—you shall see that you will. I hope for you to be in every state in the union and in Europe—Honey, you don't know how I love you! You mean all to me. I hope I can make a living for you and make you happy. I want to see you so I weep.*

*Yours always, Stuart*

Jesse was not quite ready to admit he was one of those mortals who'd trade one year in California for one moment in Kentucky. California was a wondrous whim-wham, but he'd be homesick before too many suns set over the Pacific Ocean. He was a newlywed who longed for his bride in Kentucky.

*March 9th, 1940*
*Y.M.C.A*
*Sacramento, Cal.*

*My dear Deanie:*

*March 21st will be my last talk and believe me soon as it's over I'll be rolling back to Kentucky fast as the train will bring me. When I see you again, I'll simply follow you—love you—until you drive me away. Deane I'll love you to death. Honey I can't tell you how much I do love you! Am I in love with you? You ought to know! You are all there is in the world for me except writing and my farm.*

Jesse was proud of his family, and he was eager to bring Naomi into the Stuart fold. He was the kind of man who'd leave his parents for a time, but he'd not abandon them in the days of their advancing years.

*You'll like Mom if you can ever get acquainted with her and find out the really fine person she is. She is without prejudices and will not do anything to hurt one—not even one of her own children even if that child is wrong. My dad is terribly blustery and bad to talk and swear. Don't pay too much attention to him for he's violent tempered.*

*Yet home means everything to my Dad—with all his troubles (and he finds them and enemies too if he has to snatch unseen enemies and troubles from the thin air) he can laugh. He has a good sense of humor. Mom hasn't so much. You know we laugh and talk a lot at home. I'm glad you went out home without me. I want to let you see and feel your own self.*

*My debts will be wiped away this spring—I believe. If I keep going as I've been going since last December I'll make about $5,000 this year—not counting my novel which I pray will sell well and to the pictures.*

*But as you say, regardless of sales, of money or worry—let's be together—love a lot while we still have youth with us.*

*Always, Stuart*

Jesse often thought of himself as the mongrel dog, Jerry B. Boneyard, one of God's more audacious critters. These animal world fables delighted audiences and they begged for more. Jesse Stuart was a new dog coming around the corner of a Kentucky cabin, and his lectures turned into goodtime hambones. It improved book sales considerably, and hard-earned money began to roll in.

*March 11th 1940*
*Y.M.C.A.*
*Sacramento, Cal.*

*My dear Deanie:*

*You sweet thing—goodness—when I see you I'll love you to death. You spoke of money's being a "medium of exchange"—all that I know is, it comes in so damned handy that I need more of it and want more of it especially right now—and $600 isn't going to stop my going after more—yes—more.... I can see the light now—not so much of the old indebtedness darkness.*

*Life is great with you; life is glorious; life is everything. It means more to me to live now than it has ever meant. I'm so happy with*

*you; I'm so much in love with you that it hurts, for everytime I've
ever hurt you, I'm sorry.*

Jesse's gushing about his bride and his young celebrity rank was like a
new oil field discovery, his own publishing Spindletop.

Esquire...*has definitely taken "The People's Choice" and "Ox"
and "When the Hen Crows." Go send him* [Esquire] *"Bud." You
know how to do it. If "Bud" needs to be re-typed have Blanch to do
it. You check over it afterwards. I hope he buys it in addition to the
three stories he has bought. I don't want him to substitute it for one
that he now holds. "Bud" will sell someday—and I need stories on
reserve all the time. I've just finished a good story.*

*Also, I sent a story to Blanch to have retyped—"Love is Where
You Find It." Send this story to* [Collier's Magazine]....

*He asked me to see this story again...get it away soon as possible.
And I told you to look among the carbon copies of my new stories
and find "The Last Round-Up"—have Blanch to make a new first
and carbon copy of this story for* Collier's *lost the copy I sent them.
And send this story "The Last Round-up" to* Collier's *again. They
want to see it. That will make 3 stories with them for
consideration—will have a good chance. And I'm going to do three
more on the* Collier-*order while I'm here in California. I hope
Colliers act swiftly. I believe this is all for the stories.*

*If* Esquire *sends "Knot Holes in the Planks" home, I'll place it
sure as the world in the* American Mercury. *It's another story that is
going to sell. I've done too much work on that story for it not to sell.
Pretty soon the novel* [Trees of Heaven] *will be rolling out. Then
we'll hear what we'll hear—but it won't matter much. It soon dies.
Look how I was blasted over my first book* [Man with a Bull-Tongue
Plow] *by a lot of people. But it goes on and I go on to write more.*

*I'll be home a few days before April and it is the time I've wanted
to be home. We'll spend day after day in the hills when the wild
flowers start blooming and we'll manage to do something then and
there that you once suggested. Do you remember?*

*Always your, Stuart*

*March 12th 1940*
*Y.M.C.A.*
*Sacramento, Cal.*

*My dear Deannie:*

*....This letter will be brief. First, I want you to send "Knot Holes in the Planks" to me...I want to revise it coming back on the train. Also send, "I Didn't Steal Their Briar-Scythe," I think you'll find it in the table drawer. I must keep new stories in reserve. I've done two crack stories since I've been here. I have another one started.*

From time to time Jesse acknowledged the disturbing condition of his heart, an on-again off-again indication that he might be pushing too hard, needed to slow down and smell some flowers.

*My stomach is in top condition—never any more fluttering spells with my heart. It was caused by drinking coffee—not too much coffee but one cup will do it. I've drunk tea all the time on this trip— only one cup of coffee and I was sick the night after I drank it. I've never felt much better than I feel now. I weigh 191 ½ pounds stripped. You see I've lost a little excess weight since I left Greenup and I feel better without it. If the stories I'm writing now don't sell, I can't write a story that will sell.*

*Soon as I get home, I'll put more stories and poems on the road. We'll have four poems in April number of* Harpers. *So the tide moves in. Tomorrow, I go to the University of California. I come back to the "Y" (here) day after tomorrow—pick up mail—pack and move on to Stockton, Cal.—there for a night and day—and then to Pasadena where I hope letters from you will be waiting. Hold all mail, after about March 18th....*

Jesse was a raw Kentucky boy in a new world of pastel shades, cool Pacific breezes, and an openness to replace the insularity of Appalachia. The golden state would attract Iowans too, Mexicans, and Orientals. Jesse was drawn to it the way a hungry bear discovers an unexpected honeycomb. Still, Jesse's heart would always be in Kentucky.

*March 17th 1940*
*Pasadena Young Men's*
*Christian Association*
*235 East Holly (Civic Center)*
*Pasadena, California*

*My Darling Deanie:*

*I want to tell you that you and I both come to California next spring. We're going to get enough talks so that we'll both be able to come! Think of that. I'm paving the way on this trip! Deane no man knows he has a better wife than I have and no man loves his wife more. With you, by you and for you—my life—*

*March 19th 1940*

*I can hardly wait to leave Pasadena which will be day after tomorrow. Then the long trek back across the states with a stop-over in Missouri.*

*I've inquired about living expenses out here. I've inquired about a furnished house and so on. This state is not a bad place to live and to spend a winter—in fact, there isn't any winter in southern California. The trees are shedding their leaves here now.*

*From my experiences, I believe the farthest one can get away from one's own relatives (regardless how good they are) the better one is off—so don't be surprised at any move we might make.*

*This trip is getting unbearable—and I'm getting tired as hell of it and plenty blue....*

*Your, Stuart*

Jesse's loneliness, his sweaty shirts and socks, his chagrin about who he was and who he was to become, were weighing heavily on him. He relieved his dreariness with neither drink nor sex and it became increasingly difficult for him to keep his audiences on the edges of their seats. Thoughts of returning to Naomi became his hold on his sanity.

*March 20th 1940*
*My dear dear Deanie:*
*You just think, I'll get to see you before next week end! I'll be*

*walking by your side, I think, Wednesday of next week. Honey, I'm*
*walking on the wind—just the idea of seeing you again!*

*I've been so depressed in spirit—I wonder if you've missed me this*
*time as I have missed you! I wonder if you have felt depressed as I*
*have felt. At home, I could go around and see someone I knew—and*
*here, I meet strangers at first and they become friends later. About the*
*time I know these people well enough to laugh and talk with them, I*
*have to move on!*

*This climate (I'm going in my shirt sleeves) is so warm that it has*
*made me sleepy. I can't get enough sleep. Never mind, it won't be long*
*now until I'll have to umpy-jumpy and light the fire!*

*Deane, I shall never never be away from you this long again*
*unless this country goes to war and I have to go. I'll never punish*
*myself like this—for Deane I love you more than I ever thought I was*
*capable of loving anybody.*

*....Life is so wonderful with you—I've never been so happy in my*
*life—*

*I can feel the mood you are in by your letters. Now, Honey, one*
*thing—when I get off the train—I want you there to meet me. I want*
*to see your face and I want you in my arms! That's not asking too*
*much is it? Can't you meet me?  I want to see my Deane!*

*....I come back to Pasadena tomorrow afternoon—and pack—and*
*hustle off to the Southern Pacific station where I get a bus that takes*
*me to Alhambra where I get the Southern Pacific for St. Louis,*
*Missouri—leave here Thursday evening and get there Sunday*
*evening at six—I give my talk there Monday—and then I go back to*
*St. Louis and cross southern Illinois and Indiana to Cincinnati—and*
*I hope I can ride old George* [The Chesapeake & Ohio's *George*
*Washington*] *up the [Ohio] Valley—don't know the time yet—I'll let*
*you know—this will be the last letter I'll send you from California.*

Another brief honeymoon in Kentucky was followed by another hurried
farewell, another trip, this one to the South.

*Ansley Hotel, Atlanta, Ga.*

*Dear Deanie:*
*I'm trying to get cleaned-up this morning and readjusted so I can*

*finish the last leg of this trip. I want to see you more than I can
express to you in words.*

*I feel that you are lonely too, I told Mr. MacRae* [president of
Dutton] *I would rather have been whipped as to have taken this trip.
Deane, I wouldn't be a salesman for $500 per month—I detest this
work more than any I've ever done yet—this is the honest truth.*

*I want (right now) most of all to take you long trips over the
country. And Honey, how you'll like New York—To me, it's a cage—
and will always be—to you, it will be a Gotham. You'll love it from
start to finish and you'll like Connecticut!*

*I crossed North Carolina and South Carolina last night—woke up
in Georgia this morning.... I've never seen such poor land and
miserable wretched hovels as I saw in east Georgia and within ten
miles of the city limits.*

*P.S. Have a terrible headache this morning.*

> *The Crescent*
> *New York-New Orleans*
> *En Route*
> *May 18th 1940*

*My 'Deanie'—*

*Soon, Honey soon—you with a few drops of rain and the wind of
May in your curley hair—soon, Honey, I'll be with you and you with
me—a feeling—deep of loneliness—touches me as I ride on this
train and think of you.*

*Your voice sounded great to me from Kentucky at the Prince
George Hotel—sorry you had a bad connection. You put a Clark bar
in my pajamas (you know I don't like a Clark bar.) I have never seen
your like. You know how to touch me. When I found that bar of
candy—such simple little thing—I shed tears—*

*Tonight is the first time I've had a little privacy—first time to be
able to sit down and write to you the way I want to write. I've been
dead on my feet.*

*1. Have met Sidney King Russell* [composer] *and heard him play*
Sandy River [Jesse's lyrics] *and sing it and four new songs—also his*
Song of the Hills—

*2. Have met puggie-beer drinking H.L. Menchken* [Mencken, founder and editor of *American Mercury*]*—has the bluest eyes I've ever seen—*

*3. Have bought a new suit of summer clothes—got size 44—that should be big enough—*

*4. Sales of* Trees of Heaven *and reviews have surprised me— however, you're getting more reviews than I'm getting—*

*5. Now your school is out and believe me, I'm glad—Honey, can't you pack a few belongings and meet me at Stewart's Bookstore, Louisville, Ky—May 23rd. We can go from there to Cincinnati together! I may have to go from Cincinnati to Dayton, Youngstown and Columbus—I can't and won't stay that long away from you. Duttons will have a letter there to tell me what to do.*

*I don't go to Nashville. I didn't go to Richmond but to Philadelphia instead....send me a telegram and let me know if I can expect you in Louisville—tell me if you'll be there—*I expect you! *Finish the tour with me then we'll journey East.*

*Honey I'm crossing over the green hills of Virginia on the train Tom Wolfe loved. The music is good—the music is high in the sky— but Honey, Oh—Deanie—I love you I miss you! Come straight to Louisville, Honey!* Bring our mail!

Jesse reveals his eagerness to please his publisher even if it means giving up his use of dialect that he believes is natural. He also displays his reliance on Naomi Deane to make corrections in record time.

*P.S. "The Storm" was returned from* Good Housekeeping *because of the dialect. Can't you change all the dialect and have Blanch to re- type it? Try your hand at revising a story. They've asked for its return—put the "g's" back on all the words—*

Dialect is not the only thing that troubles Jesse when he's on the road. He perspired heavily in the best of times.

*P.S. It's so hot I can hardly stand it in Atlanta—and it costs 25 cents apiece to get shirts laundried—is that holding one up in broad daylight?*

The runaway hoss's reunions with Naomi Deane are unrecorded. The coast-to-coast letter writing, overflowing with "I love you," was briefly replaced with the intimacies of conjugal bliss, but after each Kentucky honeymoon, Jesse was ready to be back on the road again. He believed his future as a writer depended in almost equal parts on writing, lecturing, and signing books. The money he made was needed for travel expenses and the accumulation of more land. It was an ill-fated combination, more than one human heart could bear indefinitely.

In New York, Jesse stayed first at the Prince George Hotel "near all the publishing houses. Cost me two and a half dollars a night." He also checked into the Woodstock Hotel, and with practiced saving of every cent, he often stayed at the YMCA on West 23rd Street. One of the letters he wrote from there was to Dr. A.L. Crabb at Peabody Teachers' College in Nashville (August 15, 1940):

> *...6,000 words on a novel today—also a few errands. And believe it or not this one-man furnace has put his pipes and cigars away— I've not had tobacco smoke in my mouth for three days. I fight to keep from being controlled by men, why should I let tobacco smoke control me?*

Naomi Deane would be waiting for him at the Ashland depot whenever the "Old George" brought the conquering hero back from New York City. She saw to it that most of Jesse's future trips would include her.

The decade of the 1940s rolled on. The Axis military machines— Germany, Italy, and Japan—signed a military and economic pact; France and Belgium fell. German troops moved into Denmark and Norway.

In November of 1941 Jesse and Naomi motored to the West Coast. They were with their friends Lena Wells Voiers and her husband Gus, who drove most of the way in their new car. On a side trip into Mexico, a tire blew out.

*Dec. 15, 1941*
*A.L. Crabb, Esq.*
*Peabody College,*
*Nashville, Tenn.*

*Dear Dr. Crabb:*

*The automobile accident was the nearest thing to death that I have experienced; though, I've been in four automobile wrecks, two train wrecks, was black-jacked and have been shot at—and missed the train that wrecked between Glasgow and Edinburgh (that killed 34) because some Scottish friends insisted that I stay a little longer and catch the next train. I'm just a lucky man. Naomi Deane has her back broken; she is in a cast and must remain in one until sometime this spring. It's been a terrible thing; and it is still bad.*

*We wrecked 130 miles south on the Texas border in old Mexico. The wreck was due to a defective casing. We were probably driving at seventy miles per hour which is not fast for a good road and a new heavy car—a Chrysler. We hadn't eaten since early morning and we were getting to Chihuahua where we could get food. There wasn't a place to eat along this forsaken highway. But we didn't get there. The car rolled over seven times—completely demolishing it— not quite—it sold for $150 for parts though it cost $1300—had about 6000 miles on it. Mrs. Voiers' (my first high school teacher) back was broken; Mr. Voiers suffered deep cuts, brain-concussion. We were all knocked unconscious—I don't know how long. I was badly bruised but pulled myself together enough to help the other three all I could. By a dilapidated bus (Mexico) we finally reached first aid—from there by a Mexican train we rode part of the night and some of the next day—finally reaching a hospital in El Paso, Texas thirty-some odd hours after the wreck.*

*When we crossed the border I had six dollars. I had had enough money to bring us home but by the time I "paid off" in Mexico—I was about done for. Others wanted money that I didn't pay—just promised—and it's only going to be a promise to that bunch of chislers. I had three checks amounting to $125 in my pocket but couldn't get them cashed in El Paso. No one could identify me. I* *wanted to wire for money—still no identification. I showed them my registration card—on the newsstand was a story of mine in* Esquire *(Dec.) also poetry—a story of mine in the Jan.* American Standard magazine.*Yet this didn't identify me. Though I showed them three books that I had written and a copy of* Adventures in American Literature *(pub.* Harcourt Brace*) with one of my stories; yet, I wasn't identified. I learned I wasn't well known as a writer right then. But I happened to have a copy of* Trees of Heaven *with my picture on the jacket—this identified me until I could wire home for money. Soon as I got it, we left Texas. And when we saw the tough-butted white-oaks in southern Indiana—trees that are so familiar to us growing on the steep Kentucky banks in both western and eastern Kentucky—we almost wept—we were getting home.*

*My sister is here with us. She's a nurse in Ironton, Ohio—but they dismissed her so she could stay with us until Deane is able to stir again. I have to be around to help turn Deane in bed for the cast will weigh from 65 to 70 pounds...all of this trouble has me very upset. Best wishes to you and Mrs. Crabb from Deane and me.*

*Sincerely, Jesse Stuart*

Compounding her injury, Naomi was pregnant. She began her successful convalescence at W-Hollow, first in the heavy cast, then in a brace. The pregnancy proceeded normally, Jesse and Naomi's only child, Jessica Jane, was born August 20, 1942, and all four passengers in the car wreck recovered at a time when another event was overshadowing almost everything else in America.

# WORLD WAR II

*It means misery and pain and suffering*
*for a lot of our boys...*

Senator A.B. Chandler
Lexington *Herald-Leader*

*December 7, 1941.*

At the time of the Japanese attack on Pearl Harbor, Jesse Stuart was already thirty-five years old, and he didn't have to serve in the military, but he would volunteer because patriotism was a family value inherited from his ancestors. Jesse's brother James served aboard an LST (landing craft) in the South Pacific, and he saw action from Bouganville to Okinawa. Jesse, referring to the enemy as "those slant-eyed sons of bitches," let it be known that he intended to do his part to assure an American victory.

He was temporarily thwarted by a combination of bad weather on the farm, a sputtering of his passion to achieve permanent status as an accomplished writer, and a faltering heart that was sending him distress signals.

The war years were frustrating for Jesse, and he seemed to have temporarily lost his creative touch. He became uncertain and apologetic. He longed for approval and acceptance.

The New Year 1942 began with a shocking letter from Jesse's New York agent, Annie Laurie Williams. At first, it appeared that Stuart may have committed plagiarism.

Annie Laurie was the bearer of the bad news:

*Henry LaCossitt* [associate editor] *of the* American Magazine *has just called to tell me the following.*

*After the* American Magazine *published your story DEATH TAKES NO HOLIDAY letters began coming in from their readers saying this story was the same story, with a different background, as one of de Maupassant's stories. So many of these letters came in that Mr. LaCossitt decided to investigate. He went through his volume of de Maupassant and finally came across one of a group of stories entitled FEAR and, in comparing your story with this, he says there is no doubt but they are the same story. Neither he nor I believe for one moment that you would take a de Maupassant story and dress it up with a different background and sell it but we do feel that under the circumstances you should tell us how you happened to write a story so nearly like the de Maupassant one. Could it be that you heard someone tell the story and did not know it was one of de Maupassant's stories?*

*Mr. LaCossitt is in a very embarrassing position and said he would appreciate having you write a letter to me, or to him, giving us your explanation of the similarity of the two stories. He says he has not yet taken it up with the business manager of the* American Magazine *but some explanation will have to be given in the magazine to their readers.*

On January 5, 1942, Jesse promptly wrote to Henry LaCossitt:

*When I opened Annie Laurie Williams' letter this morning I got so weak that I could hardly walk to the telephone office to call her. I've never had an experience like this one in my life—just to think if there's ever been a writer that has tried to be honest, I'm that writer. I've never had anything to hurt me like this. Right now, this letter may be poorly put together—I don't know. When I sent Annie Laurie THE MAN WHO WOULD NOT DIE, I was as thoroughly convinced that it was my own—every thought, word, sentence, paragraph—I didn't know that it was a story made over. I've not read a de Maupassant story since college days 1926-29 and 1931-32....I've never read FEAR....*

What the editor had discovered were the following similarities:

De Maupassant—"...two years ago this night I killed a man, and last year he came back to haunt me. I expect him again tonight."

Stuart—"Seven years ago on this very night I kilt a man. He comes back to haunt me on this very night every year. I'm watchin' and waitin' fer 'im tonight.

De Maupassant—"At the base of the wall and under the window we found the old dog lying dead, his skull shattered by a ball."

Stuart—"He saw the red Irish setter spralled lifelessly across the porch beneath the window with a spot between his eyes redder than the hair on his body."

While the similarities are striking and de Maupassant was one of Jesse Stuart's early literary role models—*Guy de Maupassant's THE ODD NUMBER changed my life regarding the way a story should be written*—it was apparently too difficult and time wasting to try to prove an open-and-shut case of plagiarism.

Dr. Lee Pennington, Louisville author and educator, says:

> *From everything I knew of Jesse, I suspect one would have to strain a bit to make too much of an issue of plagiarizing. Jesse wrote so much it's almost like the story of putting a bunch [of] monkeys in a room with typewriters and eventually they'd write some Shakespeare....Jesse never hesitated to write a story someone told him. I did know of an instance where Jesse was told a story which was not factual and Jesse wrote it up and then was quite upset when he found out the story had been made up. Jesse was a writer that liked to hold to the basic facts of the story.*

Jesse goes on in his three-page, single-spaced typewritten letter to explain that he was told the story by a nephew of Lena Wells Voiers and had liked it so much he wrote it while on the lecture circuit. He first sent the manuscript to *Saturday Evening Post* and *Country Gentleman*, but both rejected it:

> *Then I sent the story to Annie Laurie for I planned to have an agent and start sending stories to bigger markets. When it sold to the* American, *I walked in the wind for I was proud to sell you...*

*Mr. La Cossitt, I know that this has hurt you, that it has given you trouble. As a writer I'm ruined if you do not help me—if you do not help me defend myself....Never in my life have I swiped anything from anybody knowingly....I'll give this much advice to any writer now, that is, watch what you take when it's told to you.*

Before the letter is finished, Jesse is in near panic:

*This has done more to damage me than anything that could have happened. Many people will never think anything but what I took this story. But so help me God, I tell the truth if I have to die ten seconds hereafter—I never read de Maupassant's story FEAR in my life....This has taught me something, if it hasn't about ruined me or maybe has ruined me. I hope to God it hasn't.*

Jesse's explanation was accepted and the matter was dropped, but the story was the first and last of Jesse's short stories to appear in *American Magazine*. He was not ruined, his career as a writer had only begun, and one of his most popular articles was later accepted for publication in the same *American Magazine* ("What America Means to Me"). Annie Laurie Williams continued as his agent.

The texture of Jesse Stuart, his basic honesty and candor about his development as a writer and, yes, as plowboy self-promoter, might be missed without looking over his shoulder to his personal correspondence.

*August 24, 1943*
*Mrs. A.L. Crabb,*
*Peabody College,*
*Nashville, Tenn.*

*You know that I felt terribly bad about writing five or six letters and telling my friends that I had won the Thomas Jefferson Memorial Award.*

*It was the first thing that had happened to me for a long long time—and I'd been harboring the idea that I was "through" as a writer and this happened. I felt a new surge of life sweep through me and I was full of spirit again—And that's what made me write these letters. I've been awfully bad about bragging for awhile just after*

*some little thing happens; if I could wait two weeks after it happens,
I would not do it. But I can't wait. I get to a typewriter and write
letters and relax and feel important. I guess it's a part of my make-
up, something like breathing, that I have little control over. So, when
I brag, I'll have to ask my friends to forgive.*

*My crop this year is only fair. I've never in my life, worked harder.
I worked barehead through all the summer sun and my head has been
sunburned terrifically. My hair is not black now but a dirty sunburned brown. And something has happened to me that I can't write
anything—I wonder if it's all this sun. Last spring we had torrents of
rain and then later this summer it turned off dry as could be—and
our crops suffered in this region—then to cap that off, we had a storm
the other day and heavy hail that nearly ruined the tobacco and
flattened the corn.*

*There's not any people I know I would rather sit down and talk an
hour with than you and Dr. Crabb. If and when this war is over, we'll
get together again. We'll try to make up for some lost time. I am still
thinking seriously of doing more school work.*

*Sincerely, Jesse Stuart*

Jesse was his own pitchman, responding as well as he knew how to
requests for publicity pictures. He was conscious of the importance of his
appearance, and he wanted to create the right image.

*Dec. 8th 1943*

*Dear Dr. Crabb:*

*I'll send you the picture soon as I can. I'll have to look around to
see if I have one where I am not slouched. And I'll send one
pipeless...I think a slouched picture of me is unnatural for you know
I don't slouch very much...that I am always up and going...that I am
always moving...that it has always been hard for me to sit still in the
classroom until the class is over. And when it's over, I've always
wanted to get out and walk and walk....And as for the smoking, this
summer when I worked in the fields, I didn't use tobacco...but when I
sit at a desk eight hours at night, when I sit and think on a poem as I
have often spent eight hours on one poem in this new book* [Album

of Destiny] *I've put together...I've had to do something in the form of relaxation...and smoking has done that, believe it or not.*

The idea of smoking as an addiction as real as any drug had not occurred to many Kentuckians because tobacco was "King Burley," and its royalty was seldom doubted. In a letter to LMU classmate "Nick" Carter dated Feb. 1, 1944, Jesse, acknowledged that he had, at best, a questionable heart condition that might keep him from military service:

> *...Last Friday in Cincinnati, Ohio, I failed a physical for the Navy. I went down on high blood pressure. It was really high. I think, though I am not sure, I would have gotten a commission. I know that I was marked up for active sea duty same as James has. This month I go up for a physical for the army.*
>
> *Oh if you and I could sit before a pleasant fire and blow clouds of smoke from our pipes even for a couple of hours and talk over old times and people first and books second it would be wonderful.*

That same day, Jesse wrote a similar letter to Dr. Crabb:

> *Thank you for your letter of Jan. 24th. I'm glad you heard favorable comments in New York on* Taps for Private Tussie *for I threw everything I had into writing it. Yet, it will take some time to test its merits. It seems to me that it is hard to write a novel that will live very long.*
>
> *I got a terrible jolt last week. I went to Cincinnati to enlist in the Navy. I was trying to get a commission and I stood a good chance of getting it, but failed my physical—And it's the first physical I ever failed. My blood pressure was 170. That's unusually high for one my age. Too much smoking, too many Coca Colas and too much coffee I think have caused all this. I certainly feel bad about it and will try to bring my health back normal again. I feel tough. Yet, I go up for an army physical this month.*

Perhaps if Jesse had been under the consistent care of a pioneering cardiologist, future trouble might have been averted. In 1944 the United States was still a decade away from the establishment of the National Heart and Cancer Institutes and the American Heart Association's report condemning smoking as a critical health issue.

February 15, 1944—American bombers destroy the Benedictine monastery at Monte Cassino in Italy. February 21—U.S. bombers hit German industrial plants and airfields. February 29—American bodies lie unburied on the beaches of the South Pacific. March 4—American planes bomb Berlin. March 19—Hitler invades Hungary and Adoph Eichmann describes himself as "a butcher thirsty for blood."

Jesse wrote to Nick Carter:

> *I don't know whether I wrote you or not (for life has been in such whirl) that I passed my physical examination and will be called to the Navy shortly.*

*March 27, 1944*

> *Saturday at noon I finished with my last revisions on* Album of Destiny. *Deane and I went to New York 5th of this month, returning on the 10th and all the time I was there I worked with Dutton editors and William Rose Benet on this MS and I brought it back with me to do some last minute work. I made a few eliminations, revised a few. I think, as far as I'm concerned, I'm through with it, that I'm willing for it to be placed before the public for approval or disapproval. Wait until you read this book. You won't be reading* Mongrel Mettle *nor* Taps for Private Tussie....*I'll be on my way to the Navy, Thursday at dawn, I leave Greenup, KY. Report at Huntington W.Va. then I report at Louisville, KY and from there, I think Great Lakes Naval Training Station near Chicago—though I'm not sure—I dread the boot training at my age* [38 years old], *but I hope to make a good seaman....I want to walk around and look at these old immortal hills before I go—for here I was born and have lived all my days.*

With *Taps for Private Tussie* royalties rolling in, Jesse enlisted in the U.S. Navy, March 31, 1944, his blood pressure having mysteriously improved. In his boot camp uniform, a seaman recruit at the Great Lakes Naval Training Center, he appeared woefully out of character. Not until he was commissioned (thanks at least in part to his degree from Lincoln

Memorial) did he look a better part.
June 6, 1944—
D-Day!

>*June 7, 1944*
>*Dear Nik:*
>
>*I finished "Boot training" early last month but I'm still held at Great Lakes—awaiting something—I don't know what—awaiting for the place the Navy chooses to put me. I happened to be one of the oldest men in my company—and, though, I don't think I'm old, I'm probably a little old as compared to the mass of men in the Navy, though many are older than I am. I'm in here to do my best. I can still fight...I'm a seaman 2nd class.*

>*June 13, 1944*
>*Dear Nick:*
>
>*...I went to Cincinnati, Ohio on 35 liberty hours over this weekend. Deane met me there. I went over 300 miles and she traveled approximately 150. She didn't bring Jane since we weren't sure of a room for baseball is at its height in Cincinnati and nearly all the hotel rooms were filled. But the U.S.O. got us a room. Nik I never knew how sweet hours of freedom were, for I always took them for granted, until I got into the Navy. Now it is drill and work and one naturally looks back to his family—every married man here does the same thing! Those hours with Deane were precious hours!*
>
>*The Navy holds me here for something. My company is already scattered over the U.S. or the high seas! I don't know where they've gone! I'd like to know! I asked for the battleship Wisconsin soon as she's finished. But officials here asked me to take public relations and I wouldn't take it! I'm not sitting on my tail behind a desk! In very polite English I let them understand this.*
>
>*My brother James is on the high seas and probably, as near as we can learn, is in this [South Pacific] invasion—and...my three sisters are making shells in a defense plant. Are we in this war? I'll leave it to you. I owe a great debt to America for it gave me a chance to live, to grow and to learn....Naomi's brother Malcolm Norris, a*

*submariner, was lost at sea.*

Jesse would not remain an enlisted man very long. He received a commission, and in the summer of 1944 he appeared with authors Louis Bromfield and Carl Sandburg at a Book and Author War Bond Rally in Orchestra Hall in Chicago. Three million dollars in war bonds were sold that evening. Jesse was proud to be an American and a Kentuckian, and he also took abundant pleasure in what he deemed was equal footing with two Pulitzer Prize winners.

Jesse no longer felt the odd man out.

Lt. J.G. Jesse Stuart was assigned, in 1944, to the Writers Unit in Washington, D.C.; his job—the creation of Navy pamphlets. The assignment was a far cry from his writing on leaves in W-Hollow, and even though he had said he wouldn't do public relations, he was maneuvered into it.

At first he was located at the Bureau of Aeronautics; the following year he was transferred to the staff of Naval Aviation News. He was clearly out of his natural element, but he did his part with military writing and patriotic fund-raisers. Since fate had decreed that his younger brother James would lay his life on the line in the South Pacific, Jesse would do what he did best—write "Uncle Tim Tussie" columns and make personal appearances.

One of Jesse's World War II short stories, "Beyond the News in Still Hollow," is included in *The Best-Loved Short Stories of Jesse Stuart.* In this story of bedrock patriotism, a Highland sheriff, Enic Bradley, is looking for a young man, Crooks Cornett, to serve him with a warrant for draft evasion.

> *"Mr. Cornett, did you get the cards notifying Crooks he was called?" Sheriff Bradley asked.*
>
> *"We never go to the post office," Jarvis said. "We never git any letters. We don't take any kind of papers. No ust to. Not one here can read."*
>
> *"Then you've never been to the post office?"*
>
> *"When did ye go to Piney Point last, Ma?" He asked Mrs. Cornett.*
>
> *"One of the youngins was over thar last Christmas," she said.*
>
> *"The cards have been sent since then," the sheriff said.*

*"Who sent the cards?" Jarvis asked, looking at Sheriff Bradley suspiciously.*

*"The U.S. government," Sheriff Bradley said.*

*"What does the govern-mint want with Crooks?" Mrs. Cornett asked, looking directly at Bradley.*

*"Wants 'im for a soldier," Sheriff Bradley said.*

*"We haint at war again, air we?" Jarvis asked.*

*"You don't mean to tell me you don't know we are at war?"*

*"I didn't know hit. Who air we a-fightin' this time?"*

*"Germany and Japan."*

*Crooks Cornett comes in from a day of hunting land turtles.*

*"Sheriff Bradley has come all the way from the county seat to see ye," Jarvis informed his son. "He says our country's at war and Uncle Sam wants ye fer a soldier."*

*"When does Uncle Sam want me?"*

*"Right now," Sheriff Bradley said.*

*"When did the war start?"*

*"Over a year ago," Sheriff Bradley said.*

*"If I'd a-knowed hit I could a-been fightin' a year," Crooks said. "Do ye want me to go tonight?"*

*"In the morning," the sheriff said.*

*"Will Uncle Sam have ye if ye'r fifteen?" The boy second in size asked Sheriff Bradley. "I'd like to go with Crooks," he said. "Would ye keer if I'd go, Ma?"*

*"Not if Uncle Sam needs ye."*

In October, Naomi and Jane came to Washington and moved into an apartment that Jesse had found across the Anacostia River. Jesse and Naomi's spirits soared. They wouldn't see Aaron Copland's ballet "Appalachian Spring" debuting in New York, because they'd soon be living their own Appalachian spring in their own W-Hollow.

The war, at last, had turned, and the sweet smell of victory and cherry blossoms was in the air. Churchill, Roosevelt, and Stalin met at Yalta; U.S. Marines raised Old Glory over Iwo Jima; General Douglas MacArthur returned to the Philippines; Gen. George S. Patton led his Third Army across the Rhine; and President Franklin D. Roosevelt was reelected to an unprecedented fourth term. A little known senator from Missouri, Harry S. Truman, was elected Vice President, no one thinking the unthinkable—that a little, sawed-off farm boy and later unsuccessful haberdasher from Lamar, Missouri, could be swept upstream into the Oval Office.

On December 16, 1944, Glenn Miller was missing on a flight from England to France, and Christmas that year wouldn't be the same. Like Jesse Stuart, Glenn Miller was loved by people hungry for uncomplicated lyrics and understandable tonality. Both men were naturals. One would be lost over the English Channel, the other destined to travel many more miles until his own rendezvous with what the poet Edmund Charles Blunden called "Death's shadow at the door."

> *Jan. 25th 1945*
> *3539 A St., S.E.*
> *Apt. 204,*
> *Washington 19, D.C.*

*Alfred Crabb, Esq.*
*Peabody College,*
*Nashville, Tenn.*
*Dear Dr. Crabb:*

*In August I was given a commission and sent to Washington (of all the cities in the U.S.) to the Navy Dept, where I was put on some rather tedious work. By that I mean, it's a little hard to do—a type of work I wanted to get away from—I didn't want anything inside. I asked for the sea, the fleet—I asked for it but the Navy decided for me what I should do. So I am here, doing my best.*

*Dr. Crabb, our county has about 25,000 people in it, we have about 2,500 in service. Of this 2,500 over 100 have been killed or they are missing—a few are in German and Japanese prison camps. About 40 of the boys killed and missing, I taught in high school. I remember them as children. So when I saw the first casualties reported it burned the hell out of me—blood pressure (yes they turned me down when I enlisted and said there wasn't a chance for me)—blood pressure 170 or 180, or no blood pressure—I got in— and, though they turned me down when I tried to enlist for officers training, I got in as a boot. I went on a diet to get my blood pressure down. And it was still high but I talked like hell to get in—keep this mum for something could be done to the doctor.*

*I have the deepest feeling about the boys I knew and taught—they hadn't received as much from America as I have and yet they were dying for her. And then the feeling I have in my brain and heart for this country—I wanted to go to bat for a county, my county (and none of this damned toy-flag waving patriotism either) that has given me a chance in life. That's all I asked—I didn't ask for that—I just took it—But what I'm trying to get at it's worth fighting for and dying for, so I asked for the sea—anything—and what ever they put on me I'm not grumbling though the way many things are done I'd do them differently and with more speed.*

*When I came here I thought they were going to send me to a carrier in the Pacific in autumn—then I thought (and it was intimated to me) it would be in this month. Now I'm told it will be later. Deane and Jane have been with me in Washington since October—after our being 8 months apart.*

*As for writing—well, it's over right now—I don't have the time to do the things I want to do. If I did do something I doubt that I could get it published. Duttons have been out of paper.* Head O'W-Hollow, Men of the Mountains, Man With a Bull Tongue Plow, Trees of Heaven *are sold out and out of print.* Album of Destiny *was out but they managed to get some paper and now it's rolling again in cheap paper. Only* Mongrel Mettle *and* Destiny *are salable now—there may be a few* Beyond Dark Hills *but I doubt it. Duttons told me they wanted a book from me in 1946—preferably in autumn at that, so—*

*Before I close this letter, I must tell you about James. I've not heard from him for some time, 3 months. But he was in the Leyte and the Luzon invasions. My sisters (all three) are still at the shell plant. Our farm (Dad is trying to keep things together) is growing up. But we'll clean it up when the war is over.*

*Best of luck to you and Mrs. Crabb. I know you feel uneasy about your only son. My father has been in bed—he claims with the flu— but it's mostly worry so Mom writes me. But we'll go through with*

*this thing, maybe, sooner than most people think—and without*
*compromise to the German and Jap—we'll beat their ears down*
*until they won't rise again. The Japs once pickled their enemies*
*ears! Let them pickle ours if they dare.*

*Sincerely, Jesse Stuart*

On April 12, 1945, a great shadow fell over the entrance to the "Little White House" in Georgia. President Roosevelt unexpectedly died there, and there was crying in the streets of the capital city and throughout the land. Six days later American journalist Ernie Pyle was killed during a battle on Iwo Jima, and there were more tears in Indiana and beyond the rivers from the Hudson to the Colorado.

V-E day came the following month and in August the Enola Gay's belly-doors opened, and atomic bombs fell on Hiroshima and Nagasaki. Japan surrendered on the battleship *Missouri*. The little farm boy from Lamar had let it be known that the buck would stop at his desk. He accepted both credit and blame for taking the world into the Nuclear Age.

Naomi suffered a miscarriage in the autumn of 1945, and the last Christmas in Washington, D.C., was all the more bittersweet. The family was deeply saddened by the loss of the child, but the war was over and Jesse was discharged from the Navy two days after Christmas.

A photographer took a picture of Jesse, Naomi, and Jane with the U.S. Capitol in the background. They were smiling. They seemed at peace. They were a picture for Norman Rockwell.

It was a brilliantly slender passage of time.

Jesse's splendid naval officer's uniform was saved, and one day it would be headed for immutable life on a mannequin standing in a corner of the Jesse Stuart Foundation bookstore in the former post office building on Winchester Street in Ashland. Today, seeing it there, the likeness provides another dimension to the Jesse Stuart persona: more than the creator of Sid and Uncle Kim Tussie, Uncle George, Uncle Mott, Aunt Vittie, Grandpa, and Grandma in *Taps for Private Tussie*, Jesse was an American citizen, proud of his country and the values he believed it embraced. His was unrestrained patriotism, and he had been willing to give his life to preserve it. So too was his brother James. Both survived the war. Both returned to Kentucky to resume teaching.

When Jesse came back with Naomi and Jane to their vacant home in W-Hollow in 1946, he had a stronger conviction about his life's work and the role he would play in education and literature. But he wouldn't slow down.

Jesse wrote furiously in buzzing fits and starts, his stories and poems appearing in *Reader's Digest, Esquire, Saturday Review,* and *Progressive Farmer.*

Meantime, in the real world, Governor Simeon Willis, a Republican, wrote to Jesse and apparently offered him the presidency of Murray State Teachers' College. The fact that Jesse Stuart would be offered a college presidency may strike some as highly improbable. Yet Republican Governor Willis had grown up in Greenup County and served as principal of South Portsmouth High School before he was twenty years old. He and Stuart had several important things in common: both revered Greenup County as their abiding sense of place, both loved books, and both relished fine cigars properly clipped and lovingly lighted. It was perfectly natural that in the middle of his 1943-1947 term Governor Willis would invite a political ally such as Jesse to come and spend the night at the mansion in Frankfort, the very least he could do for his loyal and famous political supporter. Jesse was putting the final touches on *Foretaste of Glory,* but was obliged to accept Willis's invitation.

Following a robust Kentucky breakfast, Jesse sat down with the governor to talk about the possible candidates for the Murray State presidency. But Jesse didn't have advanced degrees, and quite likely Governor Willis had invited him to come to the Capitol as a trusted consultant. Maybe Willis hinted, "How about you for the president's job, Jesse?" And Jesse could have replied, "Naw, sir, it's too political and too far from Greenup County." A likely explanation is that Jesse turned it down because the State Board of Regents could oust him, since it held a Democratic majority and such a majority was inevitable in a traditionally Democratic state (at that time).

It's also possible that Jesse exaggerated the plausibility of his own nomination. The fact is, he did not become a college president. He was, however, offered a faculty position at Columbia University in New York, but he turned that down too. A central part of Jesse wanted to replant and husband his roots in W-Hollow—the place he called his "fountainhead." Instead he finished *Foretaste of Glory* and set off a storm of protest that nearly drove him out of Greenup County.

*Foretaste of Glory*, published by Dutton in 1946, turned out to be remarkably popular or unpopular, depending upon whose character reputation was being gored. The novel angered many in Greenup County because Jesse portrayed several local people as fundamentalist, sin-infested hypocrites. The book's characters, some of whom were as identifiable as they were laughable, believed the phenomenon of the northern lights—the appearance of the *aurora borealis*—meant the end of the world: Judgment Day! The citizenry became as wacky as many of the characters in *Taps for Private Tussie*.

Kentucky literary historian William Ward observed that "more judicious readers may have felt that the character portrayals [in *Foretaste of Glory*] did not go below the surface but existed primarily for the laughter that comes from exposing the foibles and frailties of men and women in their unguarded moments."

There were days and nights when old demon "Writer's Block" came pounding on the door. Other writers were hard at work in their places midway of the twentieth century, and competition for publication and awards was increasingly intense. Robert Penn Warren, Tennessee Williams, James Michener, Carl Sandburg, Ernest Hemingway, and Archibald MacLeish won Pulitzer Prizes. T.S. Eliot, William Faulkner, and Hemingway won Nobel Prizes.

In the late 1940's, Jesse shared the stage at the University of Kentucky with renowned poet and critic John Ciardi. A question arose concerning the merits of Margaret Mitchell's *Gone With the Wind*. Ciardi dismissed it as second-rate, but Jesse replied that he wished he'd written it.

What's to be said for Jesse's popularity growing like a beanstalk from the soil tilled in *Man with a Bull-Tongue Plow*, *Taps for Private Tussie*, and *Foretaste of Glory*?

While the litterateurs played violin, Jesse played fiddle.

*Tales from the Plum Grove Hills*, a collection of Jesse's short stories, appeared in 1946 while he was again teaching and struggling with the idea that would become, in 1949, his crowning achievement—*The Thread That Runs So True*, published by Scribner's after Dutton turned it down. The National Education Association voted it the most important book of 1949. In the *NEA Journal* appeared these words:

> *Comes now the adventure of a young teacher told by a born story-teller whose writing has the rugged freshness of his native Kentucky hills....It should help us to understand that whatever we do in home, church, or business must begin with sound education.*

In Jesse Stuart's own words in the book's preface:

> *When I began teaching, the schoolroom was not supposed to be a very interesting place, and this great profession was looked upon by many as being something of secondary importance. Now, the interest of all America is focused upon America's schools and their importance to our survival as a nation.*
>
> *No one can ever tell me that education, rightly directed without propaganda, cannot change the individual, community, county, state, and the world for the better. It can. There must be health, science, technology, the arts, and conservation of all worthwhile things that aid humanity upon this earth. And there must, above all, be character education.*

It was a message that Jesse Stuart delivered personally to hundreds of audiences across the nation—his bags packed, unfinished manuscripts nestled against his chest, his heartbeat becoming increasingly erratic.

After William Feakins' death in 1946, Jesse signed a contract with the Harald R. Peat Company, which specialized in Distinguished Platform Personalities. Headquartered on West 45th Street in New York, Harold and Grace Peat fostered and encouraged Jesse to become one of their top performers. They stoked the fires of publicity for their W-Hollow nest egg, and Jesse held up his end of the bargain—long train rides, modest accommodations, shared expenses, and extended periods of time away from home.

Naomi wrote to Mrs. Crabb in Nashville, April 16, 1947, the letter revealing her uncomplaining nature. While Jesse was moving from city to city, lecture platform to lecture platform, she had to care for her young daughter.

> *Dear Mrs. Crabb—It was nice to receive the clippings and your good letter asking us to visit you when Jesse comes to Nashville. Jane and I are not coming with Jesse. He left Sunday night for four lectures in Ohio, Illinois and Michigan. He will return to us Friday and leave soon again to be in Nashville Monday—he goes on from there to Blue Mountain* [College] *then to* [the University of] *Mississippi. I'm sure you will agree that is hardly a trip for Jane and me. We keep hoping we will get to come sometime when he isn't so rushed.*
>
> *I'm sure your Tennessee is lovely—We are enjoying our Kentucky hills right now, too. Every season brings new delight to Jane—She is four and a half now—and so awake to everything.*
>
> *Thank you for thinking of us and asking us to come— it will be a pleasure to accept again sometime.*
>
> *Sincerely, Naomi Deane Stuart*

In the summer of 1949, Jesse and Naomi joined Lena Wells and Gus Voiers on a trip to Europe. In the picture taken on the *Queen Elizabeth,* Jesse appears confident and relaxed, eagerly anticipating revisiting the Old World culture he had first experienced on the Guggenheim Fellowship. For Naomi Deane, it must have been a high point in her life, which had begun so simply in rural Greenup County.

Upon their return they were greeted with the good reviews of *The Thread That Runs So True.*

The Peat speakers' bureau urged Jesse to stay on the lecture circuit:

> *Everywhere you have been, regardless of the price paid, reports have been the same. Committees have loved you and have felt rewarded for having had you on their program.*

Speakers' fees were ringing the cash register with dollars unheard of for a poor boy from W-Hollow.

Harold R. Peat wrote Jesse near the end of 1950:

> *When we booked you for the American Association of School Administrators at Atlantic City for next February 18, 1951, this was your first $500 date....we saw coming to light that which we have always believed that someday you would be right up there at the top getting the fees that you justly deserve. Then came the San Antonio $750 date. Now we have advertised you around before convention groups all over the country at fees of from $500 up for late spring engagements, and today came an acceptance from the California State Congress of Parents and Teachers to be held in Los Angeles on May 4th....We urge you to accept it because then you will have had the top teacher groups from the Atlantic City Convention to the California Convention.*

Jesse was pinching himself to be sure it was actually true, and he shared his excitement with the teacher who had turned him around when he was a frustrated schoolboy.

*Riverton, Kentucky*
*November 13, 1950*

*Dear Lena Wells:*

> *...When I first started speaking, I got for a talk exactly ZERO. I paid my own way, gave it, paid my way home. This for the first 35 or 40 talks. First pay I got $2 expense money. Then I got $3 and many talks for $5 and I'd love to know how many $10 talks, $12, $15, $20, and old $25...$35, $40, $50 and even on the West Coast, that far from home, I got on my first tour $50 and $75. Not one for a $100. So I had to come a long way. It took me 15 years. And many people, especially around here, laughed at me. I know it. I paid no attention. They* [the Peat agency] *plan not to book me, unless it is some special place, next year under $300. And they can book all I'll be able to give at this price and above, above, above. And you know this is something for me. Because all of my life I made very low wages at the work I did. Highest in school work of all administrative jobs I*

*held, $200 per month. That was as a teacher in Portsmouth High.*
*Labor, highest, steelmills $4 for ten hrs. Lowest, twenty five cents a*
*day on farms.*

*I doubt I'm worth what I get for a talk. But people are willing to*
*pay it. I write you all this for I think you should know.*

*I tell in my talk to teachers that the reason I am speaking to them*
*is the result of teachers. They had a hand in shaping and making me*
*what I am. And this is true. Parental influence and good teachers*
*make men and women.*

*Sincerely, Jesse Stuart*

*Clearing in the Sky* (short stories) and a novel, *Hie to the Hunters*
appeared in 1950. Then followed *Kentucky Is My Land* (poems) in 1952,
the juvenile novel *The Beatinest Boy* and a novel *The Good Spirit of Laurel
Ridge* (1953). And then there were two more juvenile novels, *A Penny's
Worth of Character* (1954) and *Red Mule* (1955). The themes were
constancy, loyalty, honesty, and love of nature. Jesse's fans rushed to buy
them before they went out of print, *Kentucky Is My Land* an irresistible title
for the down-home faithful.

Naomi accompanied Jesse whenever it was possible, but she had so
many responsibilities at home, not the least of which was raising and
schooling Jane. On October 31, 1951, Naomi wrote to Lena and Gus
Voiers:

*On Sept. 26 we went to New York by train. Came home for one*
*night—Oct. 5. Then on Oct. 6 we left by car for Ohio, Indiana,*
*Illinois, Iowa, Wisconsin, and Minnesota. Beautiful weather and*
*scenery. Jesse spoke to teachers and woman's clubs. We had four*
*days in Chicago and four days in Springfield, Ill. Then two days*
*between talks.....We reached home Saturday night and Jesse leaves*
*tonight by train for Worcester, Mass. And Pittsburgh, Pa. I've got to*
*stay home a little and plant some jonquils and iris.*

*Jesse will write you the election news and gossip. I never pay any*
*attention to it nor do I discuss it. Come and see us when you can.*

*Every good wish, Deane and Jesse*

Naomi Deane's letters illustrate her desire to live the fullest life possible as wife and mother; Jesse's correspondence seldom strayed from his passion as an artist with a permanent place in literary achievement.

> *November 9, 1951*
> *Dear Lena Wells:*
>
> *After all, in America, as writers go, I'm far from being a major writer, even if I am classed, a few times, in the top ten! All my work is on one little county in Kentucky! I didn't take myself too seriously. I know we live (how good to live) and die and leave a little something behind us. I'd love to burn it all and wipe the slate clean—But I can't now, I've gone too far!*
>
> *Sincerely, Jesse Stuart.*

> *July 28, 1952*
> *Riverton*
>
> *Dear L.V.:*
>
> *Very soon I'll go on the road again. In fact, I've just got home. Deane went with me to Peabody College, Nashville, where I read two papers and lectured—I also spoke at Western Ky State College, Bowling Green, and taught in a writers' workshop in Morehead.*

On one return to W-Hollow, there was a meeting with Naomi and Calvin Clarke, their tax attorney and financial adviser. The runaway hoss emerged with what should have been a sobering realization: "I'd spent as much as I'd made and I felt very badly about it. Deane and I came away after seeing facts and figures, disgusted with ourselves."

In a letter dated May 12, 1954, Jesse told Lena Wells: "We're not making enough—only to break even. This year I'm worth $700 less than last year—and I had two books published. I went that much into my savings."

Yet he would not ease up, despite Naomi Deane's entreaties:

> *I haven't wasted or spent anything foolishly. Just come home as fast as you can. I miss you so much. You know how I hate for you to go to town even.*
>
> *I'm looking for you home—I love you and need you. I know you*

*have to be away but I also know the house--—no matter how nice we think it is—it's just no good without you.*

*It's good to know you love me. It makes things a little—no a lot easier here. I hate for you to be away. You can't imagine what it's like here without you. Knowing you as I do I don't think you would stay here without me. I'd do it only for you.*

Naomi Deane wrote Lena Wells on October 31, 1953:

*He was in the Chicago area on Oct. 23—had 3 talks—9-11-and 2. Tried to get home—I met a plane in Huntington, a midnight train and he rode a bus from Cincinnati to Portsmouth 12 to 4 A.M....Jesse left Monday for Columbus on the 27th. Oklahoma City the 30th. Hattiesburg, Mississippi Nov 3. Madison, Tennessee Nov. 7. Huntington W. Va. Nov. 9. Then home until Nov. 19, Des Moines, Iowa.*

From January to October 1954, Jesse's voyage on the "river of earth" included a series of sudden chest pains and trips to hospital emergency rooms, EKGs and conflicting diagnoses, multiple doses of nitroglycerin tablets and Scotch on the rocks. Jesse had failed to heed a letter from one of his tell-it-like-it-is fans, the gist of it forwarded to him by Naomi Deane:

*W-Hollow*
*Saturday night*
*Nov. 11, '46*

*You have a letter here from...Illinois. It first made me mad. Then I thought about it and she's right in more ways than one in the way she blesses you out. I won't send it to you—it will make you mad. But here's one quote "Jesse Stuart, I say to you, get your big fat ego away from the tea cups and women's clubs and titillating worshiping women folks. Go back to your hills. Get out your imagination dust off the good old boy meets girl plot - falls in love and gets her...What are you doing making book reviews? Any fool can read a book—But only Jesse Stuart can do the above order. I challenge you to do it? You must!"*

Eight years after receiving and ignoring this warning and all Naomi's pleas that he slow down and take better care of himself, Jesse was again on his fevered way.

Naomi was increasingly fearful. Once, in a letter, she bared her soul to Jesse:

> *I don't know what would become of me without you. I seem to get along pretty well for a few days—then something comes over me. Today I feel nearly as sad—sick—or despondent as I did where you were away last year and I stayed in home and was sick. I think it's just knowing you are away. You know I tell you when you are here that I haven't a worry or a fear. When you are away it's entirely different.*

On October 7, 1954, despite all her misgivings and fears, Naomi drove Jesse to the airport in Huntington, West Virginia, for his fateful flight to Paducah.

# HEART ATTACK!

*He it is also that is born each instant in our hearts:*
*for this unending birth, this everlasting beginning, without end...*
*this is the life that is in us.*

Thomas Merton
*The Seven Storey Mountain*

*Pray!*

Jesse waved goodbye to Naomi and boarded Eastern Airlines flight 461 at midday on Wednesday, October 7, 1954. The plane climbed above the scarlet foliage of the Tri-State hills and reached out beyond the narrow mouth of Big Sandy River. If clouds were favorable in the sweet plowshare fields of Heaven, Jesse could look down on W-Hollow and Plum Grove Cemetery.

*To see these rugged hills of home again*
*Before uncertain flight through troubled skies,*
*To be where autumn wind sends down red rain*
*Has brought me moods and hot tears to my eyes.*
*These are the jutted hills that nurtured me,*
*That gave me substance since my life began;*
*Within whose bounds I have known liberty*
*As much as any mortal on earth can.*
*I have stood here when other winds have blown*
*In seasons past to watch rain-dropping leaves;*
*Now I recount with pleasure days I've known*
*Before a change to scenes beyond the seas.*
*Upon this earth, beneath these clouds of fleece,*

> *I wish I could command this time to stop*
> *That I may know again these hills of peace*
> *Where only leaf-blood trickles drop by drop.*
>
> *Kentucky Is My Land*

On the knifing edge where the plane's wing met the air and folded it back in vapor, Jesse might still be remembering his mother, Martha, laid in her grave on Mother's Day, 1951.

As a child, he had once asked her:

> *"Can God ride on one of the white clouds up in the sky?"*
> *"Yes, God can do anything."*
> *"Well, God is a great man if he can do things like that. But I am afraid some of these days he will fall off the clouds and hurt himself when he falls to the ground. Then without God the earth will come to an end."*
>
> *Beyond Dark Hills*

Some youths might work in earnest to build snares for chipmunks, bring them home, and be surprised to see the creatures die trying to escape captivity. Other young people might cup lightning bugs in their hands, put the insects inside empty mayonnaise jars with perforated lids, and wonder why the fireflies lost their luminescence so soon.

In *Beyond Dark Hills*, Jesse remembered how he'd used cane seed to trap hungry birds in winter. He returned to his mother to ask her about what he had done:

> *"God didn't kill me and I caught his birds like the cat. Now what is he going to do about me catching these birds?"*
> *Martha patiently replied:*
> *"You are not accountable for all the sins you do now. But you will be when you are twelve years old. All of the sins you make now, me and your father will have to suffer for them. You are accountable to us and we are accountable to God."*

Jesse replied:

> *"Then I'll turn the birds loose for I don't want God to get after you and Pa about it like he would a cat."*
>
> *Beyond Dark Hills*

As flight 461 climbed through the clouds, moving down the Ohio Valley, Jesse may have thought of Naomi, Jane, and Mick, hearts still beating in the House of Stuart with its windswept glass so streaked by singular uncertainty. He may have wondered if he, Jesse, would one day die suddenly, his heart surrendering and shutting down, fluttering, flashing pictures of a life incomplete. Of late, there'd been those troubling chest sensations, sometimes turning to damnable pain.

In February, Jesse had written to Lena Wells:

> *Over the strenuous hard autumn, and the month of Jan. of this year, I went for my physical checkup and found my heart skipping sixth or seventh and often both, beats....Book Sales are, and have been for four years, in such bad way, lectures the same after expenses, that I came out about even last year. We had planned to go to Europe this summer. But no Europe for us.*

Jesse Stuart was a sick man, sicker than he knew.

The dread of dying had teased and tormented him since those first awkward, fervent poems he'd written in *Harvest of Youth*.

### Silent Earth

> *How silent, the countless billions who have died.*
> *They cannot speak to tell us where they lie.*
> *We who tramp above them, how are we to know*
> *Who lie beneath our feet where sawbriars grow?*
> *We only know men born are men to die*
> *And they too will ride, if the dead must ride,*
> *Out past all space and where all time is vain;*
> *Where their rich dust will be a hidden urn*
> *That will not hear, nor see, nor even know*
> *If the beat upon their face is rain or snow.*
> *Why should it matter? They cannot return*
> *When they have given up the body and the brain.*
> *Yet deceiving is this epitaph I found:*
> *"How oft and sweet is sleep beneath the ground."*
>
> *Harvest of Youth*

Who among the House of Stuart would be the next to fall?

The Eastern Airlines plane retraced from above the clouds the lonesome highway miles Jesse had once hitchhiked when nearly thirty years before, as a youth seeking a new life in college, he'd headed westward toward Morehead, Winchester, and Lexington. He was acutely aware of the burning moment, as if his Maker might suddenly confront him: "Come Home, Jesse. This is the end. You've had your beginning, had your chance, now it's payback time, and I'm here to collect what is mine."

Jesse was not the kind of airline passenger who would fall asleep before the plane lifted from the runway and not wake up until the wheels screamed down in puffs of blue smoke at his destination. He was constantly at work: "I had with me three books to read, four stories and a dozen poems to revise," Jesse recalled in a story he would later write for the *Saturday Evening Post*. He simply refused to misspend one moment of precious God-given time. Jesse's inner drive filled both time and space to the outer limits.

At Louisville's Standiford Field, Jesse boarded Eastern Airlines flight 157 for the continuing southwesterly descent to Evansville and another change of planes—this time to Delta Airlines flight 395 to Paducah, home of another cigar smoking humorist, Irvin S. Cobb. Born in the century before Jesse Stuart, Cobb was applauded nationally for his autobiography, *Exit Laughing*. He died ten years before Jesse's 1954 arrival in Paducah. Irvin S. Cobb was laid to rest in Oak Grove Cemetery, his granite monument bearing the words "Back Home."

Harold R. Peat, Inc.—"Distinguished Platform Personalities"—had Jesse booked the following morning, October 8, to address the First District, Kentucky Education Association, at Murray State Teacher's College. It was to be "An Hour with Jesse Stuart," for which he would be paid $500, a handsome honorarium in 1954, one that fed upon itself because a portion would be added to Jesse's ability to buy another piece of W-Hollow land.

Then, after Murray State, with hardly a chance to catch his breath, there'd be another $500 speech in the afternoon of the same day at the Illinois Education Association's convention in Flora, Illinois: Topic— "Education and American Democracy." A Cessna 180 charter would be standing by to whisk the famous plowboy across the Ohio River to Flora, approximately one hundred miles north of Paducah.

Fannie B. Rawsom, traffic manager of Midwestern Aero Service in Illinois, sent confirmation to Jesse and the booking agent in New York:

> *Since Murray, Kentucky does not have an airport, the nearest point we can land is Mayfield-Graves County Airport, which is approximately 20 miles from Murray. You stated you could not leave Murray until 11:00 a.m. on October 8. Therefore, we will pick you up at Graves County Airport at 11:45 a.m., giving you time to drive from Murray to this Airport, and arrive in Flora, Illinois, at approximately 12:10 p.m. This will allow you ample time to drive to your destination in Flora by 1:30 p.m. on October 8.*

The bull-tongue plow was cutting a deep furrow, and tight turnarounds left few moments or inches for a faltering heart.

> *I liked speed. I was a speedy American. I was getting into the swing of a life that had crept up on me more than I knew or even thought. I drove myself to push my work. When I saw the boys on the road going here and yon to lecture, we often had time for a few words with each other in the lounge car of a fast train that thundered across America. America was our lemon all right....Naomi was the first one to meddle with me. She said, "Why are you always in a hurry? You're even in a hurry to eat! You'd better slow down." She's the only one who ever tried to halt me. I told her I was pushing on only three fronts now: writing, lecturing and farming—tree farming, for I set 22,000 trees the last two years. I'd be too old to reap the benefit of these trees. But somebody would. I'd never been a selfish guy. Naomi shouldn't comment. I was forty-seven, but mom's ancestors averaged ninety-two. I told Naomi so. And she said, "Yes, but their world was different. It was a quiet country world, like you were born and grew up in."*
>
> *Year of My Rebirth*

The speaker's bureau arranged for another "Education and American Democracy" speech for Jesse one week later at the Tennessee Education Association meeting in Memphis: *Lecture to run about an hour...informal dress...speaker will be met at train if necessary...$400.*

The Peat agency had arranged Jesse's previous speaking season at the same whirligig pace. From September 29, 1953, to January 20, 1954: Bedford and Bloomsburg, Pennsylvania; Syracuse, Goshen, and Alfred, New York; Battle Creek, Michigan; Muncie, Indiana; Columbus and Cleveland, Ohio; Oklahoma City; Hattiesburg, Mississippi.

On one day alone, October 23, 1953, Jesse was booked for Joliet, Aurora, and St. Charles, Illinois—9 a.m., 11 a.m. and 2 p.m.

> *At your early convenience, will you please sign and return to us the duplicate copy of this letter? As additional engagements are booked, we will be in communication with you. With very best wishes.*

New York understood one thing: Jesse Stuart had become a booking agent's plowshare in heaven. When he went to the post office in Riverton, there was usually an egg basket overflowing with mail for the writer who once sold eggs at seven cents a dozen to buy stamps to mail out manuscripts. Jesse went on to become the Riverton post office's main reason for being. He once figured he had written six thousand letters in one year. "If I continue buying postage at the rate I have been for the past ten months, I will have spent somewhere between seven and eight hundred dollars for stamps."

M.O. Wrather, public relations assistant to the president of Murray State, wrote Jesse: "I will arrange to meet you at any place you suggest. Mrs. Wrather joins me in inviting you to spend the night of the 7th in our home. We really would like to have you."

Jesse dutifully strode off the plane in Paducah, where advance publicity described him as "The American Robert Burns." Jesse felt good about that because at last, maybe, it was rock-solid validation of the Guggenheim Fellowship that had sent him to Scotland to search for Bobby in 1938. Both Guggenheim and Jesse understood that the true value of the fellowship has ever been to search for oneself in the best context for humanity.

The greeting party from Murray State was warm and anxious to please. The drive down through McCracken, Graves, and Calloway Counties to the Murray State campus gave Jesse an opportunity to see mile after mile of harvested acres of soybeans, corn, and flue-cured tobacco unlike anything a hillside farmer could imagine back at W-Hollow. "You ought to know what we'd done with it, if we had it!" Jesse would rue.

After spending the night in the Wrather home (he did not sleep well), a short walk away from the center of the campus, Jesse confidently strode out on the spacious stage of Lovett Auditorium and was introduced by Murray State's president, Ralph Woods. Jesse nodded to the standing-room-only applause of more than 2,300 teachers—who were actually *seeing* the disciple who five years before had come down from the mountaintop where he'd written America's educational declamation, *The Thread That Runs So True*. There he was in the flesh, the author of the enormously funny *Taps for Private Tussie*, and there was the youngster who had assembled his 703 sonnets in *Man with a Bull-Tongue Plow*. There was the recipient of the Guggenheim Fellowship!

Look how tall he is! His physical presence! Lord have mercy, he's a hunk! Just like the picture taken of him sitting on the bench outside "The Hunkstand" in Harrogate, Tennessee—the generous smile, the handsome suit of clothes, the white handkerchief spilling from his breast pocket, ankle of one leg crossed at the knee of the other leg like every self-respecting red-blooded American. He's Hollywood if ever there was one. Neither Will Rogers nor Billy Sunday would have attracted greater applause at Murray State than the bigger-than-life teacher from W-Hollow.

The sound system was not the best, but Jesse didn't need juked amplification. Never mind that his voice was not deep, it had an insistent, piercing quality that could reach the farthest corners of the main floor and the balcony of Lovett Auditorium, built in the '20s with its black leather seats and deco chandeliers. There was little air stirring, which made Jesse sweat even more as he warmed to the task of "An Hour with Jesse Stuart."

The speech was old-time Jesse, filled with down home stories to keep the audience laughing. The plowboy wove his Horatio Alger boyhood-to-adulthood story with accounts of the Nest Egg, the rooster who overcame all odds until he finally fell victim to a fierce-eyed owl in the middle of a stormy night.

"Think of that," Pa had said. "A rooster game and powerful as Nest Egg would be killed by a little screech owl no bigger than my fist."

Scholars might read a death message in this tale of the survival of the

Highland-fittest: Jesse the proud cock of the walk, then death striking without warning in stygian shadows.

No matter the seriousness of the storytelling, audiences from Cadiz to Calloway County had laughed when Jesse, like a cannoneer, lit the fuse and showered the landscape with colorful slices of his life back home in W-Hollow.

> *There's a time in life when you have to decide what to do...I packed my clothes up...my mother said, "Jesse, where are you going with that suitcase?"..."I'm leaving home"...my mother laughed like I'd never heard her laugh in my life...she said, "Go ahead, go out and see what it's all about"...so I went...missed my dad...he came around the ridge...I went up the holler...no money...universal language is music...I heard music on the street corner...I went to it...they had just fired the man that took up the tickets at the Merry Mix-up...asked for the job...got it...went toward Cincinnati...learned enough about the Army at Camp Knox to make me join the Navy in World War II...blacksmithing not for me...the dream was out there...hitchhiked...Morehead State looked too big for me...Kentucky Wesleyan was no place for me...they didn't have what I was looking for...went to Berea College...who are you?...told the dean who I was...he said, Do you drink?...I said, Naw, Sir, I don't drink...he said, Do you smoke?...I said, Naw, Sir, I don't smoke...he said, Well, we've got one-hundred and four on the waiting list at Berea College, you come back next year...I said, Let me tell you something...there's not a gonna be any next year at Berea College for me, if there's a school gonna take me...Ah, he said, You're positive aren't you?...I said, I sure am...he said, There's a school in East Tennessee by name of Lincoln Memorial University and we've got a man outta Berea College acting president down there...I said, How's the fastest way to get down there?...he said, Catch a train in another hour...had enough to get on...sat up all night...got off at Harrogate, Tennessee...registered under a tree with a man who had a head like a pear—little end was up.*
>
> *Audio tape in Murray State archives*

Two-thousand three-hundred teachers howled with laughter. The air was electrified. You could *feel* it.

Later Jesse would say there were *four* thousand in the audience, a forgivable case of tall tale extravagance. He even had his audience in stitches as he recalled the 1932 Wesley Hall fire at Vanderbilt. While the old building housing the Methodist School of Divinity burned, Jesse was splitting his britches trying to save his John Fox Jr. thesis. More laughter, despite the seriousness of the fire and the consequences of losing the thesis. Jesse said that was a big part of the reason he didn't receive his master's degree, and that too turned out to be funny.

Jesse flailed from the lectern that Friday morning like the winds of Hurricane Hazel roaring with 100-mile-per hour winds across the Caribbean. The hydrologic cycle was humping as it does with no respect for humanity. Jesse said teachers were the eye of the needle—but the eye of the storm in the Gulf and in a man's heart could not be turned around.

Jesse hailed teaching as the "greatest profession—the greatest of them all because all others must pass through it." He called for "evangelism" and, as reported by Dix Winston for the *Paducah Sun*, Jesse said, "I prefer a C student with good character to an A student with poor character," and the crowd cheered its approval. It was the down-home, groundbreaking theme of *The Thread That Runs So True*, and the teachers knew it to be a certainty. It was high time somebody in Frankfort woke up and took notice.

"Ignorance is dangerous...ignorance is the greatest evil," Jesse boomed, sweat beginning to roll from his forehead.

Most in the audience were thrilled by Jesse's passionate outpouring. Those who'd heard him before called it "one of his more vigorous" talks. Interlaced with homespun humor, the speech gathered power like the hurricane about to make landfall. Jesse was roiled. He knew he had his soul-mate teachers in the palm of his hand, and he wasn't about to let them get away without a good head rubbing.

Hardly anyone suspected something had gone terribly wrong in Jesse's heart. How could such a thing be? He was the teaching profession's mountain, the man of the hour. He might've rolled right into the governor's mansion. Wasn't Jesse every bit as much the heart and soul of Kentucky as "Be-like-your-pappy-and-vote-for-Happy" A.B. "Happy" Chandler? Why, Jesse ought at least to be the Commonwealth's Superintendent of Public

Instruction.

Near the end of the "Hour with Jesse Stuart," members of the platform party began to wonder if he was having some kind of speech difficulty.

He was sweating so profusely.

His hands were shaking.

He'd given many such stem-winding, slung-twice stumpings, often two in one day, even three in one twenty-four hour stretch, but this lecture was more than even he could bear.

Jesse had disregarded his doctor's repeated warnings to ease up. Hadn't Naomi pleaded with him to slow his pace? Angina attacks were becoming more frequent, but Jesse and even his doctor dismissed them as "muscular" spasms.

He managed to finish the speech, and there was a thunderous standing ovation. Eltis Henson, Murray State's Director of Field Services, assisted Jesse as he struggled to maneuver the eighteen paces toward stage left. His legs felt like splayed and splintered tulip poplar posts. His hands were like large, fluttering leaves. Henson had his arm around Jesse to help him down the four steps from the podium. Teachers who rushed forward and crowded around him just to speak to him and to get his autograph, maybe only to touch his sleeve, began to realize he was in serious trouble.

*I didn't have time to meet them. I had to hurry.*

Jesse needed to be outside, needed fresh air, needed medicine—and didn't he need to get to the Graves County airport where his charter plane was waiting to take him to his next speaking engagement that afternoon in Flora, Illinois? The clouds—what about those towering formations and passageways filled with pressure? Was God sitting up there somewhere? Was He watching? Or just waiting to see what one of his children might do with the captured birds?

*The chartered plane was waiting. I had to be on my way to carry the ball for the schoolteachers of America.*

Yes, Jesse, that is true, but only partly right. A line has been drawn, and you'll not cross over it the way you've planned. The speech in Flora, Illinois, today is one you'll not be making. This game of capture the bird like a cat is a game you'll not be playing again for a while.

The fiddler has spoken.

Martha Guier, executive secretary to M.O. Wrather, Murray State's Director of Public Relations, remembered that she was standing behind the registration table in the lobby of the auditorium. She recalled, "Three weeks before the scheduled date, Jesse sent word that he wouldn't be able to come. Then one week before the scheduled date he sent word that he would be there. His doctor had checked Jesse and cleared him."

After almost fifty years, Martha Guier remembered how Jesse and Eltis Henson "whizzed by," lurching, reaching, stumbling down the front steps of Lovett Auditorium, not quite making it to a waiting car. Eltis Henson did all he could to help the six-foot-one, two-hundred and twenty-five pound storm cell that was about to burst.

*Heart attack!*

*My feet went higher than my head. "I will not die. I will not die," I said to myself as I went down.*

Eltis Henson and a college student got Jesse into a car and drove him to the Wrather residence, where the call was placed for an ambulance.

As word spread, teachers who'd listened spellbound to their hero were stunned into silence, then tears, then gasps, and disbelieving whispers.

"Jesse has collapsed."

"Oh, no!"

"Dear God!"

"Heart attack!"

"Telephones started ringing," Martha Guier remembered.

Paramedics arrived at the Wrathers' and took Jesse to Murray Hospital on Poplar Street, where doctors quickly placed him under an oxygen tent. The arteries of the pounding heart in the plowboy had their furrowed limits no matter what he or any doctor might think.

The attending physician was Dr. Hugh Houston. Diagnosis: posterior coronary occlusion with myocardial infarction—blood clot. Jesse's condition: critical. It was doubtful he would survive. He was sedated enough for sleep.

It was early afternoon when the call went out to W-Hollow, but Naomi could not be reached immediately—there was no telephone at the W-

Hollow home. Someone in an automobile raced to the house and told her the bad news. As soon as possible she left for Murray. The worst of her fears seemed likely to have happened. In the days to follow, she and other members of the family arrived in Calloway County and stood at Jesse's bedside. They understood that it was problematic as to whether he would live, even though his words at the instant of the attack had been: "I will not die...I will not die."

Jesse Stuart was only forty-six years old—and now each of those years would be represented by one day in intensive care—one year, one day, one year, one day.

> *When I woke up, my wife, doctor and nurse were standing around my bed. I was breathing good fresh air like that I'd switched on in a plane at about two miles up. Good, clean, fresh oxygen. I lived in this tent for over three weeks. I had nurses around the clock for a month. I'd never noticed nurses very much. They were white-uniformed angels of mercy now....For thirty-five days I couldn't feed myself. I lay flat on my back forty-six days. I had to learn to walk again.*

Naomi had written in letters a week after the heart attack:

> *So glad to have your letters. Am not allowed to dictate much now.* [Jesse] *Will not be allowed to sit up in bed any until November 1. Must stay in Murray Hospital until last of November....Jesse is holding his own. He rests and is always glad to see Jane and me. He is still on the critical list and the crisis is not past. Jesse knows of your call and letter but he must be kept very quiet.*
>
> *Will have to make many changes in living. Have always been as you know a strong active man but barely missed death in this instance.*

Another letter in October:

> *Jesse is still improving nicely and that is wonderful news to us.*

October 19:

> *Dear Lena Wells and Gus: I'm Jesse's nurse today from 3 to 9*

*p.m. He was out of the oxygen tent yesterday, last night and all day today. He still has two special nurses and will be on the critical list until Friday but he is so much better...I am happy and content wherever Jesse and Jane are. Here's a message from Jesse.*

*When I was stricken I never thought of hell or heaven, loved ones or friends, but I thought this, "I am not going to die." For the next 20 minutes I suffered something hard to describe. I had no pulse or blood pressure when admitted to the hospital. In September I was a strong man. In October I am thinking of the changes I am going to have to make.*

October 26:

*After this week they were [to] start letting Jesse dangle his feet over the bed...next week get him up in a chair maybe. All this he looks forward to eagerly. Last night he slept all night long without even one capsule.*

"Toward the end of the forty-six day stay in Murray Hospital, I went to see him," said Martha Guier, who retired in 1988 after forty-two years with Murray State University. In her later years she accepted an invitation to visit the archives where scrapbooks of pictures and published clippings are preserved in the Jesse Stuart Collection.

*Murray adopted Jesse and was very supportive of him. He thought of himself as a teacher. I didn't particularly like his* Taps for Private Tussie*—it didn't hit me right—I was no judge of Jesse as a writer, but as a man he was fantastic, a motivator. He couldn't sit still...hands flailing...lot of energy. He was down to earth. He loved people.*

After Jesse's return home he was confined to the big Lincoln bed, and a "No Visitors. Doctors Orders" sign was pounded into the ground where the walkway leads to the house. Dr. Charles Vidt had determined that even well-meaning visitors caused Jesse's blood pressure to shoot up with the natural excitement of his fiery temperament.

When he was not staring at the ceiling, Jesse could part the curtains and look out.

December 2, 1954: a letter to Gus and Lena Wells Voiers:

*...I'm not allowed to write a letter by Doctors' orders, nor to have company except members of family for 5 minutes each but I'm writing you to say I'm alive and thankful to be. I've had to fight to live. This has been my hardest fight. I'll be in bed a month more—3 more months doing very little—6 months on top of that before I stir normally again—no coffee, tea, Cokes, smoking. Never again. Deane has been and is under a terrible strain. 100's of letters are here to be ans. This is all for this time. Sincerely, J.S.*

December 14, 1954:

*...When I wrote you and a few other letters before Dr. Vidt came out here, put me back in bed and stopped all letters! This morning he was here for two hours and he gave me permission to write two or three letters a day....See, my heart tested perfectly up until last March. It skipped a few beats due to overwork. But I've had the best health and have been strong as a lion. Had a good heart too! For I almost came back from the dead. See, I had chest pains and tried to tell two doctors but they told me—they intimated it was in my head—And gave me a "clean bill of heath" which almost sent me to my grave.*

Two days before Christmas 1954, Jesse could tell there was an unusual amount of traffic going and coming from his father's home further up the hollow. His doctor brought the word to him.

"Jesse, your father has died."

Jesse cried.

*I still find it hard to believe he is gone. This is why I think I hear him when it is only the wind in the willow leaves. I think I hear his hoe turning the stones over again in his corn row. How can he leave this world where his image is stamped so indelibly upon everything? He is still a part of this valley, just as it is still a part of him.*

*God's Oddling*

From this day forward, Mick and Martha slept side by side atop the hill in Plum Grove Cemetery, God rode and ruled the clouds, and Jesse was responsible for himself with a measure of independence he'd not quite known before.

# NO VISTORS—DOCTOR'S ORDERS

*It might be said that the river flowing by is the present time,*
*upriver is the past,*
*and downstream lies the future.*

Harlan Hubbard
*Shantyboat: A River Way of Life*

*Flow!*

Naomi Deane believed in Jesse the way a Highland wife believes she has a rockbound duty to care continually for her family. She unselfishly set aside her personal hopes and desires—in 1955, she became Jesse's full-time nurse.

In January, Jesse was allowed to dress for the first time following the heart attack. Then he went outside his house for the first time, as he later described in "My Heart Attack and I" for the August 13, 1955, issue of the *Saturday Evening Post*:

> *...today, I saw the first butterfly....I'm not pushing on all fronts now. But I'm still ambitious. America is not my big lemon. Someone else can have the juice. And someone else will have to run with the ball for the schoolteachers of America while I sit on the side line. I am getting back to the old life I knew that made me a man.*

February 8, 1955. Naomi wrote to Lena and Gus:

> *Everyday brings Jesse nearer to being his old self (to me). We went to Dr. Vidt last Wednesday and there is still marked improvement. Monday we went to Dr. Dole for an eye examination and although Jesse must wear glasses—he says he has good eyes—*

*healthy eyes. Our plans for the future will not include any travel very far from home and from our doctor. Jesse says he does not want to plan on European travel for a year or two and I know he is wise in his decision. We are still very close to his serious attack and I will never forget the anxiety I knew the first 10 to14 days....I am doing every little thing the doctors tell me to keep Jesse. It is so wonderful to see him return to his old self again....As ever, Deane.*

There was nearly a year of confinement in the big Lincoln bed at home in W-Hollow, the rambling house spilling over with books, manuscripts, letters, and blank pieces of paper crying out for words. Naomi Deane hovered like a mother hen feathering her Nest Egg from the gathering storm. She eyed the circumstances and tucked tighter her conviction that without her there was literally no hope for Jesse.

The sign pounded into the ground outside the walkway leading to the Stuart home—"No Visitors. Doctors Orders"—was no public relations gimmick to capture a photographer's attention to fill newspaper space. It meant exactly what it said. Jesse had narrowly escaped death, and he was a long way from being out of the Seaton Ridge woods.

Unannounced visitors to the house had been a constant problem. The devoted from many states, many countries and conditions, often popped up out of nowhere to knock on the door or peep through the windows. For loyalists, Jesse and Naomi's house had become a shrine, a place to come to and at least to take pictures for family albums. With meteoric fame comes adulation that sometimes knows no bounds. In time the hero worship becomes a nuisance even for someone as outgoing and welcoming as Jesse Stuart.

Think what teaching too often has become in the twenty-first century.

Schoolteachers dutifully show up in classrooms, going through the motions of state-controlled curricula, understandably losing patience with beleaguered students and parents anxiously awaiting the best grades for the least amount of work. Most want something vaguely and forlornly called "self-esteem"—but how many would want "to run with the ball for the schoolteachers of America?" Oh, there'd be some, but they'd soon become "agitators" and "nonconformists," and they'd be penalized for disobedience.

One year after the heart attack at Murray State, Clyde C. Ball of the Associated Press wrote: "As a country-school teacher, high-school principal, and...superintendent, Stuart often encountered violent opposition to his educational reforms. He was beaten, shot at, and threatened.

"Yet, at 48, he has lived to see many of the reforms for which he fought adopted. The school-tax dollar is now more equitably divided, to the benefit of rural and city pupil alike. The antiquated, politically chaotic school-trustee system has been abolished.

"Many of Stuart's old pupils have become teachers. He is proud of their work."

Naomi had the patient wisdom to encourage Jesse to begin keeping a journal. It would not be easy, because after the heart attack he had to learn all over again how to use his hands. The writing would be a gradual process, but as the months went by, the journal became the basis for one of Jesse's most popular and revered books, *The Year of My Rebirth*, published by McGraw-Hill in 1956. Jesse dedicated it "For All Who Have the Will to Live."

> *At the corner of the house I paused and looked down at the stream which runs under the house. In the early days when we lived here, Dad hewed a log and put it across this stream. We walked over this footlog on our way to the barn. On the other side, now our front yard, used to be the garden where my father, mother, and I worked together.*
>
> *Once my world had been the American skies, the long train trails that span the continent, the ribbons of highway across this vast and beautiful America. My world had been a thousand friends in a hundred cities, ten cups of coffee and loud talk until three in the morning. Now my world was reduced to my home, my farm, my hills. I lived more closely with my wife, my daughter, my animal friends. I thought more deeply of my God. My heart went back to these.*

Jesse wrote a letter to Peabody Teachers College President Henry Hill on April 7, 1955, six months after the heart attack:

> *...This thing certainly hit me unexpectedly. And I've really had an uphill fight to live. I've had 4 doctors, 2 at Murray, one at Louisville*

*and one at Ironton, Ohio, and each has marveled at my recovery. So
I say this can happen to anybody, especially the ones who have
ambitions to write books and be college presidents and doctors and
the vanguards of men of the spirit who dream and work for a better
land and uplift of its people.*

October 15, 1955, was Jesse Stuart Day in Kentucky, proclaimed by the
governor, and a memorial was dedicated in Greenup. The solid granite
shaft on the edge of the courthouse yard symbolizes the belief of a grateful
community that Jesse Stuart was a champion for his Highland people. The
inscription on the monument reads:

*By your own soul's law learn to live,
and if men thwart you, take no heed.
If men hate you, have no care.
Sing your song, dream your dream,
hope your hope, and pray your prayer.*

The year after Jesse's near fatal heart attack, Naomi drove him from W-
Hollow to Ashland and left him at the train station while she went
shopping. He wanted to meet the new trainmaster at the Chesapeake and
Ohio terminal.

Jesse took a seat on one of the backbenches of the waiting room. He
was all alone. He was breathing the air of the waiting room for the first
time since the heart attack, as in the days in the '30s when he first boarded
the *George Washington* to talk to stuffed-shirt publishers in New York.

Chester Powell, the new terminal trainmaster, usually visited the
passenger station around noon, when #3, the *Fast Flying Virginian*, came
smoking in. The train was switched into two trains; one continued on to
Cincinnati and the other went to Lexington and Louisville.

*One day when I was at the station looking after Number Three, I
observed a man sitting on one of the benches on the back side of the
waiting room. I became conscious that he was looking at me and of
course as you know when that happens you automatically find
yourself looking at the person who was looking at you.*

*After the trains had gone and the crowds dispersed, the gentleman
came up to me, offered his hand, and said, "You're Chester Powell."*

*He meant it as a question. I responded that he had the right man, and he said in a strong voice, "I'm Jesse Stuart."*

*He said he had read in the paper about my promotion some time ago and wanted to meet me. We talked for about an hour and could have talked all afternoon if either of us had the time. Let me say here that Jesse did most of the talking.*

*In our talk we found out that both of our fathers had been C&O Railroad employees in the track department and it seemed that knowing that brought a bonding that developed in friendship.*

*"I'd better get out there and watch for Naomi," he said, "She went up town shopping while I stayed here to meet you."*

*We shook hands again and said we hoped to see each other again and often, and he was gone. I had asked him for his address and I shall never forget his tone of voice when he said, as if everyone who wasn't living under a rock ought to know, "I live in W-Hollow, in Greenup County."*

*I wrote Jesse a note the last week of February, 1956, and told him I had bought a new Oldsmobile and I would like to come down and show it to him. I received a phone call from him in which he said he would be anxious to see my new car and that I should come on down and allow plenty of time for the visit.*

*"We have some things to talk about," he said.*

*I drove down to W-Hollow on either the first or second of March, 1956. I remember how cold it was and that a brisk wind was blowing. He watched for me, I suppose, for as soon as I pulled into the driveway he came out of the door putting on his jacket. He got in on the passenger side and we shook hands.*

*He commented that, I "sure had a pretty car." I was particularly proud of the power windows and seats. He worked the windows up and down and the seat back and forth several times then reclined his seat and said, "Let's go!"*

*I thought he did not look well and seemed tired but he insisted on driving over to Greenup. He wanted me to meet the people that ran Leslie's Drug Store. They carried all of Jesse's books for sale.*

*When we got back home and stopped in the driveway, I asked him what he thought of my car.*

*"Oh," he said curtly, "It's nice but I wouldn't have it. You'll have nothing but trouble with all these gadgets."*

*He invited me to go in but I made some excuse of needing to go on. Then he said, "But you said you had all the time in the world when I asked you to drive over to Greenup!"*

*I went in.*

*Beside the front door, sheep bells hung on leather straps. He rang them and explained that he had brought them home with him from Scotland. At the ringing of the bells Mrs. Stuart opened the door and he introduced me to her.*

*"This is Naomi Deane," he said, "my good wife of many years." She welcomed me in and took my coat. Two well-worn chairs sat in front of the small fireplace, which was blazing, and the March chill I felt in my bones soon went away. We were both cold from standing so long on the porch looking at those bells.*

*But the thing that really got his attention that day was when I told him my mother's parents were second generation Scots. When I told him my grandmother's maiden name was Alexander, he immediately said, "Oh, from around Aberdeen, I bet." I told him I had heard that and standing there in the cold he gave me a guided tour of Scotland.*

*There was something else he explained to me about the bells. He said, in his teacher like way, that the bells were of different sizes and were designed to make certain sounds so the shepherd could communicate with his sheep since there could be several flocks grazing in the same pasture. He wanted me to touch the bells as he told the story. One was the size of a half-dollar, one the size of a quarter, etc. Then he told me something I will never forget.*

*He said that when wolves were about, starving wolves, and it was evident that they were going to attack the sheep, that an old sheep would stray back from the flock and sacrifice his life for the rest. "Jesus did the same thing for mankind except he was young and that made the sacrifice even more meaningful."*

*We sat quiet for a few minutes watching the fire jump with the tug of the wind, then settle back down. I had told him early on of my interest in poetry. "Scots are all poets I think," he said. Then he asked me to recite one of my poems. I did, but when I had finished, his only comment was that he understood what I was saying.*

*I had brought some of my work with me with the purpose in mind that he would be my critic and tell me as Emily Dickinson once pleaded— "Tell me if they are worthy."*

*He destroyed that notion when he said that a writer writes first and foremost to himself. He doesn't need some critic telling him if his work is all right. He said further that the only critic he was interested in was the one who "reads my work and puts out his money to buy it. That is the person I am writing to please."*

*I got the message. No one ever to my knowledge won an argument with Jesse. As for my poetry, I wanted so badly for him to give me his approval, but he did not. All he would say was "You have to write what you feel and know about, and you have to write a poem over and over until it becomes you and you become it."*

*I wanted more but I can remember him saying on that occasion, "And that is as plain as I can make it."*

*It may not be religiously sound to say this, but I hope to see him again some day and read my poem "A Kentucky Morning" to him and tell him that he influenced it and that it did take me twenty years to finish it. I am sure he would call Naomi over and say, "Did you hear that?" Then he would slap me on the knee and laugh. He loved to laugh. He said laughing was serious business and was not to be put aside just so we could have serious thoughts.*

*Presently, Mrs. Stuart came into the room. She was carrying a large round tray loaded with a pitcher of hot tea and lots of good things to eat. Both of us stood and Jesse picked up a small table and placed it between our two chairs to support the tray. She explained that the biscuits were left over from breakfast, and then she said something that really impressed me.*

*"This blackberry jam was made from berries Jesse picked last summer."*

*My thought was that she loves him so much that the important thing about the jam was not that she had cleaned the berries, cooked them, and put them into jars all on a hot summer day, but that Jesse had picked them.*

*Afterwards, he took me through the house and showed me the places where he wrote. He showed me some of Edgar Lee Masters's manuscripts. I asked if I could see one of his. He showed me* The Good Spirit of Laurel Ridge.

*We had stopped on our way back from Greenup at a little cabin not far from Jesse's house, and he introduced me to an elderly gentleman by the name of Theopolis Akers— 'Old Op' to his friends—the hermit of Laurel Ridge. He was a steadfast believer in the world of spirits. As I was holding the manuscript I ventured to ask Jesse what he thought about the "spirit world."*

*"Every true Scotsman is a believer in the spirit world," he said and grinned.*

*When it came time for me to leave, Jesse walked with me to the car, talking in his agreeable manner, and after I got into the car, he closed the door himself and said, "Thanks for coming by." That was the line from the poem I had read to him. I never forgot that and I used it as the title for my second book of poetry.*

*He invited me to come back later in the month when the ground would be warmer and when there were so many things to see. I did go back in early April, and we walked and talked until I was exhausted. He never stopped talking, telling me the names of vines and little flowers. He would pick up leaves very gently and show me little flowers just peeping their heads up. Then he would lay the same leaf back over them. I suppose the little flowers knew themselves when to push the leaf away and show themselves to the world. He didn't say that but I think that was his message.*

*One morning in late summer 1956, I called Jesse's home and Naomi answered. I had heard Jesse was not feeling well, maybe depressed. I asked if I might speak to him, and she said let me get him for you. I am sure he will want to talk to you, then she whispered, "Would it be possible for you to take him for a ride, he needs to get out."*

*I said, I could and would. I heard her say, "Chester's on the phone and wants to talk to you a minute."*

*There was some hesitation, and he said into the phone, in a gruff voice, "What do you want?"*

*I thought about telling him, we'd talk another day and hanging up, but I decided perhaps I could help him, and so I said, "My friend, I'm having a light day and wanted to drive up the Big Sandy a little ways, and I would enjoy your company, providing you could leave the bear at home."*

*He laughed a little and said, "I'll be ready by the time you get here."*

*We got together about eleven o'clock, and after shaking hands (we always shook hands when we met and when we parted), he said, "How far are we going, I can't be gone all day."*

*I assured him we would work on his schedule, but knew down deep that he just wanted me to know that he was in charge.*

*We drove through Catlettsburg and took Hwy 23, which ran parallel to the Big Sandy River. Actually, the destination I had in mind was Louisa, where a fellow by the name of Hinkle, an old retired cook on the C&O extra forces (camp cars) ran a motel and restaurant.*

*About ten miles south of Catlettsburg there was a little community called Burnaugh. A few houses, and a big general store. We were perhaps about five-hundred feet from the store when Jesse ordered me to stop the car. I pulled over and then he told me to back up, which I did. "Stop," he said, which I did, and he got out of the car and called to an old fellow sitting peacefully on his front porch minding his own business.*

*"Come down here!"*

*The old fellow got up and said, "What do you want?"*

*Jesse didn't tell him what he wanted but just repeated what he had said. The man got up and slowly walked down the driveway, and I decided to look the other way, but I heard Jesse say, and I think these were his exact words, "When did you decide to give your farm to the state?"*

> *"I ain't giving nothing to nobody. What gave you that idea?" he retorted in a voice equally as loud as Jesse's had been.*
>
> *"Well," Jesse said, "I see these erosion places are washing your soil down into the state's ditches and they come with machines and dump trucks and haul it away to make somebody else's farm to make his land richer."*
>
> *Then Jesse did the strangest thing. He tried to shake hands with the man. The fellow refused and told Jesse to mind his own business, turned on his heel and went back up the hill. Jesse got back into the car with the most pleased expression on his face and seemed happier the rest of the day. I was up that way in the fall and saw that the man had indeed sown some fescue and was getting a good start.*
>
> *Interview*

Clearly, Jesse Stuart needed to be active. But hardly anybody imagined that he'd become a high school principal again. Naomi Deane protested, as she had with Jesse's sheep raising project, but scolding would not suffice— her husband was a man of action. The writing of *The Year of My Rebirth* was like a second-stage booster engine on a dubious space voyage.

In 1956-57, he again became principal of McKell High School, and his experiences would became the pages of *Mr. Gallion's School*, published ten years later. The principalship lasted one year. Jesse was fifty years old, and the management of a troubled school was simply too much for his damaged heart. It was time to return again to W-Hollow to write and farm. There'd be new opportunities if only he would listen to Naomi and his doctor. Stepping back from the daily pressures of students, faculty, superintendent, and school board would lead to the 1958 publication of *Plowshare in Heaven*, a collection of short stories, which he dedicated to Oscar Sammons. The tales in the book ranged from the ripsnorting "Zeke Hammertight" to "The Devil and Television," a feast of humor and exaggeration.

Two years after the heart attack, Jesse and Naomi took a "Sentimental Journey," which appeared in the October 28, 1956, issue of *The Courier-Journal Magazine*. They walked the old W-Hollow path toward the one-room Plum Grove schoolhouse:

*I stopped under an oak. I had this thought. This oak is our
community and each leaf is one of us. We are tied to each other as
the leaves are tied to this tree.*

*It was wonderful to walk this path again where I walked to school
with other children. There were so many things to see. On this path I
had found knowledge not in books. I found this where the wind was
fresh and clear of dust. This wind was good to breathe, for the
wheels of an automobile had never rolled over this land. I walked
over it with a new hope and a new song in my heart. My prayer was,
I wished every youth in American could be privileged to walk over a
path similar to this one I had walked over and see what I had seen.*

Jesse's health had broken down through a complex web of compulsion
and relentless passion combined with a daring disregard for wellness. Too
often, perhaps, before the heart attack, he valued almost everything in
terms of quantity: lift more, run harder, lecture more, talk faster, write
more, write faster, publish more. Quite possibly his Achilles heel was his
addiction to giving "talks."

Jesse told Lena Wells, "With all the good reviews *The Good Spirit* has
received in leading papers it's sold so far 7,000 copies. I worked 26 months
on it....Figure ten percent of the sale of a book and my agent's fee ten
percent of that and you'll see why I have to give talks."

After a brief time with Scribners, Jesse signed on with McGraw Hill,
where Ed Kuhn was his patient but demanding editor. The relationship
Jesse enjoyed with Kuhn was illustrated in a letter to Jesse in 1955. Kuhn
had waded through several of Jesse's submissions and then gotten down to
no-nonsense evaluating: "If there was anything wrong with *The Good
Spirit of Laurel Ridge*—which was a *fine* novel, still selling about a
hundred copies a month—it was a relatively weak story line. Characteriza-
tions were excellent, background colorful, setting original. But was perhaps
less convincing and compelling than it should have been."

The year would dawn when a Nest Egg would come home to roost just
as Martha had predicted.

*July 26, 1957*
*Dear Lena Wells:*

*...If one lives by faith, knows his heart is morally right as I know mine is, then he has strength. I don't know fear. I give them honesty, integrity and the right things to make people first and writing incidental. A great writer should be a great man....I'll go to Louisville for physical exams in early August. Four talks are pending if I pass exams. But I'll never go an hour again. Yes, I've gone an hour and 45 minutes and people didn't move out of their seats—not one of 700+ left....*

*P.S. Have a 100 letters or more to answer. Books to write. Stories, articles to do to get back into the game. But watch and see, I'll be there. God knows an honest man after he sees into his heart.*

In 1958 Jesse appeared on Ralph Edwards's popular television program "This Is Your Life." Jesse was tricked into believing that he was flying to the West Coast for a Heart Association fundraiser. Everything went as the television producers planned, and Jesse was on stage with Naomi Deane, Jane, brother James, and Jesse's lifelong friends "Nick" Carter and Harry Harrison Kroll.

That summer '58 Jesse taught in the Graduate School of Education at the University of Nevada in Reno.

*Dear LW & Poppie Gus:*

*...The fact is, I'm the most over-loaded teacher on this Campus. I think this, and without roses to myself, they've found me to be the most versatile here. At least they think I am. In the six weeks I'm here, I'll have to read at least 250 papers, teach (and prepare) for a 60 hour load. In addition give five talks. We like it very much here. You know why. Where is there a climate like this one? Yes, we can stay on if we want to or I can come back next summer but doubt that I'll do either. The S's have other plans if they work.*

*All the best, Sincerely, Jesse*

The last three decades of Jesse's life—1954-1984—were shadowed and framed by six heart attacks (or seven, depending upon who counted the nitroglycerin tablets), strokes, and numerous complications. Naomi again warned him that he should slow down, but that would've been about like trying to tell the Ohio River to flow backwards.

*June 29, 1959*
*Dear L.W.*

*Hope I will be able to be at Berea. Took a recent checkup, which was merely routine and an EKG showed a partly "block" of artery in heart. This week and next are crucial ones for me. I've always been able so far to find some magic escape. Now, I'm in pajamas resting in room here, no company, am allowed only a fountain pen and a few letters per day.*

*July 11, 1959*
*Dear Lena Wells:*

*Can't be at Berea. Hope now soon I'll be able to go to Louisville to see my doctor there. And, of course Bardstown is out. This is some blow to come right now. But I'll pull out of it. I have a "branch block" to the heart which cuts off one third of blood supply—Only rest cures this. How long it will take I don't know. But it can and will be done.*

*July 21, 1959*
*Dear Lena Wells and Gus:*

*It makes me sick because I couldn't be at Berea. I helped Dr. Weatherford get some of his speakers. Wish I could have been there. I would have done my best to uphold my side of the ledger. The paper read, probably fell flat. If I could have read it and could have spoken between the lines, as I planned to do, it would have been different....I would have liked to have seen Wilma Dykeman and Jim Stokley and of course, Jimmie Still and Harriette Arnow—would have like to have seen everybody. Gus, writing is a hard way to make a living but, honest, it's like politics or poker, you once get into it, you can't get out. And to cap it all, your record trails after you. Whether good or bad, long after you're departed from this mortal world....P.S. I can't get out of the house. Can't have company. Wish I could do both. Have been in one month plus....*

*September 1, 1959*
*Dear Lena Wells:*

*...Regarding RPW* [Robert Penn Warren]*....He has gone East, has*

*become one of those of a school, who believes it takes a little filth for filth's sake, to sell a book.*

*....I believe we should write life just about naturally and tell the filth by implication, if and when it must be told. If it were my book, I wouldn't blame you. Youth are having a hard time as is and to see their elders, especially their teachers do this, they accept it as a matter-of-fact. I have been under the impression that the trend is in reverse. Well, what ever I do from here on, regardless of trends and sales I'll be what I am and to hell with that kind of writing, filth for filth's sake.*

*Sincerely, Jesse Stuart.*

*P.S. Neither James Still or I would do this kind of writing and we're fast becoming little unknowns but there will be a brighter future for both. Lets hope.*

Robert Penn Warren's biographer, Joseph Blotner, has explained and defended him:

> *Sexuality permeates the novel [The Cave, published by Random House in 1959] not only in the revealed consciousness of each character but also in the coarse and explicit language of country people who reminded some readers of Erskine Caldwell's Tobacco Road....This quality provided a convenient club for those who had no sense of the novelist's fundamental intentions and little appreciation for the versatility of his prose.*

*September 8, 1959*
*Dear Lena Wells:*

> *There was a review* [of The Cave] *on the bookpage in Sunday* Courier-Journal, *by a man who said he was a friend of RPW (one, perhaps who is on the C.J. staff or, perhaps teaches at the University of Louisville) and his review said publicly just about what you write to Margaret Willis and what you have written me. I've not read the book and right now am just coming to life enough to do a little work each day on something I have been working on. It may be six months*

*before I get to read it. The book presumably was based on Floyd Collins and a [cave]—the one he's in...in Western Kentucky around Mammoth cave. But he moved it to eastern Tennessee. There are no caves, that I know in that area except Cudjo's Cave, on LMU property, near Cumberland Gap. It's a small one. So East Tennesseans will be displeased with that kind of writing about that area. They'll never refer to it with pride. In fact, they won't claim it. But his reason for doing this is, I believe, he's afraid of suits....*

*Warren was reared by a schoolteacher mother and a banker father in a small [Kentucky] town on the Tennessee border above Nashville. His people were conservative, smart, and religiously Methodists. He's of old English stock.... He writes to sell, Lena Wells. He writes what the people want....So, is he smart? Is it money? His friends say it is money. I don't know. He is one of my teachers. I had him at Vanderbilt. He didn't grade me too highly. Not as high as you did.*

*September 19, 1959*
*Dear Lena Wells:*

*Before we could get away to Ironton this morning where I went for a medical checkup and an EKG at the General Hospital (Ironton)— A couple from Minneapolis, Minn. Pulled in here. Mr. & Mrs. Roppe (Norwegians) stopped. He'd had two heart attacks and had read The Year [of my Rebirth] (thought it a great book) and his wife works for Dayton Bookstore in Minneapolis. She was telling me about a Ky. writer, RPW writing one of the filthiest books—one she couldn't finish—and on the strength of his name—publicity from publishers on said book—they ordered 200 copies. I just let her tell me about RPW—Then she said they returned 175 books to publishers and kept 25. Believe me, this is a slap....I told her I knew RPW—he'd taught me at Vanderbilt. This was all I told her. Said she: "I don't care who he taught. He's written the dirtiest book I ever started to read."*

*Sincerely, Jesse*

*P.S. I hope to get enough health to finish one and I hope this won't be said about mine.*

Harcourt, Brace and Company published *Adventures in Reading: Olympic Edition*, with an introduction by Jesse Stuart, excerpts from which appeared in the March 14, 1958, issue of *The Courier-Journal Magazine*:

> *I think all high schools should strive to create the balance of scholarship and athletic ability, which the Greeks once had. Good sports are as important to the development of the body as good reading material is to the development of the mind. I want all my pupils to be interested in sports, and to play at least one game well.*
>
> *Writing has never been a task for me. Writing has been enjoyment. I have laughed and wept with my characters.*
>
> *During my career I have written many things about teen-agers. Perhaps some of my best writing is about them. The reason I've written so much about teen-agers is that I know them. I've been close to them for so long a time that they keep me young as the years go by. I like the teen-age period. It's the time when we want to turn the earth over to see what is under it.*
>
> *I believe education and educated people will save us from world catastrophe. When people are educated and become enlightened, then—and only then—will we have a better world.*
>
> *The world of books is the most remarkable creation of man. Nothing else that he builds ever lasts. Monuments fall, nations perish. Civilizations grow old and die out. And after an era of darkness new races build others. But in the world of books are volumes that have seen this happen again and again, and yet live on, still young, still as fresh as the day they were written, still telling men's hearts of the hearts of men centuries dead.*

Jesse had taken this message out into the world far beyond W-Hollow. He would soon be on his way to Egypt.

# THE BROTHERHOOD
# OF MINSTRELS

*He never wanted to hear young people
from eastern Kentucky apologize for being from eastern Kentucky—
that they could do anything—
that the key to it was education.*

Judge Sara Combs
concerning her husband,
Gov. Bert T. Combs
(Interview)

*Sail!*

The 1960s begin:

The Statue of Liberty flame illumines another new decade...
harbormaster record keepers in lower Manhattan sort through outbound
traffic manifests...deck hands coil their mooring lines...the Hudson and East
Rivers flow into the choppy North Atlantic...headwaters meet the
ocean...bonds of isolation are released...another torch is about to be passed.

John F. Kennedy is elected thirty-fifth president of the United States...
Camelot dawns...the age of innocence precedes by nearly a half-century the
time of nine-eleven and America's invasion of Iraq...Columbine and CNN
have not yet compressed the consciousness of the United States.

The public issue of tobacco, the Burley variety grown in Kentucky, is
still measured, in 1960, in terms of family farms, quotas, and a complicated
system of price supports. Nicotine addiction and its fatal consequences are
slowly beginning to be heard of from Lexington to W-Hollow. The

After *Taps for Private Tussie, The Thread That Runs So True,* and *Album of Destiny,* Jesse wrote children's books: *The Beatinest Boy, Huey the Engineer,* and *A Penny's Worth of Character.* From book signings to speakers' platforms, Jesse Stuart resonated with the faithful in his audiences, who loved to hear him unwind and recall the early days of growing up in his beloved W-Hollow.

Jesse's barnstorming across America, his relentless pursuit of just one more speaking engagement, led to his first heart attack in the autumn of 1954. He collapsed after an hour-long stem-winder at Murray State, and it was a miracle that he survived. He spent a year of recovery at W-Hollow and kept a journal, which became another book, *The Year of My Rebirth.*

**M**ore heart attacks followed in the 1970s and 1980s, but Jesse stubbornly clung to life. He wrote the autobiographical *The Kingdom Within* and *If I Were Seventeen Again*. Paralyzed on the left side, he sat in his wheelchair, puffed his cigar, and thought of ways to give a gift of land to the Commonwealth of Kentucky he so dearly loved.

"What will happen to the land when we are gone?" Jesse had wondered aloud in the autumn of his life.

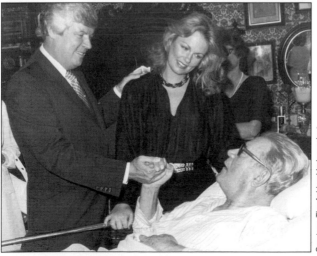

**F**ormer Gov. John Y. Brown and First Lady Phyllis George Brown came to W-Hollow to present Jesse with the Governor's Distinguished Service Medallion. They also thanked him for making possible the Jesse Stuart Nature Preserve, where white-tailed deer step warily through billions of fallen oak leaves, where wide-eyed bullfrogs croak...where the good spirit of Old Op laughs past the sourwood trees.

Courtesy *The Courier-Journal*

Naomi Deane stood by Jesse the way a Highland woman guards her man. She was there for all the days in the wheelchair, and she visited every day during the two years he was comatose in the Jo-Lin Health Center across the river in Ironton, Ohio. She rode in the hearse that brought him home to Kentucky, in 1984, and the last words she spoke to him at the graveside were: "Goodbye, Jesse." Naomi Deane died in 1993, and she is buried beside him in Plum Grove Cemetery.

JESSE
HILTON STUART
AUG. 8, 1906
FEB. 17, 1984

NAOMI DEANE
NORRIS
STUART

*Courier-Journal* and *Louisville Times.* In that 1972 book, Creason wrote:

> *Nearly 40 years ago when Stuart, then a Greenup County teacher, had advocated changes in education—consolidation, elimination of the trustee system—he was branded a troublemaker out to wreck the very school system that had educated him. He was forced to back his convictions with his fists on numerous occasions.*

Joe and Jesse bonded. They were good old boys in the best sense of the phrase, in the salad days before political correctness.

Each in his own way, driven by inner voices, the two bards of the people, *by* the people, and *for* the people, roamed the 120 counties of Kentucky, searching for one more face, one more handshake, one more story fit for telling. Jesse and Joe liked to be with people who seldom if ever made headlines—they were the grassroots nobodies who might be mentioned on an impersonally-written obituary page, but like as not with a name spelled wrong.

Jesse Stuart and Joe Creason were card-carrying members of the brotherhood of minstrels, the *meistersingers.* Five centuries after the invention of the printing press, they were the poet and the journalist unacclaimed by the literary critics but revered by the folks "down home." Jesse and Joe also had faltering hearts in common.

Their friendship ended too soon.

Joe died of a heart attack while playing tennis, August 14, 1974, in Louisville.

Born in 1918 in Benton in far-western Kentucky, Joe Creason was buried in a small cemetery by the side of the "old" road in Bethel, near the home place of his wife, Shella, in Bath County. Joe's favorite tree, the Kentucky coffee tree, grows from his grave—not visible from the "new" KY 11, which bypasses to the west. It's as if the highway designers didn't know, or perhaps discounted, the importance of Joe Cross Creason to the Kentucky he loved.

Jesse Stuart and Joe Creason were two Kentucky writers who shared the commoner's touch without pretension, without fol-de-rol. Whether you lived in Louisville or W-Hollow, Benton or Bethel, Cairo, Egypt, or East Cairo, Kentucky, you didn't have to work overtime to understand the writings of these two *meistersingers* who loved people, especially Kentuckians. Joe and Jesse were self-appointed ambassadors for the Commonwealth of Kentucky.

Joe's description of Jesse in 1960: *He does everything with the overwhelming determination, enthusiasm and intensity of a man killing snakes. To that end, Stuart doesn't have just one book currently ready for market—he has five in various stages of completion. All five could appear this year.*

One of the five books was *God's Oddling*, which Jesse himself called:

> *...the one book I have wanted most to write all my life. It is about my father, Mitchell Stuart. It is for him, too. Even though my father was unable to read or write anything but his own name, I believe he was a great man. He was great in spirit and great in his influence upon others. There is no other man that I have ever loved or respected more. When I set out to write this book, I discovered that I had already been writing it all my life, for I had written poems and stories and articles about my father from the time I started writing.* God's Oddling, *then, is the harvest of all my writing seasons. It is the best book I could write, and I hope it is worthy of the man I have tried to portray.*
>
> *The title of this book,* God's Oddling, *comes from something my father used to call my brother and me. For years he used to call me "oddling" because I had gone away to school and become a writer, and because I didn't smoke the tobacco we grew or drink the mountain liquor brewed nearby. I was recovering from my heart attack when my father died. During those last days he used to come visit me at my house, and he still called me "oddling." It was then, just before he died, that I thought my father was one of God's Oddlings, not me. He was a proud, independent man, who always made his own decisions and went his own way. He was a very gentle man, too. He was an oddling, all right.*

The word "oddling" is not to be found in either the *American Heritage Dictionary of the English Language* or the *Oxford English Dictionary*. "Oddling" is an Appalachian adaptation of Middle English (1100-1500), *odde*, and Old Norse (1100-1300), *oddi*—meaning point of land, triangle, or odd number. Shakespeare's *Merry Wives of Windsor* delights in "divinity in odd numbers, either in nativity, chance or death." The roots of Appalachian speech reach far back in time—Jesse and his father Mick preserved the richness of the language of their people and the period in which they lived.

Joe Creason had visited at W-Hollow in the early spring of 1960, and *The Courier-Journal* photographer James N. Keen took pictures of Jesse and Naomi poring over maps and travel books—*Cairo and Environs* and *The Egyptian Revolution*. The pictures are an invaluable source for visualizing this diminishing time, 1960, in the lives of Jesse and Naomi. Jesse didn't look like somebody who six years before had suffered a near fatal heart attack. Naomi appeared resigned, accepting of reality. Her husband never ceased to amaze her.

There he is—Jesse looking to the left with his right forefinger pushing up his cheek in a moment of finding a thought to gather it in; then, looking to the right, the palm of his hand giving his leonine head a place of comfort; then, both hands locked behind his neck in a posture of reflective openness beside the shelves of books, books, books. Joe Creason and James Keen captured the essence of one of Appalachia's stout-hearted men.

The other pictures portrayed Jesse as he was seldom seen by outsiders. His trust in Joe Creason's judgment made an essential difference. There's a view of the shack where Jesse "stores his manuscripts." Another picture inside the building shows shelf upon shelf of magazines with stories he wrote, first editions of his books, and "originals of book illustrations." One of the "outsider's books" on a shelf is John Steinbeck's *Tortilla Flat*. Still another picture shows Jesse wrapping the manuscript for a junior book, *The Rightful Owner*, preparing it for mailing from the post office in Riverton to his publisher on the East Coast. Original manuscripts and "poems scribbled out on any kind of scrap paper" line the walls like a tornado's wildest dream come true.

The invitation to go halfway around the world to Egypt had come to Jesse from the president of the American University in Cairo, Dr. Raymond L. McLain, who during the post-World War II years had been president of Transylvania University in Lexington when that fine liberal arts school was struggling to stay open. Dr. McLain's reputation for innovation had succeeded in rescuing Transylvania, and his fame had widened to an international level. The appointment of Jesse Stuart to teach in Cairo for one year was as inspired and potentially fruitful as it was daring. After all, Jesse might show up woefully unprepared for Middle East culture shock. He might try to stand toe-to-toe with President Gamal Abdel Nasser or take it upon himself to sit on the edge of his desk and blow smoke in his face. Anybody who knew Jesse knew the only way he could possibly be was, simply himself.

In the summer of 1960, Jesse, Naomi, and Jane boarded the Italian liner *Augustus* at Pier 84 in New York, bound for Naples. The voyage was a fairyland of sunrises and sunsets. The time in Italy was brilliant and unforgettable, superb moments with plenty of good food and fine cigars to close each day of new discovery.

The Stuarts arrived at Alexandria on the *Esperia*, August 24, 1960, and soon they were as much at home as if they were on the bluffs overlooking the Ohio River where it loops northward at Riverton and rolls on toward Portsmouth.

> *We lived on the side of the island facing the Nile Hilton Hotel. We lived on the second story of a seven-story stone house where we could stand on our balcony and throw an apple core into the Nile near the bulrushes where it was said Pharaoh's daughter found Moses.*
>
> My World

Jesse was not an "Ugly American," but some of his New World critics and the watchful eyes of the Nasser regime might have questioned the assertion. It's highly unlikely the new Central Intelligence Agency, established in 1947, had used Jesse as its agent, although his patriotism was well known. In *To Teach, To Love*, Jesse wrote

> *When I first looked into my students' faces, a new fear struck me. Some of the countries from which they came were hostile to the United States. Had national attitudes rubbed off on these young men and women? Would personal hostilities nullify my efforts to reach them?*

Contrary to the *Ugly American* stereotype, Jesse settled in, watched, listened, and had the good sense to reason that there might one day be "One World," but for now Egypt was Egypt and Kentucky was Kentucky. He began to compare what he was seeing and hearing with his growing concern that in America there might possibly be too many rebels with doubtful causes.

> *In America students don't love a school this much, not any more. Many American students dread the start of a school year. They remain at home until the day of registration. Here they wanted to live on the campus. I didn't know that Muslim girls didn't date boys as girls do in America. I didn't know marriages for young couples were arranged by their parents and many a groom and bride didn't see each other until the day of their wedding. There were many things I needed to learn about this world.*
>
> To Teach, To Love

Jesse was a learner, the kind of man who comes upon a point of inquiry, picks it up like an apple fallen from a tree, examines it for possible worms, then voraciously bites into it. He might even relish the core and seeds, saving the woody stem for thoughtful chewing. Or coming upon a wetness by the side of a hill, he might imagine that there was a hidden spring waiting to be discovered, and he would take a long-handled shovel to dig for the water that had percolated up there. He understood the importance of freeing every drop of water and nourishing each square inch of soil.

> *We had come eight thousand miles to this little three and one-half acres of American University college-campus freedom which was locked in with a big padlock. But freedom cannot be held behind a gate. It jumps over a fence and becomes a fresh-blowing wind. Freedom can start from my tongue that can generate hot words for a hot wind. It can start from many tongues. And to hell with the stooges and spies! I'll teach school when the teaching starts.*
>
> To Teach, To Love

Jesse laid to rest speculation that his trip to Egypt had been handsomely covered by a propagandistic U.S. government or some Ford or Rockefeller foundation with a hidden, built-in agenda. He was paid $5,000, less than he had made when he was principal at the McKell High School in South Shore, Kentucky, in 1956-1957. Jesse said in *To Teach, To Love* he had taken hold of the opportunity "to help the people, and by doing so to buy goodwill for our country."

But Jesse, the devout Protestant Republican, was incensed about the election of JFK.

*November 10, 1960*
*Dear Lena Wells:*

*Did you ever think you'd live to see the day we'd get what we've got for the White House for the next four years? Can you believe it? Let's start work before he's in to send him back to Boston to cut coupons from his bonds....He's one joker the majority of Americans will hang their head in shame over in the next four years! Now, who'll occupy the White House. What kind of a crowd? Don't tell me money doesn't speak in America!*

*November 10, 1960*
*Dear Gus:*

*Happy to have your letter but distressed to learn—or even think— a recession is in sight. My book published now—G.O. [God's Oddling]—I hope will pay back the forward M.H. advanced me while I was working on another book. Now, I expect a loss of $2000 or more in this teaching assignment. Magazines are out of the picture from here. No sales. No talks which bring in from no fees to good fees. So my income is already down. Then when we go home we have to buy a car and a truck and start all over again and send Jane off to school. If books don't sell—and they're luxuries and people don't have to buy them—so we can't expect it....Eisenhower has given us two terms with dignity—and our country has been prosperous....I wonder what we are in for in the years ahead.*

*Sincerely, Jesse*

Jesse's unorthodox teaching, which had endeared him to so many in Kentucky, was like an unexpected, comforting breeze in the Sahara and Libyan deserts of turmoil and tradition. An example of Jesse's oasis can be appreciated by listening to a conversation recalled in *To Teach, To Love.*

*In my creative-writing class, I had Ibrahim Nimr, a large friendly Sudanese who sat in the front row. I also had him in one of my education classes. He was as dark as a moonless winter night, with the gentleness of a lamb. I was very fond of him. He had not enrolled in my writing class but had not missed a class since it had begun the second semester. When a student read a poem he liked, he was all smiles, showing a mouthful of white teeth.*

*I made it a point to get better acquainted with him. I learned he was a member of one of the 140 tribes which made up the twelve million population of the Sudan. I learned his 140 tribes all spoke different languages too. And I learned Ibrahim was a schoolteacher. But I wondered why he liked our writing class so well.*

*"May I?" he asked, handing me a sheaf of something at the end of a class. "I'd like to show you."*

*"Sure," I said. "I'd like to see."*

*I opened the sheaf, and I got a stack of two dozen pen-and-ink sketches of the Sudanese. This man was an artist.*

*"Where did you study art?" I asked him.*

*"I never studied art, sir," he said. "I just like to draw in my spare time."*

*"Have you been the one doing all the drawings on the blackboard before this class begins?" I asked him.*

*"Yes, sir," he replied.*

*"What else do you like to do?"*

*"Write poems and stories!"*

*"Have you got any with you?"*

*"Yes, sir, but they are written in Arabic."*

*"Can you translate them?"*

*"Yes, sir, with some help. My friend Omar El Reedy is helping me."*

*Omar El Reedy, a Muslim despite his last name, was writing some of the finest lyric poetry written in all Egypt. He was in this class too.*

*"How much verse have you written?"*

*"Enough for two or three books if it's good enough to be published."*

*"And what about your stories?"*

*"I have many."*

*"I would like for you to join this class and make credit hours," I
said. "I'd like to have you. You're the kind of student I'm trying to
find."*

*"I'd like to be in here," he said. "I'd like to register if I can."*

*"I think this can be arranged," I said. "I'll see the registrar."*

It could not be arranged. More correctly, it wouldn't be. Jesse's written
request that Ibrahim Elawam Nimr ("Son of the Tiger") be admitted to his
creative writing class was denied by the Committee on Student Standing.
Jesse seethed, but he refrained from using a chain saw on the committee
chairman's door.

*Son of the Tiger came to the door of the English class. He stood in
the corridor.*

*"Come in," I invited him.*

*He smiled and walked in. I didn't tell I had received a copy of the
committee's letter.*

*After the class was over he walked up to my desk smiling.*

*"Now, you come back to this class," I said. "You don't get credit
when you audit. You don't pay. You just be my guest."*

*Son of the Tiger understood.*

*To Teach, To Love*

In the mysterious land of the Nile, the longest river in the world—4,160
miles long, 1,820 miles longer than the Mississippi River—United Arab
Republic President Gamal Abdel Nasser laid the cornerstone for the Aswan
High Dam, impounding water for Lake Nasser, modern source of electrical
power and irrigation. In the Valley of the Kings, in the vast expanse of
Upper Egypt, farmers still used ancient traditions of plowing with oxen.
These determined agrarians turned the topsoil for a new generation.

In W-Hollow, future impoundments of water eventually would seal the
fate of Cedar Riffles, where frogs would no longer *too-deep, too-deep,*
minnows would lead their schools to upstream pools, and water moccasins
would glide harmlessly to up-country headwaters.

The Egyptian civilization, dating back to 3,000 B.C., with its thirty
dynasties, represented a daunting reality for a Methodist born two
millennia later on Cedar Riffles in Kentucky.

Teaching methods in an authoritarian society were unlike the freedoms taken for granted in the United States. Jesse Stuart understood, and he had the good sense to watch what he said and to take special precautions—the way a moonshiner might when Prohibition revenuers showed up and rushed to governmental judgment.

Jesse wrote in *To Teach, To Love*:

> *I couldn't stand up and voice my opinion about what was right and wrong the way I could in America. I would have been arrested. No one could speak against the government. It had the final say, the final word. And my wife and I, before we could teach there, had to become temporary citizens of Egypt. This was so our earnings could be taxed.*
>
> *Even our school paper and magazine,* The Scarab, *had to be read and censored before publication. These young and old Americans who bellyache about freedom in America should try being in a dictatorial country such as Egypt now and then....I disposed of the notes I used in my classes even though they contained nothing critical about Egypt. Since our fireplace wouldn't work, I took them down to the Nile, right in front of our home, where Moses was said to have been found in the bulrushes, and here I cast my notes upon the water. I left no traces of my scribbled handwriting. I learned fast. I learned the color of the galabias* [djellabas, Moslem-world garments] *the Egyptian CIA wore. They were very often on our campus.*

Jesse Stuart, the writer/teacher/farmer, had no choice. But he remembered his Robert Browning, no matter the restraints of dictatorial decree.

> *Ah, but a man's reach should exceed his grasp,*
> *Or what's a heaven for?*

While Jesse was teaching at AUC, Naomi taught at a private elementary and secondary school in Cairo, and Jane began her freshman year at AUC. Possibly it was one of the most personally rewarding experiences in the Nest Egg family of Stuarts, and Jesse made sure that Browning's reach extended beyond Egypt.

*We spent Christmas and vacation days, and even long weekends, traveling with our daughter Jane to other countries. We often flew up to Beirut, Lebanon. We visited Saudi Arabia, Jordan, Syria, and the Holy Land. When the school year was over we spent most of the summer visiting European countries that had been part of the Roman Empire.*

*...I've returned to countries I had visited, and I've traveled to many more. I've traveled in ninety countries altogether, some only once, some as many as sixteen times. Now I feel definitely that I know what my United States is. Again, I have said many times on the platform when I have been questioned about the United States, "If you have traveled and have found a greater country than the United States, tell me where it is, and I'll cancel everything I'm doing and be there in a week!"*

*Certainly we make mistakes in America. And we'll go on making mistakes. Certainly we have problems in America. We've had so many I wouldn't know what to do without them....The United States is a people's dream. We live better, have better food, better schools, better roads, more vehicles, more merchandise for sale in our stores than any country I have ever been in. We have more and better farming, the greatest farming in the world. No country has better trained school teachers and better schools, from kindergarten to the graduate level. Too many Americans don't realize what America means to them and to the world.*

*To Teach, To Love*

The Middle East pulled Jesse back a final time in the '70s when he made his last pilgrimage to the distant lands of memory, writing in one of his farewell books, *My World*:

*One evening in the summer of 1972, Naomi and I sat on our balcony watching the boats on the Nile. The feluccas were going upstream, for this is the way the wind blows constantly. Their sails were spread and full of wind. Other boats came down with the current. Transportation on the Nile, the wind taking the boats up and the current bringing them down, hadn't cost anything as long as there had been an Egypt.*

*I told Naomi that I'd like to return to Egypt and teach again at AUC. I had never taught youth as bright, youth who had more respect for education, school properties, and their teachers. Of course, not all the students enrolled at AUC came from Egypt. Some came from Arab countries in Africa and the Middle East, from Europe, and some from the United States. They came from all over the world.*

*"But time is fleeting for us," Naomi reminded me. "We don't have enough time left to live all the places you'd like to live. I doubt we will ever live here again. But we can return for visits."*

*All around us were the lights of Cairo. The lights loomed up and made a bright canopy in the sky. Higher up there was another canopy of starlight. Down below us flowed the mighty Nile, the most famous river in the world, loaded with traffic that would be moving all night and all day tomorrow. I'd like to live in Cairo again, beside the Nile in Zamalek on the Island of Gezeriah, and teach at American University in Cairo.*

My World

*I loved the masses in Egypt. The fellahin who have farmed the Nile Valley for five thousand years are the best workers in the world. All they do is work. They hardly know they have a government. When the masses in Egypt become educated, Egypt will change. It has to change to keep pace with an ever-changing modern world. I wonder what students I taught there thought when Apollo 8 went around the moon. I am sure they rejoiced and remembered that a free man from a Western-world society was for a time in their midst.*

To Teach, To Love

While he was in Egypt in 1960, Jesse received word that he had been awarded a $5,000 fellowship from the Academy of American Poets. He would formally accept it after his return home.

*April 9, 1961*
*Dear Lena Wells:*
*In NYC we have to stay over a few days for the award will be presented to me there. I think this is the plan. Not a big affair but a*

*minor little thing for the biggest achievement ever—that is for me.
Twenty seven years, 1600 poems published and nothing—then the
award of all awards dropped unexpectedly into my lap—Life is
great, Lena Wells: Live it fully and while you can. The years grow
shorter for all of us.*

*Sincerely, Jesse*

*May 25, 1961*
*Dear Lena Wells:*

*If I go away again it will be for one semester or less. I have a
contract here for U. of Alaska for twice as much money as here and
half as much teaching but I've not signed it. I'm taking the year at
home and taking but few talks. I've got books to write—yes, more of
them. I know what goes into a book and what one subtracts from a
person. And I know I'm not the top apple on the tree but those in KY.
and this has been said, who write a book to knock one off "the
pedestal" (I have never known I was on one) will have a fight on his
hands—for I know my destiny. It is to knock no one off a pedestal but
to lend each a helping hand—when and if I can. But I know time is
fleeting and I have so much to do. I can see five more books—maybe
six—two of these are ready. Another one will be shortly.*

*Sincerely, Jesse*

Jesse, Naomi, and Jane arrived back in the United States on July 12,
1961. He went to work immediately to complete the manuscript for *Hold
April*, poetry that would live as long as readers reach for eternal spring.
Biographer Everetta Love Blair called this volume "a collection of poems,
which might be called the summation of his lifetime of poetic thought."

Blair recalls the letter Jesse wrote from Cairo to his old Vanderbilt
mentor, Donald Davidson:

*Twenty-seven years ago, I got the Jeanette Sewal Davis Prize of
$100, and 1957 or '58, the Lyric Magazine prize of $50. Never
dreamed such as this would happen to me! Well it has! Over 1600
poems, and I've never budged from what I believed about poetry—
that it should communicate—I wouldn't become a part of a school. I*

*never gave an inch from what I believed....Well, now, this—God has let me live for something!*

*May 5, 1962*
*Dear Lena Wells and Sir Poppie Gus:*
   *...We've been almost too busy to live. Why have I been busy? Improving this farm and buildings. I've done the planning. Help is limited and expensive. But we have done valuable things. Valuable for here and for the place....Have revised very much, the book of poems—almost to perfection. Have cut a novel down since last October from 1020 to 688* [pages]. *Have selected stories, poems, excerpts from books, (each one third) have written forewords to each—what caused me to write each—have written general and advanced questions to stories and excerpts of books—all told almost 200 pages of writing since Oct. 1961. In addition from 6 to 8 talks per month. Even taking the tour for the USIS, going from Country to Country will be a rest! So you see what I'm up against. In addition I write 25 letters per day. Receive more than I write. I've used Sundays to work trying to get caught up....we've had two years of income tax to make out. Egypt put me behind.*

*June 2, 1962*
*Dear Lena Wells:*
   *Have just listened to some old recordings and they bring back another world you, Gus, Deane and I used to know—a good world it was too. We traveled by train with smoke billowing to the skies— trains making every little stop—If by car we went over a lot of dirt roads. Today our world would be a strange one to youth—but it is a world youth of today might like better than this one we have. And everybody read magazines and papers then. Everyone had his favorite magazine. He read his books too. So, we've witnessed a changing world and have adjusted accordingly—even some of the things I wrote yesterday—are outdated today. The language has even changed. But, change or no change, we'll be brave in a changing world and follow where she leads—rejoicing as we know! There's only one time for this—it is now! Your philosophy—make*

*every day count!*

*Sincerely, Jesse*

In the years 1962-1963, Jesse embarked again, this time on a seven-month World Lecture Tour sponsored by the United States Information Service. He took his *Man with a Bull-Tongue Plow* message to Beirut and Tehran. It was a period of continued relative innocence, before the age of almost daily terrorism.

From King's Palace Hotel, Athens, Greece, Oct 23, 1962:

*Dear Lena Wells and Poppie Gus:*
*...We were from the time we left NYC 24 hrs. getting to Tehran 10,000 miles away. In Iran I gave ten lectures—besides meetings with educators and writers and a few social events—and we traveled 2500 miles inside Iran by plane, train and car. Then to Egypt for 15 days and I have 19 major lectures to student groups in their largest schools...and I had conferences with their cultural clubs with educators—besides social events—meeting with my former students—so 29 lectures in a month besides other events, made it a busy one.*

Camelot would soon come crashing down, innocence would be as lost as a deer in an Appalachian spring. Marilyn Monroe committed suicide on August 5, 1962..."Freedom Riders" were attacked in the Deep South...The United States and the Soviet Union danced on the edge of nuclear holocaust...And on November 22, 1963, President John Fitzgerald Kennedy was assassinated in Dallas, Texas.

The clock also ticked for Jesse Stuart.

*August 30, 1964*
*Dear Lena Wells and Sir Poppie Gus:*
*...We're back from a 17 day tour and 3715 miles. Deane did the driving—and I did the speaking—almost covering Florida....I spoke at Ft. Meyers—near there at Lehigh acres. Then to Sarasota—then to Jacksonville where Hurricane Cleo was coming up the coast to pay a visit. Everything was cancelled. And we pulled out when the Hurricane was 40 miles away. We drove west to escape it—then up*

*through Georgia to Chattanooga—and from there home.*

Jesse and Naomi revisited Cairo and spent a month in Greece.

> *There is a little Greek restaurant...just under the bank and above the Aegean Sea. Naomi and I found this restaurant when we first visited Greece together....We ate octopus tentacles and seaweed soup here. It was so good we've been back every time we've been to Greece....Attica, which produced the world's most learned men, would be my choice spot to live outside my native Kentucky and the United States....On the southern tip of old Attica I could have fruit, grapes, olives. I could grow a garden. All of this would be fun. No wonder so many people from Western countries, young people and old, live on the Greek mainland and on the islands. What a beautiful, clean country!...An ancient country with one of the greatest civilized people who ever walked on the face of the earth. The Egyptians educated for death. The Greeks educated for life.*
>
> My World

On to West Pakistan, India, Thailand, the Philippines, Taiwan, Japan, and Korea. In Dacca, Naomi learned of the deaths of her parents in a car accident—her father had been killed instantly and her mother died later. Naomi returned home and Jesse continued the tour.

The decade of the 1960s included "Jesse Stuart Day" at the University of South Carolina; dedication of the Jesse Stuart collection at Murray State University; five honorary doctorates (Marshall University, Northern Michigan University, Murray State University, Berea College, and Pfeiffer College); Author in Residence at Eastern Kentucky University; and a tour of Europe and Africa.

Published books during the 1960s included *Huey the Engineer, A Jesse Stuart Reader, Save Every Lamb, Daughter of the Legend, My Land Has a Voice, Mr. Gallion's School*, and *Come Gentle Spring*.

*Huey the Engineer* and later *A Ride with Huey the Engineer* demonstrate Stuart's desire to reach and resonate with a youthful readership. He uses his own humble beginning to teach a lesson of respect, adventure, and pleasure—

> *Ever since he could remember, he had dreamed of some day being able to see what lay outside of Clearwater Valley, Every day, for the two years he had been going to school, he would hurry to the tracks just above the Three Mile Station to watch Huey, the Engineer, drive his Engine No. 5 along the Eastern Kentucky Railroad.*

*A Jesse Stuart Reader* is a convenient way to sample the life's work of the "Writin' man from W-Hollow." The collection begins with "Nest Egg" and includes seventeen other short stories—"Battle With the Bees," and "Old Op and the Devil." This volume includes excerpts from *God's Oddling*, *The Thread That Runs So True*, and *The Year of My Rebirth*. There are twenty-six of Jesse's thousands of poems, including "Our Heritage"—

> *We are a part of this rough land*
> *Deep-rooted like the tree.*
> *We've plowed this dirt with calloused hand*
> *More than a century.*

> *We love the lyric barking hound*
> *And a piping horn that trills.*
> *We love our high upheavaled ground,*
> *Our heritage of hills.*
>
> 

*Hold April*

As a book title for a collection of short stories, *Save Every Lamb* symbolizes Jesse's approach to his work and his life, which are inseparable. He throws nothing away, counts each human being as intrinsically valuable, and savors the thought of heavenly days to come. *Save Every Lamb* was recycled from Jesse's first novel, *Trees of Heaven*. Culling, pruning, and weeding do not seem to hold much appeal for Jesse Stuart.

*Daughter of the Legend* is the idyllic story of a Melungeon girl, a descendant of the "lost tribe" of East Tennessee. Neither the writing nor the legend upon which it is based is every man jack's cup of joy. Jesse Stuart collectors prize it, loyalists place it high on their list of "Jesse's books I have read and loved," and some may wish there'd been a more unflawed effort. As Jesse consistently made it clear, he didn't write for critics.

*My Land Has a Voice*, published in 1966, is a rich sampler of short stories—"Corbie," "Red Mule and the Changing World," "A Mother's Place Is with Her Son," "Judge Ripper's Day," and "Remember the Sabbath Day and Keep It Holy." The tales illustrate the vigor of Jesse Stuart's creativity: "Corbie" symbolizes individuality and the need for special education; "Judge Ripper's Day" is a comical fable of lying, mean-spirited deceit, and Judgment Day restitution; "A Mother's Place Is with Her Son" recalls Martha Stuart and how hard she worked before she died:

> *You boys must not forget it takes work, sweat, and honesty to make you amount to something in life.*

*Mr. Gallion's School* suggests the possibility of an author in his twilight years trying, after almost twenty years of repeated heart attacks, to extend the life of something as monumental as *The Thread That Runs So True*. The same freshness was not there and a weakness was beginning to show.

Jesse Stuart toiled, all right, but his heart was never the same after the first major coronary he suffered at Murray State. One thing was certain: as long as he could write, his will to live would be as strong as the creature that pulled the bull-tongue plow. He might talk about dying being a natural thing, but he'd fight every step of the way to the grave.

*Come Gentle Spring*, another collection of vintage Jesse short stories, concludes the decade of the '60s, foreshadowing the final decade of writing, which included a variety of less vivid work, from *To Teach, To Love* to *Dandelion on the Acropolis*.

In a letter to Roland Carter, dated January 22, 1965, Jesse acknowledged the inevitable:

> *Oh, if I only knew I had 21 more years ahead of me! I'm afraid I haven't! So in these years to come, those left, you can expect books from me. I'll be pushing what I think is the last lap. I'll give it all I have.*
>
> *Sincerely, Jesse*

# HEADLONG RACE WITH
# THE TICKING OF THE CLOCK

*Gertie held the Bible open at Ecclesiastes...*
*"One generation passeth away,*
*and another generation cometh....*
*All the rivers run into the sea; yet the sea is not full;*
*unto the place from whence the rivers come,*
*thither they return again."*

Harriette Arnow
*The Dollmaker*

*Pay heed!*

In a dream, a telephone call had come from his agent in New York City. Jesse later recreated it as a fictionalized conversation in a small allegorical autobiography, *The Kingdom Within*, published by McGraw-Hill in 1979. It's not clear whether the dream preceded an oncoming seizure or if the opposite was true—faltering heart, hallucination, then the made-up telephone call.

"We have just received word from Stockholm that you have won the Nobel Prize for literature!" exclaims the voice in the dream.

"My 'barnyard, redneck, hillbilly' books linger on, refuse to die, and win prizes," replies Jesse in his flight of fantasy. Since no Kentuckian had ever won this highest of honors, why not Martha and Mick's first-born son?

One of his most ardent biographers, Everetta Love Blair, had extolled in 1967: "This writer predicts that Jesse Stuart may well win the Nobel Award for Literature some day." To some, if not to many literary minds, such a prediction as Blair's and such reveries as Jesse's might seem as far-fetched as any W-Hollow Nest Egg tall tale ever told.

But what if it was no more than a fantasy in the mind of a Kentucky

Highland plowboy? If Browning's words ever meant anything—"A man's reach should exceed his grasp"—then it was theoretically and spiritually possible that Jesse Stuart might one day be summoned to Stockholm or, short of that, maybe, just to Heaven—one place being about the same as the other for most writers anywhere in the world.

For Jesse, the decade of the '70s was a headlong race with the ticking of the clock and the heart.

Summer 1970: Eastern Kentucky University sponsored a creative writing conference featuring Jesse Stuart and a relatively little known but critically acclaimed Kentucky author, Hollis Spurgeon Summers Jr., author of *City Limit* and *Weather of February*. Born in Eminence in Henry County ten years after Jesse, Dr. Summers taught creative writing at the University of Kentucky, 1949-1959. Summers with a Ph.D. from Iowa, and Stuart, with his bachelor's degree from Lincoln Memorial, had at least one important thing in common: they were patient with their pupils, both men, in the tradition of Kahlil Gibran's The Prophet, teaching by not teaching:

*"For the vision of one man lends not its wings to another man."*

Neither pedantic nor professorial, Stuart and Summers wanted their students to be in touch with their "inner kingdoms." As Hollis Summers liked to say, everybody should allow themselves to "sit free," comparing it to the feel of the motion of the schoolyard swing—a child's or a grown person's rear-end firmly in place, feet pointing outward, mortal body arcing through time. Jesse should have listened and heeded this part of his co-leader's advice!

On the evening of January 3, 1971, Jesse and Naomi had invited Delmar and Mary Hamilton to join them at home for drinks and a steak dinner.

Biographer Frank N. Leavell describes what happened:

> *As they were enjoying some delicious steaks and fine conversation, Stuart suddenly slumped down in his chair with a cardiac arrest, which means that his heart just stopped beating. With the reflexes of an athlete, Delmar dragged his body to the floor and started pounding his chest with cardiopulmonary resuscitation while Mrs.*

*Stuart called an ambulance. By the time the ambulance arrived, Delmar had succeeded in reviving his heart. Without Delmar's training and quick thinking, the story of Stuart's life would have ended here. The ambulance rushed him to St. Mary's Hospital in Huntington, and from there he was transferred to the University of Kentucky Medical Center in Lexington, where the experts decided he was too weak for open heart surgery.*

Jesse was strong enough to persuade Naomi to smuggle into his hospital room no fewer than fourteen unfinished short stories. Then, after his release from the hospital, Jesse's doctor recommended that he take a trip but *do no writing!* That would be a little like telling Jerry B. Boneyard to walk while all the other dogs were running hell-bent for varmits.

In March of 1971, Jesse and Naomi departed on a three-week Caribbean cruise. Shortly before docking at Port Au Prince, Haiti, Jesse was seized with the sweet urge to write. Disregarding his doctor's strict orders, he used up all Naomi's and his stationery and then went looking for pieces of paper wherever he could find them. According to Jesse, other passengers were complaining that they didn't have anything to write on—he had commandeered it all! By the time the luxury liner completed the voyage, Jesse had written three hundred pages in longhand, which was the first rough draft of his next novel, *The Land Beyond the River*.

*The Land Beyond the River*, 380 pages, begins with utter despair.

> *We waited for Poppie to return from Ohio where he had gone to find fame and fortune....“I have to give up here in my native state of Kentucky,” Poppie had said....“We've gone from farm to farm— eight farms since we've been married—and I can hardly keep the starvation dog from our door. So, I'm off to Ohio to look around for a farm. I want Social Security or welfare and old-age pensions which are all better in that wonderful state, so Uncle Dick told me”....But Poppie said, last thing before he went to Ohio, his Old Family Cemetery...was where he wanted to be buried when his life's trials and tribulations were over.*

Jesse's campaign against the welfare system, his strong Republican, entrepreneurial, Horatio Alger self-reliance was a 1973 refrain of the 1943

*Taps for Private Tussie.*

Published in 1973, *Land Beyond the River*, came with a picture of Jesse on the back of the jacket—half-smoked cigar lodged on the right side of his puffed out lips—forehead deep with creases—hair in a lengthening wave hanging above the left side of the worried face—eyes in doubtful shadows—double chins down—huge hands gripping knees like an aging Rodinian thinker.

He was simply not well, and he appeared to know it.

*The Land Beyond the River* found itself adrift in a sea of Watergate, the end of the war in Viet Nam, and the removal of Sioux Indians from Wounded Knee—circumstances over which Jesse had no control. Reality bulldozed Jesse's poetry and fiction.

That same year Jesse's *Come to My Tomorrowland* was published, the eighth and last of his children's books published during his lifetime.

The 1973 Nobel Prize for Literature went to Australian Patrick White, while Jesse was receiving an honorary doctorate from the University of Louisville, followed by four more honorary doctorates—Morehead State University, Ball State University, Ohio University, and Transylvania University—making a total of sixteen. This much recognition was redeeming, given Jesse's failure to complete his master's degree.

Beginning on the eve of 1970 and continuing through 1977, Jesse conducted creative writing workshops at Murray State University. Martha Guier, not soon to forget the October 1954 morning in Lovett Auditorium when Jesse suffered his first major heart attack, recalled with fondness that her father, Quint T. Guier, enrolled in his first Jesse Stuart workshop. Mr. Guier was eighty-nine years old, and he was ninety-four when the last workshop was held in 1977. Mr. Guier exemplified the natural respect older people held for their hero from W-Hollow. These were Old Guard members of the brotherhood and sisterhood of "true Kentuckians," that mysterious quality defying definition.

Irvin S. Cobb had come close: "The Kentuckian is more a Kentuckian than he is a Southerner....From center to circumference, from crupper to hame, from pit to dome, he's all Kentuckian."

In 1973 Jesse's doctors had confirmed another heart attack, but surgery was not believed advisable. The episode forced the cancellation of a trip to the Congress of World Poets meeting in Taiwan, but it didn't prevent Jesse from writing furiously in the car on the way home from the hospital in Lexington to the comfort zone in W-Hollow. In that same autumn of his medical malaise, Jesse was back in King's Daughters Hospital with yet another heart attack. It was as if he was trying to set a new endurance record for overachievers.

Jesse was sent home with the usual warnings, and he was able to spend another Christmas at home. Through it all, he kept writing, blip or no blip on electrocardiogram screens. Jesse and Naomi rescheduled their trip to the Far East, a thirty-seventh wedding anniversary gift to themselves.

*The Seasons of Jesse Stuart*, an autobiography in poetry, was published in 1976, the eighth volume of poetry published in his lifetime.

Sam Piatt wrote a seventy-first birthday story (Jesse called it his seventieth) for the next day's issue of the *Ashland Daily Independent*. It is the best, last personal account of the man from W-Hollow talking introspectively about himself, his writing, his life in the here and now, and his rendezvous with the hereafter:

> *I shall never retire. I can't retire. If I could forget all the ideas in my mind and on these little scraps of paper in every pigeonhole, over each room in this big house—I find them and I keep finding them....There is not any way I can stop their coming. They enter my brain and they stay there until I dispose of them....The idea is the thing....They come in a classroom to me when I'm teaching a class. They come to me riding on planes. They come to me in our car when my wife is driving.*
>
> *Before my cardiologist stopped me from driving, Naomi used to ask me to get from under the wheel and let her drive. This was when I pulled the car over on the berm, took out my little notebook and recorded an idea. They came to me on ships at sea. They came to me at parties when everyone was having a good time but me. I was disturbed in my mind. They've come to me in dreams. I've gotten out of bed and recorded ideas in my notebook which I later wrote and sold to magazines. There is no way I know, even if I wanted to, to fence ideas out of my mind. There isn't any fence to hold them. There*

*isn't any defense against them.*

*There has never been enough time to write all the ideas I have had, to teach all the years I have wanted to teach, to see countries in the world that I have never seen—countries I want to see and feel I must see before my departure from this world.*

*Time, now, not ideas—which I have aplenty—is my greatest raw material to utilize to the fullest extent as best I can. Time, the raw material I have left, to use to the best of my advantage.*

*Right now in my life is when more people want to meet me, want to come to our home in W-Hollow for a brief visit, or even a longer one. Right now I must be interviewed and fill in questionnaires for books that are being written on me. Eight books have been published on me. Two more books are ready to be published on me, at any time. Two more books have been written and are at the publishers, awaiting rejection or acceptance, while another book is being written....so much to do and so little time than when I first began writing. In younger years I had so much time for writing and teaching. This is certainly not true now.*

*...I have been a busy man, a very busy one, never taking time for vacations. The last twenty-three years of my life I've had to work under a handicap, having had six heart attacks.*

*...All of this is like other dreams I've had. One of these dreams has been a repeated dream. That there isn't anything wrong with me but it was only a dream I had of having six heart attacks and having to take medicines to keep alive, from seventeen to twenty-three pills per day over a period of twenty-three years* [a total of approximately 167,900 nitroglycerin tablets]. *Even after one of those dreams, I dreamed I was back playing football. Such wonderful, pleasant dreams that it was tragic for me I had to awaken to reality—to know my dreams were only dreams and without truth.*

*Does an author reach a peak?*

*I have book manuscripts ready, waiting to be published—a novel, short story collections, two essays, and more poetry. I can produce at any moment a publishable manuscript from my reserves. I have always kept a reserve because with a reserve—which is like a deep bench in baseball or football—an author has a better chance of being published.*

*And this is the way it has to be about retirement. I know part of that which is in my head has to be released on the written page, revised, then published by a good name publisher on the published page. My words on the printed page always look so much better to me than the way I write them in longhand. They look better when I have typed on the clean white typewriting paper—the best that money can buy.*

*Not only are these ideas in my head for short stories, poems, essays and four or five novels, but I have little notes on single scraps of paper clipped together and in pigeonholes all over this place. No one can take my notes, read them, and know what I've meant for a story, essay or poem. I only write down in one of my notes what will remind me of the thought I had when I got the idea. When I see these words there is a reawakening in my brain of the thought or thoughts I once had and I immediately go to work.*

*Each scrap of paper with an essay, short story or article idea will be approximately one day of work. This is the process of creation and not revision. Often when I revise I do more rewriting. But I do get story, article, essay on paper and there is no one, no one on this earth to decipher my thinking, not even Naomi Deane, who is closer to me than any person. She can't decipher my ideas but she can follow my revision with her own, the last once-over to improve the written piece. She can also give titles, which is the most difficult thing for me in all of my writing.*

*In writing four or five novels—I'm not sure about one—I've never made any notes. These are in my head. Once in an interview I told the interviewer about these. He was the only person I've ever told and when he interviewed me the second time, within a year, he asked me about these novels. I asked him what novels? He told me what they would be about and it was true. I had told him too much about them. I have regretted telling this much about novels I plan to write. I shouldn't have done this. I don't know what made me do it. What I plan to write has always been my secret. I direct a creative writer workshop but I was never a participant in one in my life and I wouldn't be. The only place I want readers to read me is on the printed page after I am published.*

*With all the ideas I have now for poems, stories, essays, articles, novels, and assuming that I don't have any health problems, I estimate it would take me four years—and I'd have to give up traveling, except, perhaps, one brief journey per year to some distant part of the world, Australia, New Zealand, southern countries in South America and island groups. Not Greenland as I had once planned due to my body's circulation of the blood. This visit, despite my longing to see it, would tax my heart too much in its arctic chill.*

*So must I continue to plan for and to work for the oncoming four years, if they are allotted to me? Shall I put myself on a schedule and do this writing? Maybe, and without the hopes of getting most of it published in my lifetime. I don't think of publication when I write. I think of writing the story and getting it on the typewritten page.*

*I let the publication take care of itself at some later time when my mind is calm and I feel like relaxing. Which is always a good feeling for me, since I seldom ever feel like relaxing.*

*Birthdays! Birthdays! They roll on like heavy wagon wheels into the writer's unforeseeable destiny! These measurements of time make one sad and in a somber mood! This is if he has planned in his lifetime to make his life count. It reminds me of a line in an old church hymn my father used to sing: "Work for the night is coming, when man's work is done."*

*What bothers me most, and I have given this much thought, pondering over my novel ideas and shorter ideas many times, is what is the quality of the ideas I want to get on paper. What value will they be on the printed pages for future readers? Why do I think these have to be written? And I do know no one but I can decipher my notes and write what I have to write.*

*Will what I have to write be literature? Will it be worth saying? Am I, I wonder, an eccentric to think nine-tenths of what is written is fluff—that it has no lasting value? Why will I write what I think is quality, buy paper, pay to have it typed, conserve my precious time, if it will not sell? Say flash-in-the-pan, sensational magazines wouldn't have it, even if I offered it to them, which I don't.*

*Yes, I think it pays. At least I will have made a good honest try for lasting quality. I've had several of my stories over thirty years old sell to quality magazines and later be reprinted in secondary and college textbooks. Good, lasting quality creativity is above monetary values, even in the author's lifetime.*

*I have, also, been lucky enough in late years to live very well and to travel to parts of the world I've wanted to see.*

*I know if I do not put my collected ideas on the written page there is no one else who can do this for me. If I don't do this it will never be done. I think my ideas are good enough to be given a trial of the test of time. If I live, breathe, keep my health to a modest degree, I'm going to see that they get this test, even if they're not published in my lifetime. A few of these ideas are like perishable vegetables. They have to be taken care of now. There are no more like them where these came from.*

*Seventy years of my life will not have been frittered away. They will have been utilized to the fullest. Then, why should I fritter away the last ones I have to live? I could have a stroke, of which I have fears. I could have another, a seventh, heart attack, and it could be fatal. In my mother's family of five, four of them went with cerebral hemorrhages, which concerns the heart and its allied causes. My father and his four brothers and two sisters went of heart attacks. I do not plan to go with either. I do not think about it. I plan to do the work I have planned ahead.*

*I have to do it. I shall make every effort. If I live, keep moderate health and have the time, I shall do it.*

*I'm always glad to have that task ahead, know what I'm going to do and do it.*

A violent storm, or so it seemed, jolted Jesse in his sleep about four o'clock on the morning of April 15, 1977. The blow was neither wind, nor thunder, nor lightning. Lord God, it was the blocking of the flow of blood welled up by aging arteries into and out of a badly battered heart.

March 18, 1978: Jesse suffered a stroke while watching the University of Kentucky-Michigan State University televised basketball game. He spent the next three weeks in intensive care, a blear of time in which fact and fiction rolled in and out like ocean waves on a crumbling beachfront. The message was clear from the lighthouse, but Jesse Stuart chose to hear what he wanted to hear, feel what he wanted to feel. The passion to write from his kingdom within may have dimmed and flickered, but the spark of creativity was not yet extinguished.

Hell hath no fury like multiple heart attacks scorned!

Jesse was paralyzed on his left side. A hospital bed was arranged for him in the master bedroom, and he was virtually bedridden for the rest of his life. Dr. McWhorter prohibited visitors until well into June. But none of this kept Jesse from continuing to publish his newer works:

*Dandelion on the Acropolis: A Journal of Greece* was published in 1978.

*The Kingdom Within: A Spiritual Autobiography*, the last novel to be published in his lifetime, was issued in 1979. Perhaps McGraw-Hill published *The Kingdom Within* knowing that it most likely would be Jesse's final novel. There comes the day of calculated reckoning: will this be the last morning risen? Will this be the last speech given? Will there be a sudden collapse and dying as Vice-President Alben Barkley had done in that April of 1956 after saying, "I'd rather be a servant in the house of the Lord than to sit in the seats of the mighty"? And what of one mortal man's mind? Would his Cedar Riffles run dry? Minnows no longer school for lack of water? Frogs no longer *"too-deep"*?

*If I Were Seventeen Again and Other Essays* would be published in 1980, but the next four years became less like an ocean wave and more like fog descending upon Cedar Riffles. It would steal in softly like Sandburg's little cats' feet at Christmas time, like Browning's "natural fog of the good man's mind."

> *What is he buzzing in my ears?*
> *'Now that I come to die,*
> *Do I view the world as a vale of tears?'*
> *Ah, reverend sir, not I!*

*The Kingdom Within* is a capstone to a career cursed with repeated heart attacks, but Jesse had the strength to write it down on paper. Nitroglycerin tablets and Scotch, which one of his doctors had prescribed, was not thought of as unusual therapy at the time. It was believed to be as good a medicine as any at a time predating routine open-heart surgery and pacemaker implantations.

It was no dream when she led him from the house to the car and leaped in beside him. Her hands gripped the steering wheel, and the white Cadillac roared out of W-Hollow to KY 1, up to U.S. 23, then right at speeds of more than one hundred miles an hour.

> *"I'm in pain. Drive! Drive! Drive! I don't care! Drive!*
> *"This is all this car will do! Auckland* [Ashland] *is close!"*
> *"It had better be!"*
> *He had drained the glass.*
> *"Are you wide awake?"*
> *"As much as I ever was in my life with this—continued pain. I can't take much more. If I give up now I'll die!"*
> *Jean* [Naomi Deane] *pulled the white Cadillac on the east end of the Kingston Hospital's* [King's Daughters Hospital] *emergency loading and unloading ramp. Here the patients were taken in when they arrived. Here they were rushed through in emergencies. Jean came to a sudden stop by skidding the wheels and leaving rubber tracks!*
> *Twenty miles, twelve minutes!*
> *"Pain lessened?"*
> *"It's still with me."*
> *Jean got out and opened Shan's* [Jesse's] *door.*
> *"Hurry, emergency," Jean shouted.*

The fictive autobiographical book *The Kingdom Within* is as remarkable as it is memorable, but mainly it has been read and treasured by Jesse's most ardent followers, those who've read beyond *Taps for Private Tussie* and *The Thread That Runs So True*. In *The Kingdom Within*, Shan Powderjay (a name Jesse frequently used to represent himself) welcomes home his "head children" on the imaginary day of his funeral service. The "head children" were his "story people" and his "poetry people," and he wants them to be there when he's laid to rest. Yet at the same time he would witness it too, as if he were a ghost.

> *When he walked up on the Plum Grove Hill, which was a low hill surrounded on three sides by valleys, he could look in all directions at the low-lying hilltops under the blue high dome of April sky. To his right was the white stone Plum Grove Chapel with a spire on the top and a cross on the front. There it was, the cross, a symbol, his symbol. He never wore a cross in his life. He didn't have to wear one for a symbol. His was implanted within him. His was invisible. The Kingdom was Within him. A cross didn't have to be worn to show who he was. His Kingdom Within him had decided everything he had done.*
>
> *There would be a stone up for him at Plum Grove in the Powderjay plot, close to his mother, father and brothers, and it would have his name, dates of birth and death. Shan knew what his epitaph would be. He had written it* [with a little help from Robert Burns and John Masefield] *while he was in college but he didn't know he was writing an epitaph.*

> *The Kingdom Within*
>
> *If there is life beyond the grave,*
> *He lives in future bliss.*
> *If there is not another world*
> *He made the most of this.*
>
> *Harvest of Youth*

In his first book, *Harvest of Youth*, Jesse crossed the line of plagiarism. As a college student he presented these four lines as if they were his own, giving no credit to Burns for the last two:

> *If there's another world, he lives in bliss;*
> *If there is none, he made the best of this.*

Jesse spent eleven days in intensive care and eleven days in a private room at King's Daughters Hospital in Ashland. On the day of his release, his doctor gave Jesse a little lecture, a bit like shooting a B-B gun at Brer Bear's backside.

*"Follow your diet, take your medicines as I have prescribed them for you. Stay in your home all of May in robe and pajamas! Later I will discuss short trips out in the car in June with your wife. Don't smoke any more cigars."*

*"No more cigars....I have no desire. And I promise you, I mean this. No more of my wonderful cigars."*

*"No drinking."*

*"Yes, Doctor."*

*"No overeating."*

*"Yes, Doctor."*

*"Keep the weight down."*

*"Yes, Doctor."*

*"Don't climb steps."*

*"Yes, Doctor."*

*"Do all the walking you can do in your home and out in the yard, when weather permits. Walk on the level. Live in normal temperatures!"*

*"Yes, Doctor."*

*"Remember, we don't want that seventh attack. It could be the fatal one, you know."*

*"Yes, seven was always my lucky number. Don't worry about it. I won't."*

*"Well, this is it! Good luck to you, Shan! Keep in contact."*

*...Jean wrote a check for Shan's expenses which his insurance didn't cover. Counting what his insurance paid and he paid, he knew it didn't pay to be sick. It didn't pay financially to have the sixth heart attack. He had paid for it in two ways, cash and more heart injuries.*

*The Kingdom Within*

Jesse would be mostly bedridden for the rest of his life. But he'd doggedly muster all the strength he could to make every moment count.

# HERE IS WRITING
# THAT TOUCHES THE HEART

*Stuart...was one of Kentucky's most prolific authors;*
*and his place in the literary world is decidedly controversial.*
William S. Ward
*A Literary History of Kentucky*

*Consider!*

In *A Literary History of Kentucky* (University of Tennessee Press, 1988) the late William S. Ward assessed *Man with a Bull-Tongue Plow* as "vintage Stuart with its headlong flow of words, intense emotion, strong subjectivity, and careless attention to form. Much of the criticism of the volume was harsh but much was also warmly favorable; hardly any was neutral....some of the poems were said to have the freshness of medieval ballads; some of them, though rough, were declared to have great beauty."

*Man with a Bull-Tongue Plow*'s opening word— *"Sir"* —is Jesse's opening shot across the bow of literary criticism. He makes it painfully clear that he's not going to conform to convention: *"I do not sing the songs you love to hear."* The last two lines, the rhyming couplet of Jesse's idea of a Shakespearean sonnet—

> *And these crude strains no critic can call art,*
> *Yours very respectively, Jesse Stuart.*

Jesse has fun with the rhyming of "art" and "Stuart," and he uses "respectively" rather than "respectfully," which compounds the playful disrespect.

The second of the 703 sonnets in *Bull-Tongue Plow* continues with more rustic ramblings—

> *And may I pause to sing a corn-field song*
> *Beside my plow between the tall corn rows—*
> *And may I idle my root-plow along*
> *And sing tunes futile as the wind that blows.*
> *There may be some to love the strains that Stuart*
> *Made on Kentucky hills beside his plow—*
> *There may be some to love his rustic art*
> *And keep his futile tunes in brain and heart*
> *When he is quiet and sleeps beneath the clay*
> *And has no thought of his past yesterday.*
> *And we shall hope then for a brighter day*
> *When some young poet guides his plow along*
> *And plows upon the quiet Kentucky clay*
> *Where Stuart plowed and sings a better song!*

You either like the strained rhymes or you don't. It's not easy to find a middle ground. When *Man with a Bull-Tongue Plow* was published in 1934, critic Malcolm Cowley gave it a prominent but reserved review in the *New Republic*:

> *Here is a new sort of book about the Kentucky hills. The others were written from the outside....Jesse Stuart is a poet who lives inside the cabin and writes about the life he knows best. He writes about sidehill farmers, moonshiners and loggers not because they are picturesque but because they are his own people....At their best, his poems have the springtime freshness of medieval ballads. Their worst fault is that they are written without effort or economy. Jesse Stuart says everything at least twice.*

Jesse's repetitiousness often is as annoying as fingernails on a blackboard, but his contribution to Kentucky's and the nation's literature is as measurably valuable as any work of his contemporaries. He was connected with the real world where he was born and lived throughout his life. He tightened his belt and went to work. He leaves it to new generations of poets, novelists, and short story writers to do better work. In that sense, he is a building block, perhaps, a cornerstone.

What Jesse Stuart wanted most of all was to be "The Writin' Man from W-Hollow." His "red in tooth and claw" naturalism suggests a literary kinship with Jack London and Stephen Crane. London's *The Son of the Wolf* and Crane's *The Red Badge of Courage* were in the tradition of Theodore Dreiser's *Sister Carrie* and *An American Tragedy*. The first of the naturalists was Frank Norris, author of *McTeague* and *The Octopus*.

A definition of *naturalism*: A theory that art or literature should conform exactly to nature or depict every appearance of the subject that comes to the artist's attention; specifically, a theory in literature emphasizing the role of heredity and influence of environment upon human life and character development. That's Jesse.

All four early-twentieth-century American writers—Norris, Dreiser, London, and Crane—have enjoyed extraordinary fame well beyond their deaths, although London committed suicide at the age of forty, Crane died of tuberculosis when he was twenty-eight, and Norris died at the age of thirty-two. Only Dreiser lived a long life and continued to write until his death in 1945. Stuart's star has been waning but refuses to die out.

Biographer Mary Washington Clarke has written of Jesse Stuart:

> *Ile has not tried to be avant-garde, obscure, nihilist, precious, nor has he used any other transparent literary device to appear wiser than he is.*

Clarke's assessment, while not intended to damn with faint praise, seems to pigeonhole Jesse in a tight little corner—local colorist, regional writer, primitivist, professional hillbilly. In truth, he was some of each of these things, which makes him all the more endearing to his fans who've stuck with him because he's believable. He resonates with those who simply love him.

Another Stuart biographer, Ruel E. Foster, has judged:

> *It seems clear then that Stuart's primitivism is a natural attitude— one growing out of his way of life. It is not a romantic escape from life, inculcated by reading Rousseauesque books on the delights of untrammeled nature. For Stuart is about as honest a primitivist as we can find in our country today; he knows as well as any writer living the grimness and tragedy of life on the mountain soil. When*

*he chose it as a way of life, he was choosing something he knew.*

Write about what you know! Jesse lived by and for this truth, incorporating it into his writer's forums, presaging such gatherings as the annual Appalachian Writers' workshop at Cumberland College. One of its organizers, Professor Marianne Worthington, writes:

> *Late in his career, Stuart fell out of favor with literature scholars and critics because he was so popular with readers. More than a regionalist or a local colorist, I think Stuart was labeled even worse, a "popular" writer rather than a "literary" writer of national significance and importance.... Maybe it is better not to label him at all but to just let him "be" what he was. The editors of* Appalachia Inside Out *refer to Stuart this way: "Stuart's world has long been a familiar one to readers of Appalachian literature. A pioneer in Appalachian poetry, Stuart is noted for fidelity in representation of folklore and his fierce love of his native land."*

One of Jesse's classmates at LMU was poet, novelist, and short story author James Still, born one month before Jesse in Alabama but destined for a long life of writing at the forks of Troublesome Creek in Knott County, Kentucky. Similarities fade there. It's fair to say the two men came awfully close to being as different as oil and water—Jesse, the brash, vocal, Bunyanesque stalwart—James, the softer, quieter, more reflective member of the literary intelligentsia. Eventually Still received his master's degree, Stuart never did. Stuart soon was meteorically popular, Still eschewed popular appeal but achieved a modest following in literary circles.

Literary historian Ward has noted that Still "is totally free of the faults of the local colorists of the turn-of-the-century era, when the typical writer played up the quaint and outlandish dialect and behavior of his or her characters—and even exploited them."

Jesse was accused of doing just that, yet it seems pointless to compare Jesse Stuart unfavorably with James Still, or the other way around. They were simply two different Kentucky writers, and readers will benefit from finding pleasure and meaning in both. To ignore or dismiss Jesse Stuart while lauding James Still or vice versa is regrettable.

Jesse Stuart will be remembered as a man with an unselfish heart who gave back to life as good as he got and more. He was to *become* the thread that runs so true.

Jesse's verses were unpolished although he worked tirelessly to make them suit his purpose. He might be criticized for his crudeness, but scorned and ignored as worthless? Jesse's answer comes in the couplet to the third sonnet of *Man with a Bull-Tongue Plow*—

> *I do not care to know if this is art—*
> *These common words born in a common heart.*

His name is not mentioned, much less memorialized, in some modern encyclopedias of world literature. Names move from Strindberg to Stubbs with apologies to none. Jesse Stuart's sonnets have been rejected for their incorrect Shakespearean rhymes, for being unfashionably contrived, out-of-date, and out-of-joint, for word images repeated over and over, and for thoughts as naked as a jaybird's call.

Jesse's loyal readership knows better.

They understand he was no William Faulkner, James Joyce, or T.S. Eliot. Jesse's friends would come to know him as the W-Hollow neighbor who wrote *Man with a Bull-Tongue Plow* and to know that he was no creator of an *Absalom, Absalom!, Ulysses,* or *The Waste Land*. What's more, they didn't want him to be. They could understand Jesse Stuart, but they could hardly be expected to have the slightest idea of what Faulkner or Joyce or Eliot was talking about.

Never mind. Nobody's suggesting that Faulkner, Joyce, or Eliot should be ignored by Appalachian youth today. But neither should Stuart be forgotten.

Linda Scott DeRosier, author of *Creeker*, published by the University Press of Kentucky, remembers how when she was a little girl on Two Mile Creek in Johnson County, she wrote a letter to Jesse Stuart.

> *He was the first writer who ever seemed real to me, because I always read....it seemed to me early on that books kind of came from the heavens or some place....I had no idea who wrote some or how they got written but I knew whoever it was it was probably somebody close to God or in New York, which is the same thing.*
>
> *Books were something that I loved and lived in but they were not*

*real to me—everything was fiction....But then there was Jesse Stuart,
and by the time I first read Jesse Stuart, I must've been a little girl,
maybe 5th grade, 4th or 5th grade, something like that....by the time
I first read Jesse Stuart there was a kinship there, because he
seemed like a real person, and our teachers talked about him as if he
were a real person.*

*And he wrote about things that I'd seen. I'd never seen a city
street, for example, but I'd seen the hills and the hollers that he
wrote about. I'd seen the room that he wrote about. I'd seen the
room with the family sitting by the fire and me lying on the feather
bed, watching them sit over there and drink the last cup of coffee,
seen them outlined by the fire. And Jesse Stuart's rooms were all like
that, or seemed to me to be.*

*And he talked about...when I think of it today...images...he talked
about Christmas coming and it being cold outside and the kids being
excited but there not being all that much coming, and I always had
great Christmases, but I could see those little kids expecting Santa
Claus and Santa Claus not going to be able to come, because Daddy
was trapped by the snow someplace else.*

*Interview*

As Stuart scholar Edwina Pendarvis has suggested, Jesse may have read
well and learned what he thought he needed from Carl Sandburg and John
Donne. Likewise, his roots reach back to William Wordsworth and his ode
"Intimations of Immortality":

*Hence in a season of calm weather,*
*Though inland far we be,*
*Our souls have sight of that immortal sea*
*Which brought us hither,*
*Can in a moment travel thither,*
*And see the children sport upon the shore,*
*And hear the mighty waters rolling evermore.*

A Jesse Stuart without a Wordsworth, Donne, or Sandburg suggests a
flawed picture. Yet, it serves no worthwhile purpose to paint Jesse Stuart as
one who could do no wrong. Even when he believed his poetic powers

were the greatest, as in *Album of Destiny*, Jesse could be woefully and strangely awkward—

>           *Red Holbrook Speaks of Emanuel Frainwood's Death*
>
> *I've heard it said Emanuel Frainwood died*
> *Of a copper-jacket bullet in his brain;*
> *I've heard it said, Azelia Moore, his bride*
> *Put him to bed where he'd not rise again.*
> *Emanuel left his life in second prime*
> *And like bloodroot died early in that season*
> *To be compounded under sprout and thyme,*
> *His bride was all that could have been the reason.*
> *I've heard it said when old John Moore passed on*
> *And when Clid Claxon got too old for love*
> *Bee Moore went to the berry patch at dawn*
> *To meet Emanuel Frainwood in the cove.*
> *His youth bride would not share with her mother*
> *Emanuel's love that Fan once tossed aside;*
> *Buried by Fan, Azelia does not bother*
> *To mourn the loss of one she slept beside.*

The twelve disciples of the "Agrarian *versus* Industrial South" once represented literary mountaintop-heroes for a lonely and frustrated plowboy from Greenup County, Kentucky. They were the self-appointed, self-anointed apostles, and their soaring ideas had become southern Gospel.

Jesse Stuart dared to believe there was a place for him around the Agrarian campfire, and he was so bold as to think the trailblazers might call him in. He was wrong. He was soon to discover that he was not welcome in the Agrarian inner circle—he was barely tolerated, arguably, as an ill-prepared upstart from a distant land—of all places, W-Hollow. He was the product of one-room schoolhouses in Kentucky and a poor man's college in the "hillbilly" end of Tennessee.

Allen Tate refused to include Jesse's work in a poetry anthology, accusing him of pandering to the eastern seaboard publishing houses by stereotyping Appalachians for profit. "His dramatization of himself as the Hill-billy, for New York consumption, has disgusted me for years, and I suppose I can't be fair to his work." In regard to fairness, it seems that Tate was stereotyping Stuart, a real agrarian, not a theoretical one.

After Jesse arose from the edge of the Agrarian campfire, shook the dust and ashes off his feet, he accepted the advice of his most trusted mentor, Donald Davidson. The plowboy went home to amass the mountainous *Man with a Bull-Tongue Plow*—

> *Once, Davidson, I went to you with lays;*
> *I read you plow-boy lays no man had heard;*
> *I read you lays of my kin's rustic ways;*
> *I read old tunes to you like a fluting bird.*
> *And you did like the shrill notes of my fife;*
> *You liked the splits I wove into my baskets;*
> *And you did like the way I sang of life;....*
>
> Sonnet 579

> *....I was a man who hated silly stuff—*
> *Don't let men make a moon-god out of me,*
> *When I am dead and they can run a bluff*
> *And tell about the fool I was at tea.*
> *Don't let them sentimentalize this man.*
> *I've lived the things that I have said and done,*
> *And I did not belong to clique and clan....*
>
> Sonnet 580

Linda Scott DeRosier, "Creeker," was asked about Jesse's stereotyping and his playing straight into the hands of the stereotype merchants in New York City.

> *I think sometimes stereotypes, well, hell, they start*
> *somewhere....all of us are grounded somewhere in some of those*
> *stereotypes. Somebody once told me that Jesse Stuart's sound of*
> *people talking were only heard in* Lil Abner, *and yet I've heard those*
> *sounds, and they're in my head. We want the good parts of the*
> *stereotypes but we don't want the bad parts. And we have to be very*
> *careful because if you're going to show the truth you can only show*
> *it as you know it. And I think that's what Jesse Stuart did. And I*
> *found his truth pretty truthful...to me...I can't speak for anybody else.*
>
> Interview

"Stereotypical" includes "unoriginal," "uninspired," "unimaginative," and "threadbare." While degrees of such descriptive words can certainly be laid at Jesse Stuart's doorstep, it would be fairer to evaluate the sum of his life's work.

Robert Penn Warren wrote cautiously in the foreword to Jesse's *Head o' W-Hollow*: "...a unique book, bound for its own kind of immortality....We can readily see that it belongs to a certain genus—a genus that includes *Sut Lovingood* by George Washington Harris, *Georgia Scenes* by Augustus Baldwin Longstreet, and the ramshackle epic of *Davy Crockett*."

The comparison of Jesse with Tennessee River steamboat captain George Washington Harris and Georgia jurist Augustus Baldwin Longstreet did not suggest a recommendation for Pulitzer or Novel prize judges. The "local colorist" badge pinned to their coats—not quite dishonorable, but a second- and third-rate tag nonetheless—faintly damned all three. There have been "local colorists"—James Fenimore Cooper, Washington Irving, Bret Harte, Harriet Beecher Stowe, Sarah Orne Jewett, and Mark Twain—who have transcended their awkward beginnings. But in the case of Jesse Stuart, he had a longer way to go to reach a literary mountaintop. He just climbed the beanstalk as far as was able.

He kept writing. And writing. And writing.

"Creeker" summed it up when asked how she answered the criticism that Stuart wrote too much, was not polished, but was loud, self-inventing, not like those Agrarian intellectuals down at Vanderbilt.

> *Jesse Stuart wrote about my reality in a way that nobody else did, and I had to be grown to appreciate the others* [the Agrarians at Vanderbilt].

How would she place Jesse in the company of other Kentucky writers?

> *You never forget your first. And Jesse Stuart was my first. You love this one in this way and that one in that way.*

Literary critics have pinned the "local colorist" label on Jesse's one all-occasion suit of creative clothes because *Man with a Bull-Tongue Plow* lacked polish, *Taps for Private Tussie* was one dimensional, *The Thread That Runs So True* was simplistic, and *To Teach, To Love* was weary with overabundance.

Creeker:

> *Writing, I think, is something like, the painter comes in and you've got these tubes...you've got these tubes sitting there, and they don't mean anything, and you start splattering that stuff on canvas, but it has to be squeezed through the tube and you have to be the one to put the brush to it. And I think that some people don't like what comes up and some will. And as for local color...you know some of us come from a place which is pretty dogged bright and dark, you know there's a lot of contrast and a lot of color in our area. ...I've been all over the world, and I don't know of any place that has the range of language used in the way we use it. And very often that never gets outside. Much of it is not appropriate to say in polite company, and so we don't. But you know, the truth is, people can characterize events and human beings and the human condition in very few words that they are so absolutely precise and usually not repeatable.*
>
> *You go out into the world and each little place has its own code for the way that they communicate. So the first thing you have to do if you're going to manage to make it in any setting is to crack the code of how they communicate and an awful lot of things are communicated without saying anything.*

Edwin T. Arnold, professor at Appalachian State University, wrote in an essay called "The Canonization of Jesse Stuart" in the 1985 fall issue of *Appalachian Journal*:

> *What do we do with old Jesse Stuart? Overpraised initially as some sort of natural rustic genius, a "bardic" singer of the hills, even a reincarnation of Bobbie Burns himself, in his later years, poor Jesse was sometimes an embarrassment, a professional literary "hillbilly," a man out of touch with the times who wouldn't keep quiet.*

It's doubtless true that a certain amount of attempted "canonization" has occurred along with occasional hagiographies (worshipful biographies), but nobody ever said Jesse had no warts. It behooves the congregation to be wary despite temptations to think the "Writin' Man from W-Hollow" could do no wrong.

Frank H. Leavell, now professor emeritus at Baylor University, in his 1981 dissertation quoted J.R. LeMaster, who had a generous, even-handed historical literary perspective on Jesse Stuart.

> *The significance and purpose of the book* [The World of Jesse Stuart: Selected Poems] *are explained nowhere better than* [in] *LeMaster's own introduction. He explains that Stuart began writing poetry during the unsettled generation between World War I and the Depression, unsettled both in spiritual values and in poetic direction. Stuart followed the bardic tradition of Burns and Sandburg. These bards were singers, not philosophers—they were emotional, not intellectual—they were rural, not urban. But new poets such as Ezra Pound and T.S. Eliot changed the direction of poetry leaving Stuart and the bards out of vogue.*

Said Leavell in a recent telephone interview:

> *You'll be doing Jesse Stuart a great disservice if you try to make him a 'great writer.' He was a local colorist if ever there was one. He gave us eastern Kentucky in a beautiful way.*

Writing In his 1981 dissertation:

> *Perhaps a hundred years from now when everybody is plastic coated, computerized, and regimented, the world may return to Stuart for a W-Hollow renaissance.*
>
> *Beyond his social history Stuart will be remembered for his human values: honesty, purity, self-reliance, family, religion, patriotism, and conservation. These "old verities" are permanent. A society may neglect them for awhile, but it must return to them or wither away. Maybe Stuart will someday be remembered as the prophet who remained faithful to them during the sixties and seventies while the groups in sync fled after false gods.*
>
> *Finally, Stuart will be remembered for the myth that he has created....Abe Lincoln's rise from a log cabin to the White House is such a myth. Stuart's life has also become a myth of that American dream. And many of his stories will live as myths of such themes as*

*awakening and initiation, the cycle of life and immortality, the union of man and the land and God, and the Garden of W-Hollow.*

Wade Hall wrote the foreword to the University Press of Kentucky's 1980 reprint of *Trees of Heaven*:

*Indeed, the novel contains some of his most skillful writing—a spare, sinewy prose that can be as direct as a twelve-gauge shotgun or as lyrical as August corn tassels blowing in the warm wind. Somewhat less successful is young Stuart's experiment with narration in the present tense, a technique that sometimes produces only a strained immediacy.*

He was simply being Jesse. He was experimenting with a technique. As historian laureate Thomas D. Clark has put it: "He was Jesse from the tip of his toes to the last page he wrote."

William Ward called *Trees of Heaven*—

*...a foretaste of other Stuart novels, and the praise it received, like the faults that were found, in general typified later criticism. Readers and critics alike have delighted in Stuart's vigor and enthusiasm, his enormous flow of words and the headlong pace of his style, his freshness, the abundance of human warmth, and his portrayal of hill people and their ways. But his faults have sometimes had a kinship with his merits. The enthusiasm for his forceful flow of language, for example, has been tempered by the regret that he is not more economical in his use of words and the wish that he were a more disciplined writer, and one who revised with greater care before going into print.*

William Ward has a possible answer to the sharp differences of opinion about the literary worthiness of Jesse Stuart:

*During his lifetime he was accustomed to three critical reactions: an uncritical, almost mindless adulation that would make him one of America's great authors; an indifference close to scorn that either ignored him or dismissed him summarily as an undisciplined writer with few ideas and small literary merit; and a more temperate view*

*which had lamented shortcomings while readily citing strengths and*
*offering encouragement and critical advice.*

Ward takes the third possibility as a promising middle ground, a fair judgment affording an opportunity for a more positive outcome.

In his article "Roberts, Still, Stuart & Warren" written for the Kentucky Humanities Council magazine, H.R. Stoneback describes Jesse Stuart as "probably the single most popular writer in Kentucky history." But Stoneback, who received his Ph.D. from Vanderbilt, quotes Andrew Lytle (editor of *Sewanee Review*) as saying Jesse Stuart's writing was "heavy with the worst kind of regionalism." Jesse's submissions were rejected by the *Review* because of "too much dialect, too much attention to mountainy quaintness in his Appalachian characters, too overwritten, too sentimentalized."

Jesse's response in a 1969 letter to Stoneback:

*I know I have been considered a third rate regionalist, second rate*
*regionalist and first rate regionalist but I say to hell with all*
*this...I'm glad I have remained an individualist and not a joiner and*
*that I live within one mile of where I was born and farm the same*
*land my father and grandfather farmed. I am an honest Agrarian.*

Jesse thought it was most humorous to learn that the literal extent of some of the Agrarians was a tomato plant or two in their backyards, maybe even a flower garden. Jesse's idea of an "honest Agrarian" was to write and to farm.

Lee Pennington wrote in *The Dark Hills of Jesse Stuart:*

*Jesse Stuart has been called a "regionalist" too long. The present*
*connotation of that term indicates a lower type of writing which*
*does not reach up to universal quality and is far from the literary*
*definition of regionalism.*

Pennington recalls the Corn Island Storytelling Festival, which he and his wife Joy produced for nearly three decades:

*Critics hate Jesse, when they do, maybe because Jesse didn't*
*spend too much time worrying about what some would call his*
*"sloppy writing." Jesse wanted to tell a story and that was all that*

*was important. His stories were about as close to the oral tradition as you can get....Jesse didn't try to be oral; he just was. Now oral and written are two different beasts. The best in one is not the best in another, and there's the rub. Jesse was never very much concerned with the King's English—especially as he was capturing a speech way back up in the hollers where there weren't too many kings.*

The oral tradition is considered folk literature, and Jesse is slap in the middle. Leonard W. Roberts' *Up Cutshin & Down Greasy* and *South from Hell-fer-Sartin* (University Press of Kentucky) are good examples of the oral tradition: "Big Fraid and Little Fraid," "The Headless Ghost," and "The One-Eyed Giant." Jesse also told such stories, and he had a knack of selling them rather than giving them away.

Loyal Jones, teacher and former director of the Appalachian Center at Berea College and author of *Faith and Meaning in the Southern Uplands* and *Appalachian Values,* describes Jesse as representative of the southern poor boy class, unlike the "Agrarians" at Vanderbilt who represented the more elite South.

*Stuart's prose and poetry were in the language of his family and neighbors. It was rough-edged, and it employed regional dialect that was going out of style in literary circles. Stuart's years at Vanderbilt highlighted the class differences of the South and to a great degree between the Lowland and Upland South.*

Jesse dressed up in plus fours during his Guggenheim fellowship in Scotland, and he donned cap and gown for his sixteen honorary doctorates, but underneath remained the W-Hollow heritage: brogans, open-throat shirts, and nothing to set him apart from his friends and neighbors.

*"What then is so bad about being a regional writer?"* Frank Leavell asks:

*...the word has a bad connotation. It implies not only a restricted locality but a restricted vision. It is associated with provincialism. Furthermore, it implies a restricted appeal, that few beyond its locality would be interested in reading it...if so many of the great writers are indeed regionalists, why are they not known as*

*regionalists? The answer is that other dimensions of their works overshadow the local color, and by these other dimensions they are judged.*

Jesse's dying wish probably says to all those who would call themselves "writers," whether they be regional or global: Be in touch with what you *know* to be true, and remember, it's impossible to please everyone.

> *Take each man's censure, but reserve thy judgment....*
> *This above all: to thine own self be true,*
> *And it must follow, as the night the day,*
> *Thou canst not then be false to any man.*
>
> *Hamlet*

Billy C. Clark, Jesse Stuart's second cousin, author of *Song of the River* and *A Long Row to Hoe*, calls Jesse "one of the great American writers because of his ability to capture the land and the people."

"Stereotypical writing?"

"No truth to stereotyping in any way...somebody is always going to complain....Jesse understood people, the heart of people," says Clark.

The important thing is this: if a writer does her or his best, then no amount of criticism will make a hill-of-beans difference; if a writer does not quit, does not give up trying to be better, growth will always be possible. It could be argued that Jesse climbed as high as he could on the beanstalk, and he might have gone even higher if he had possessed a higher intellect or more professional craftsmanship. There was more to Jesse Stuart than his role as a celebrated writer.

Loyal Jones praises Jesse Stuart the teacher:

> *He was egalitarian and was quick to tell students that they could do the things he had done. His college convocation talks were inspiring to students who were unsure of their abilities. His egalitarianism made him a great teacher and educational administrator. He related to everyone and was empathetic with their problems, and yet he had the courage to stand his ground on principle. He thoroughly believed in his students and their ability to do good and even great things in the world. He revered teachers and would answer every letter from them.*

George Brosi in *The Literature of the Appalachian South*, wrote:

> *Deep down, Jesse Stuart represented the finest of rural American values. He loved the land; he loved the animals, wild and domestic; and he loved the people. He stands for a world where all live in harmony and where those, like himself, who have the humblest origins, can enjoy the richest rewards. Jesse Stuart had a very special gift that allowed him to write down his thoughts and emotions so that others could understand them, laugh with them and be uplifted by them. In a fundamental way, the richness of his poor Appalachian background transcended its poverty and enriched not just Jesse Stuart, but all who have been touched by his life and work....Stuart...had a gift for conveying mountain people whose ignorance of "civilized ways" might sometimes make them look outwardly foolish, but whose human dignity and rural values allowed them to ultimately triumph over trying circumstances.*

Hear the judgment of Donald Davidson, who encouraged Jesse not to feel guilty or defeated by his failure at Vanderbilt, but to go home and write about what he knew:

> *The readers of Jesse Stuart must say, "Here is writing that touches the heart."*

*Clearing in the Sky and Other Stories*, published in 1950, was reviewed by Orville Prescott in the *New York Times*. This collection of twenty-one short stories written in the period 1941-1950 points to one of Jesse's persistent problems—repetition of material. Yet the *Times* is generous:

> *"...to ask him to write with more depth and power, with fewer tricks and mannerisms, would be to ask him to write like somebody else. He's doing all right in his own way, hoeing his own row in his own garden. And that's not a bad thing to do in life or in books."*

In the summer 1962 issue of *Southern Observer*, Robert Avrett of the University of Tennessee reviewed *Hold April*: "*Much has happened, as man and as poet, to Jesse Stuart since the publication of* Man with a Bull-Tongue Plow....*Two fundamental qualities persist, however, in* Hold April....*Still evident are the poet's probing interest in man and his natural environment, and a simplicity of style unadorned by decorative artificialities."*

In 1979, G. Sam Piatt wrote in the *Ashland Daily Independent:*

> *"Surely, the story of Jesse Stuart, poet of the land, exemplifies the American Dream: the rise from obscure beginnings in a one-room log cabin to fame and fortune; overcoming seemingly impossible odds through determination, frugality and hard work; being knocked down by defeat but rising again to set the heels and continue the climb."*

So, why should there be another, a twenty-first century, biography of Jesse Stuart? Not to glorify him certainly, neither to canonize him, nor to set him apart as one without deficiency. What, then, its purpose? Jesse (he'd prefer that to "Mr. Stuart") is a promising starting point for the companionable study of American and English literature. Sure, one may begin with any number of better known, more gifted authors, but the volume, variety, and sincerity of Jesse's work are an inspiration to those who value simpler beginnings. *Jesse Stuart —The Heritage* was undertaken to introduce the man from W-Hollow to a new generation living in a technologically-driven century in which television dominates the popular culture and computers make hoe handles look as ancient as bull-tongue plows.

*Listen!*

If there be a resurgence of thinkers, readers, and writers from W-Hollow to Silicone Valley, and if it be traceable to any one of Jesse's books—*If I Were Seventeen Again and Other Essays, New Harvest: Forgotten Stories of Kentucky's Jesse Stuart,* or *The Thread That Runs So True*—then, by jingo, the two year journey it took to write *Jesse Stuart—The Heritage* will have been worth the ticket to ride.

# ROOM 129

*When I think of God,*
*I think of the evening sky in Kentucky.*

Jesse Stuart
*Beyond Dark Hills*

*Hush now.*

This is 1984, the winter Jesse Stuart died.

The last time Thomas D. Clark visited with Jesse was in the spring of 1980, when there was a symposium at Greenbo State Resort Park, just down KY 1 from W-Hollow Road. Sponsored by the Jesse Stuart Foundation, the four-day event was called "Jesse Stuart and the Greenbo Sessions: A Weekend in 'Stuart Country.'" There were many dignitaries there, including Harry Caudill, celebrated author of *Night Comes to the Cumberlands*. More than twenty colleges and universities were represented, including Vanderbilt, which had taken so long to realize what it had had on its threshold in 1931. The participants read papers and discussed the heritage of the bedridden climber who had failed in his youth to scale the distant mountain of the master's degree and that ultimate pinnacle—the Ph.D.

When the symposium participants took a walking tour of W-Hollow, as the group trudged up the trail past the home place, Naomi Deane singled out the Mississippi-born Kentucky historian, Thomas Dionysius Clark, then a spry seventy-seven, and asked him to come in so that he could speak personally to Jesse.

In the winter of 2003-2004, one-hundred-year-old Dr. Clark still had a vivid remembrance of the "last visit" with seventy-four-year-old Jesse.

> *I sat by his bed and talked to him about writing and manuscripts.*
> *He was lying propped up in the big bed, but he didn't move. He had*
> *a great stock of manuscripts, and I asked about them—he drew on*
> *them* [as from a well.] *We talked about the conference a little bit,*
> *some about India, and his travels. I knew him pretty well...many*
> *times our paths had crossed. Jesse was always enthusiastic about his*
> *writing and he was still enthusiastic. I had no trouble understanding*
> *him.*
>
> *Jesse Stuart had a sense of humor....He created basic, good*
> *writing, the rural life/mind folklore of his region....he glorified the*
> *common man. I was there about thirty minutes and then rejoined the*
> *group when they came back. It was not a doleful parting, but he was*
> *a sick man, a man on his way out.*

"So long," were Thomas Clark's last words to Jesse Stuart.

It was a wonder, a miracle that Jesse weathered so many cardiac arrests, possibly a total of six. Trips to hospital emergency rooms had become almost a game of Russian roulette played with ambulance drivers, doctors, and nurses. Naomi Deane, steadfastly loyal, was there with nitroglycerin tablets and Scotch tempered with branch water, but the major damage had been done with the first heart attack in 1954. No amount of "Jesse, be careful," "Jesse, slow down," "Jesse, you're killing yourself," "Jesse, we need you, man" would have made much difference. It was like trying to hold back the moon-directed tide of time.

Jesse, in 1980, was wearily winding down like a hallway clock that had been wound too tightly. He spoke to Sam Piatt about

> *...turning back the clock of time and living each silver minute*
> *over, fighting the same fights, loving the same loves. Oh, for the joy*
> *of having my first poem, my first story, my first book published*
> *again.*

But the grandfather clocks in Jesse and Naomi's home of homes in W-Hollow were *tick-tocking*, their slender Tennysonian pendulums swinging without regard for fame, fortune, nature preserve, or human compulsion.

*Love took up the glass of Time, and turn'd it in his glowing hands;*
*Every moment, lightly shaken, ran itself in golden sands.*

*Locksley Hall*

The seasons stretching from 1970 to 1984 were as painfully wrenching for Naomi Deane as for Jesse.

> *April 8, 1970*
> *Dear Lena Wells:*
> *...two dear, dear friends who mean so much to Jesse and me—*
> *what memories we have of travels with you. And how many times we*
> *say "oh—we did that with Lena Wells and Gus." We are lucky—*
> *lucky women Lena Wells. We have the "cream of the crop." Each*
> *day I say a prayer of thanks that I can share the hours with this*
> *wonderful boy of mine! He is a jewel—a gem—so kind and*
> *generous—so warm and loving. Spring is coming late this year—but*
> *when it gets warm and pretty you must come and see us—we must*
> *talk again of many things. Tomorrow we go to Louisville and when*
> *we return I want to finish my "cleaning"—and be free to enjoy April*
> *here. Take care—and remember we love you.*
>
> 
>
> *Deane.*
>
> 

During the final five years, G. Sam Piatt regularly visited Jesse and Naomi at W-Hollow. Sam became a confidant, a human being stepping aside from the veil of objective journalism to become a faithful, compassionate friend.

> *Although I spent most of my life less than twenty miles from W-*
> *Hollow, and Jesse was, in sorts, my boyhood hero, I never met him*
> *face-to-face until the spring of 1971. That was the year when Doug*
> *Everman, the editor of the* Greenup News, *sent me out to Jesse's*
> *house to get an interview. Naturally, I was a bit nervous and anxious*
> *as I headed up his front walk with notebook and tape recorder.*
> *I had read Jesse's poems and stories in my American Writer's*
> *textbook, along with those of Robert Frost, Carl Sandburg, and*
> *Edgar Lee Masters and Amy Lowell, while I was a schoolboy. Jesse*
> *had come to speak at my eighth-grade graduation ceremony at*

*South Portsmouth Elementary/High School, and he left quite an impression on me.*

*He had provided inspiration—made me aware that I, too, could make my life count.*

*At any rate, Jesse's easy, homespun ways soon put me at ease. I launched into my interview, but before five minutes had passed Jesse zeroed in on me with questions of his own: "Who was your father...what did he do for a living...where did your mother's people come from?"*

*Before I knew it, I had my wallet out and was showing him photos of my family!*

*This shows the kind of man Jesse Stuart was. He was keenly interested in other people, and that interest was genuine. He didn't stare past you, or glance at his wristwatch. He had an excellent memory—able to recall first names of students he had taught thirty years ago. And he kept track of their progress. He tried to convince them to go on to college, and even worked to get them scholarship money.*

*Once I realized what was happening, I quietly returned my wallet to my pocket and managed to regain control of my interview.*

*"Did you have a sense of doom when you went out there when he was so sick?"* another reporter asked.

*"No I never got that sense. I always, if anything, believe it or not—Jesse could lift my spirits. He never complained during this time, except one time he complained that he was having some pain in his shoulder. But other than that I don't believe he had much pain. And he kept his sense of humor. Sometimes he'd become almost childish."*

*"In what way?"*

*"Well, making up stories and talking about somebody in the county running off with somebody's wife or something of that nature, and he'd laugh. Something of the past or current events, sometimes. He just enjoyed people and coming to know all he could about them and not being able to get up and go anymore he sort of—I felt like— depended on me to keep him up on what was going on in the*

*county."*

*"In 1978, he had the paralyzing stroke. Was he bedridden as a result of that stroke? Or would he get into a wheelchair and somebody would push him outside?"*

*"Richard Prince would come. Naomi Deane had hired Richard to get him up every day at four o'clock, into the wheelchair, and I filled in for Richard when he went on vacation. He'd get his arm around Jesse's neck and then he'd get one leg in between his legs and raise him up and Naomi Deane would bring the wheelchair in from behind and set him in the wheelchair and he was happy."*

*"That was a pretty heavy 225 pounds?"*

*"I think at that time he still weighed 185, maybe 190. He wasn't wasted away by any means."*

*"Still enjoying his cigars?"*

*"Oh, yeah, I always stopped at the drugstore in Greenup, well maybe not always, but often, and bring him a Roi-Tan or he liked those Swisher Sweets. They were only about ten cents apiece, something like that, very cheap cigars."*

Jesse would coax, "Ah, come on and have one with me," and Sam would accommodate his friend. They'd know the feeling of trust that comes to good old boys in measures not understood by those outside the brotherhood. These were moments as bonding as those shared by two men on a small fishing boat drifting down Little Sandy River.

*"And like I say, he got me started back on cigarettes. I had quit maybe two years and I thought I could have a cigar with him."*

*"He said he did not inhale?"*

*"Probably, he didn't. I watched him bring that smoke in and blow out a lot of smoke, so I would say he did not inhale. With a cigar you're gonna get some nicotine in."*

At times such as these, nicotine is not an issue. If you don't inhale you're probably not going to be satisfied, but the firmness of the cigar is gratifying, and the taste tingles the tip of the tongue.

*"He seemed to enjoy just looking at it and puffing it and remembering things. He didn't smoke cigarettes, but there sare photos of him*

*with a pipe."*

*"He used cigars more for reflection?"*

*"Yeah, that's the impression I had. It seemed to help him get the juices to flowing a little better."*

*"How was his appetite?"*

*"Naomi Deane fixed some very excellent meals, and you know I got in on them a few times at the kitchen table, and they'd wheel him in and we'd have dinner in there."*

*"What was her specialty?"*

*"I don't remember on that. Things that he was brought up on. The brown beans, I know he liked those. Fried potatoes, he liked fried potatoes. Things that weren't good for his heart, no doubt."*

Correct nutrition was not an issue when each meal could be the last.

*"Did he ever talk to you, Sam, about his doctors? The relationship with his doctors? Was he kind of—his own doctor?"*

*"I don't think he put a lot of stock in doctors."*

Jesse had had five or six cardiologists, and there'd been at least five or six opinions—overlapping, contradicting, quibbling. It didn't add up to Jesse's best interest.

Sam Piatt said, *"He told me one day about the doctor who after the 1954 heart attack had told him to have a regular little jigger of Scotch."* I believe he enjoyed a few Scotches after the stroke, even," said Sam. "I recall Naomi Deane fixing him one and one for me too. Scotch and water. And she would take one too."

*"Did he talk to you about death?"*

*"No, he did not have that serious vein about him. I brought the pastor out to anoint him with oil for, you know, healing. Clyde Johnson was the minister of the Methodist Church where I attended, United Methodist Church in South Shore. And he believed in the anointing of oil and healing and he said 'I wonder why don't we anoint your friend Jesse with oil?' So, it wasn't going to hurt anything.*

*"I told Naomi Deane what I wanted to do. I didn't share it with*

*Jesse. Anyway, we arrived at the house, I don't remember when it was, '81, and Johnson brought the oil that he had, which was from the Holy Land. So we went in and Jesse never did, I think, know what was going on, because Johnson took the oil, made the cross upon his forehead and Johnson was having a prayer and I opened up one eye and Jesse's eyes were wide open—it was fright! Because he thought he was passing. I didn't think anything about it, you know, and Naomi Deane had her head bowed. And we left and I came back in the next day or two days later, and Naomi Deane met me at the door and she said 'you scared Jesse to death. Said he thought you were giving him Last Rites, said after you left, 'Will I get through the night? Will I get through the night?'"*

"What else do you believe is important for us to know about Jesse?"

"I believe he thought about the possibility of having another stroke. But he didn't know. He lived from day to day. I think he had a dream about being paralyzed down the side.

"He enjoyed the fruits of his labor quite a bit. Some books were still coming in, Dandelion on the Acropolis, *another book of essays, things that he just enjoyed. I think that's what kept him going. He held out that hope for miraculous healing. I believe that he did the PTL* [Praise the Lord television program] *and the scriptures and all.*

"Physical therapists were there to help him keep the circulation going.

"Another time, they had an old trunk they'd gotten over in Zanzibar, and they kept it there in the bedroom, and I went over and sat down on that trunk, and it creaked. I went on talking, but they weren't listening. Jesse said, 'Sammmmmm, would you mind to get off of that trunk! We got that and it's not very strong.' I should have known better than to sit down on an old antique trunk. But he was very nice about it, and they tried not to embarrass me.

"He showed me his published works and gave a little insight on his current projects. He liked to have his books where he could see them—reach out and touch them, fondle them like a loving parent. Some local critics had told me they thought his ego was too big. He *liked to talk of his accomplishments, true, but the ego was not for him.*

*"I think a writer for the* Herald-Dispatch *in Huntington put it in the best perspective. 'Jesse's ego was for his native people, the people he wrote about. He was trying to show that he, one of them, had overcome poverty and adversity to make his life count, and that they, too, could do this. He felt that they should share in his triumph.'"*

Then came a sign of the times: *Esquire* magazine celebrated its fortieth anniversary and excluded anything written by one of its former stalwarts. Possibly he was out of step with the current needs of the magazine in 1973, a year that began with a sniper firing from the top of a Howard Johnson motel in downtown New Orleans and, by the end of the year, the Pentagon reporting that since 1961 nearly 46,000 Americans had died in Viet Nam. There were many taps at Arlington, but hardly any could be heard for Private Tussie.

Jesse fired back:

*Dear Lena Wells:*

*Can you believe that I, who have had the highest number of short stories ever published in* Esquire—*58, Scott Fitzgerald with 48 in second place—and I've had two articles and 29 poems, 89 publications—would not have been reprinted in the 40th Anniversary publication. I can't conceive of this. I'm glad you're writing them. My stories in their magazine used to help sell* Esquire *in this area. I hope you write them and get some others to write them.*

*October 5, 1973*

*I never heard of anything like what* Esquire *did to me. Never! Never! A big blow in my life, but not a knockout blow.*

Esquire's decision to omit Jesse Stuart was just the kind of news his doctors hoped to avoid because they knew how potentially dangerous it could be. The television set had circumvented the "No Visitors" order and had become a fearful intruder. Naomi's challenge was to make the best of

Jesse's deteriorating heart condition.

> *October 23, 1973*
> *Dear Lena Wells:*
>     *Dr. Bray sent us directly to the Hospital from his office yesterday*
> *morning. He said Jesse has had a heart attack. He wasn't well when*
> *you were with us Saturday. Of course we had to cancel our trip—*
> *very upsetting and disappointing to us—That invitation will never*
> *come again for Jesse. We are in a private room—on a monitor—no*
> *visitors. Dr. says three weeks perhaps....*
>
> 

*Fondly, Deane*

Jesse's mind was playing games with him. He was a University of
Kentucky basketball fan, but there were limits to how late he'd listen to a
broadcast. The *Esquire* slam dunk had clearly boxed him out, unnerved
him, and caused him to write uncharacteristic letters.

> *Dear Lena Wells:*
>     *I wouldn't sit up until 2 AM to listen to any basketball game even*
> *if our Lord Jesus Christ was jumping center—despite the fact I'm a*
> *spiritual man I'd skip. As you perhaps know I've been there again. I*
> *went in with pain enough for two men to bear, but old lucky Jesse*
> *got out and got to come home New Year's eve.*
>
> 

*Sincerely, Jesse*

Four more years wended by, and Jesse weathered them, but he was like
Nest Egg warily watching for the bloodthirsty owl.

> *December 29, 1977*
> *Dear Lena Wells:*
>     *I'm home from the hospital but must remain in the house for two*
> *weeks in robe and pajamas while I recuperate. Lying in Intensive*
> *care during the Christmas Holidays was rough but I had to be there.*
> *It was the place for me to go.*
>
> 

*Jesse*

> *January 25, 1978*
> *Dear Lena Wells:*
>     *I'm staying in. I couldn't begin to shovel snow. I don't even carry*

*wood from the garage and build fires. Deane has been doing this.
She has learned how and has become a first rate builder of fires in
two fireplaces. We've not been getting out only two times since Dec.
23rd. I spent days in the hospital and house. I don't do anything
except write a few letters, watch TV and listen to radio—and this
has never been my world to do this. I've always been busy and on
the move. But now, Lena Wells for both you and me, it will be
different.*

*Sincerely, Jesse*

*P.S. We've got from 30 to 36 inches of snow in our area.*

In the autumn of 1978, Lena Wells Voiers wrote from her home in
Vanceburg a letter to her former student and lifelong friend in Greenup
County. Gus had passed on, but she had been there when Jesse needed
her—from the time she shamed him into returning to high school, to now
when he was nearing the end of his life. Yet she did not scold Jesse. She
accepted him with pride as the good man from W-Hollow.

*Judge Oscar Sammons just walked by my window on his way to
Lewis County Court House. I read in some newspapers that Judge
Sammons is resigning his job this January 1979.*

*Jesse, I think, your illness scared Judge Sammons and he wants to
retire before he gets sick too. Of course you know that you always
worked too hard as an author and a traveling lecturer.*

*I have no further comments. Just behave yourself and come to visit
me when Deane is glad to bring you.*

*Sincerely, LWV*

Jesse's memory of his teacher never wavered—she was the eye of the
needle, an essential part of the enthusiasm and the persistence of the boy who
grew up to become the man who wrote *The Thread That Runs So True*.

*You taught me in school. You have known me since I was 15 yrs
old and you were a very young woman. You have seen me grow,
come along, write books...You have been a booster, a helper, an
uplifter, a great teacher because you go back and help all of your
pupils. Not one but all. This is great teaching.*

George T. McWhorter played a key role in the acceptance of a body of Jesse Stuart's correspondence into Special Collections at the University of Louisville. He was one of the last of the visitors to Jesse's bedside at W-Hollow. Trained as an operatic singer in New York City, McWhorter had recently returned from Scotland and had made his own sentimental journey to the Hebrides.

> *Everybody loved Bobby Burns and I think Jesse desired to be loved the same way.*

There in the W-Hollow bedroom, with the sun descending over Seaton Ridge and Cedar Riffles, George McWhorter presented Jesse with a private concert of three songs: "Ca' the yowes to the knowes," "Bonnie George Campbell," and "Think on Me."

McWhorter says Jesse's favorite was "Bonnie George Campbell:"

> *High upon Hielands and laigh upon Tay*
> *Bonnie George Campbell rode oot on a day;*
> *He saddled, he bridled, and gallant rode he,*
> *Hame cam' his guid horse, but never cam' he.*

Sam was there in May 1982, and Jesse struggled to sign for him a copy of *Kentucky Is My Land*. Symbolically and rightfully, it would become one of Jesse Stuart's last signatures, a statement of belief and purpose, love and commitment.

Later that evening, May 19, Jesse and Naomi Deane were alone. He had drifted off into sleep. When she tried to wake him up, he did not respond. He was breathing, but that was all. Naomi waited. Jesse had told her he wanted to die at home, but her better judgment told her the hour had come to call for help and take him one more time to King's Daughters Hospital.

He had suffered another stroke: Jesse Stuart was pronounced "comatose."

On June 28, 1982, Naomi agreed to move Jesse from the hospital to Jo-Lin Health Center in Ironton, Ohio. He was not expected to live more than a few days. But he must have clung to an inner strength, perhaps an Old World Highland faith, taunting medical opinion.

The single-floored Jo-Lin Health Center holds solidly to hard-packed ground at the corner of 10th and Center Streets in Ironton, population approximately 13,000. The natives have descended from a mostly blue-collar tradition in this old industrial enclave of limestone quarries and coke production for steel mill furnaces. With mining as its principal identity, Ironton is plotted in a narrow rectangle across the Ohio River from Kentucky, located on the northern bank about halfway between the mouths of Big and Little Sandy Rivers. In his books Jesse sometimes referred to Ironton as "Toniron."

Ironton was founded in 1848, about the time of the publication of *Wuthering Heights* and the death of its author, Emily Brontë. Her last poem, written when she was only thirty years old, the year of her death, speaks softly to the soul of Jesse Stuart—

> *No coward soul is mine,*
> *No trembler in the world's storm-troubled sphere:*
> *I see Heaven's glories shine,*
> *And faith shines equal, arming me from fear.*

Armed from fear, Jesse answers back in plowboy wisdom and passion born of W-Hollow—

> *There are seconds in our lives that pass*
> *Us down long, dark alley ways of dreams.*
> *We drift like leaves on currentless streams*
> *Out beyond all time and whirling mass*
> *Of space. And softly we sink, and deep*
> *Beyond all time and where all time is vain,*
> *Where we give up the body and the brain*
> *And lie in peace in our dead sleep.*

*Harvest of Youth*

Emily was a shooting star across dark and lonely Yorkshire moors. In the next century, Jesse was a spectacular meteoric shower above the dark hills of Kentucky. Both poets faced the end of their lives with courage and an abiding faith in eternity. As for Jesse, many times he'd been a witness along pathways leading to death, from the sawbriars that would skin you alive to rutting bucks locking horns in mortal combat. Death was a constant specter in the hollers of Greenup County, and the last day would come to everyone. Jesse not only recognized that he was no different, he seemed to rejoice in it.

*I know that Earth will be my last lover*
*To kiss her lips will not disturb my will;*
*For others lie with her under cover,*
*Lie with her curiously still.*

*Harvest of Youth*

In 1982 *The Best-Loved Short Stories of Jesse Stuart*, selected and edited by Harold E. Richardson, appeared with an introduction by Robert Penn Warren. It would be Jesse's last book published in his lifetime. The theme of death, sunset, and return to earth is often repeated. Finally, in *New Harvest: Forgotten Stories of Kentucky's Jesse Stuart*, selected and edited by David Palmore there is the tale "Death Comes to Nicodemous:"

*"Where air you goin', By-Jacks, ridin' that poor old workin' mule to death on this hot day?" Big Brownie asks. "Ain't you got no mercy on dumb brutes in sicha weather as this?"*

*"Goin'?" By-Jacks repeats. "Ain't no one been around to see you and broke the news about Nicodemous Pratt? He kicked the bucket at four o'clock this mornin'."*

*"The devil he did," says Big Brownie. He leans back on his scythe handle and wipes the sweat with his big fire-shovel hand from his cucumber-warty red face. He wipes a stream of sweat bigger than is drippin' from the mule's bells with his index finger and slings it onto the yellow-clay earth.*

*"I'll tell you," says By-Jacks, "our days air numbered same as the hairs on our head and when the Master rings the bell it's just like a dinner bell callin' a body home from the field to dinner. I've been out all over the neighborhood this mornin' tellin' the people about poor old Nicodemous, payin' my last respects to a good man and a good neighbor."*

The author of thousands of poems, hundreds of short stories and novels, was gently laid on a gurney, then placed inside an ambulance and driven through Ashland to the bridge spanning the big river. He had passed this way many times before, but this time he was helpless as the route angled past Coal Grove to the double front door of Jo-Lin Health Center.

Inside there was a quick ninety-degree turn to the right, past the lounge where patients gathered to search longingly for familiar family faces. There were the young and old invalids in a village of the afflicted and the slowly dying. There were vacant faces and awkward disarray—a woman repeatedly knotting her fingers, another giving up trying to put a cotton sock on her foot and finding a place for it on her right hand. She smiled and waved as if she were in an owner's box at Churchill Downs, as if she had a winning trifecta.

Jesse's gurney rolled past the central nurse's station where medical records were carefully checked and dutifully filed, then, on a straight line, Jesse and Naomi went down the corridor—"the long, dark alley way of dreams"—to Room 129, on the left.

Naomi watched as the attendant guided the gurney into the small space, to the bed alongside the wide, western window, where Jesse would drift like a leaf on a currentless stream—without speaking—hardly moving—haunted, yet comforted, perhaps, by his own words:

> *...now in the end when I meet Death,*
> *if I am still young or if I have grown old,*
> *I shall not be afraid.*

For the last two years of his life, Jesse lay in a coma. Naomi visited him almost daily, and she read to him because she believed he might be able to hear her voice. It is said that the ability of the comatose to hear the spoken word is the last thing "to go." The patient does not make an outward sign—oh, maybe a flicker of the eyes that was not there before a loved one appeared. Naomi Deane never lost faith. She believed Jesse could hear her. She read him letters and Christmas cards. She played a game of thinking that Jesse would provide her with a response, and she would write it and ask for his approval. Only then would she seal the envelope and set it aside for mailing. Naomi Deane had been the driving force behind Jesse, and without her he might have been a forest fire out of control.

Now, he was barely an ember.

"He is my strength," Naomi told Sam Piatt.

> *It doesn't tire me coming here each day. Just seeing him, holding*
> *his hand, keeps my strength up....I believe he can hear me, and that*

*he understands....He gets so many letters from people we don't know,*
*and I can't possibly answer all of them, though I do the best I can....I*
*don't know how Jesse did it. He would try to answer every letter,*
*especially if they were from students....So many people don't know*
*that he's no longer active.*

That Christmas of 1982, Room 129 was decorated with wreaths made of grapevines from W-Hollow, and there was a small Swiss music box that Jesse had received the previous Christmas. It was now on his pillow. "I played it over and over for him," said Naomi, "The tune is 'The Little Drummer Boy.'" Naomi believed Jesse heard it and loved it.

Others might forget the strong young man with the bull-tongue plow and the teacher with the thread that ran so true, or they might feel embarrassed about visiting, seeing Jesse lying there, helpless in his foretaste of Glory, his kingdom within. They might not know what to say, being uncomfortable with the soundless view of him, unaccustomed to his not talking, having only themselves to find something fitting to say. But Naomi did not falter. The walks down and back up the long corridor were a time for speaking to others who sat in their wheelchairs and smiled back to her. The ends of lives marched to the beat of their own drums in a parade that knew no turning back.

"She continued to treat him as if he was going to wake up at any moment," said Jo Linda Heaberlin in her office in the summer of 2003. "Comatose patients can't speak or show any emotion. They can't let you know any of their needs."

Jo Linda is a painstaking nursing home gatekeeper who tries to understand reality and each individual patient's right to a decent parade route to the other side of the window of life.

"We have always had the philosophy to take the very best care that can be given. We feed food that we'd want to eat. My father built this facility. He opened it in 1974 and he worked here until he passed away in 1994. He named it after me and left it to me."

Naomi?

"Mrs. Stuart was gracious—she didn't expect to be treated any differently than anyone else."

Naomi came promptly throughout the deathwatch—reading to Jesse, kissing him, combing his graying hair. More than at any other time, he had become her child, yet she showed him her respect and did not patronize him. He deserved no less.

As it was written in the Book of Ruth:

> *And Naomi took the child,*
> *And laid it in her bosom,*
> *And became nurse unto it.*

Piatt remembered: "Jesse opened his eyes, yawned, and such—but there was no indication that he actually could comprehend any activity or sounds around him."

Mrs. Heaberlin took from her desk the priceless gift she'd received from Naomi—a first edition of Jesse's autobiography *Beyond Dark Hills*, the rare McGraw-Hill first edition copy with richly marbled end-leaves. Naomi made sure each Jo-Lin employee had a copy, Jesse's words as prescient as they were when first published in 1938:

> *The voices got thinner and thinner on the night wind.*
> *And finally they died away....*
> *The wind rattled among the dead cornhusks where*
> *the corn had been topped.*
> *The milkweed seeds blew out in a white thinness on the blue air.*

Jo Linda escorted her visitor to Room 129 to show where Jesse had lived those bewildering final moments of his life. The patient now occupying the half of the room nearest the sundown view said he didn't mind that the visitor would want to know how it might've looked when Jesse was there—the seasons from spring to winter on the other side of the window pane: bird feeders, six pigeons fluttering away, maintenance crews coming and going—and after the sunset, a new moon rising, Orion the Great Hunter on guard to protect the defenseless.

"How long have you been here?"

The man seated in a chair looked away from the television screen, his daily entertainment.

"Ten years," the man replied with a friendly smile, hands folded in his lap.

"Have you heard of Jesse Stuart?"

"Yes."

"Have you read him?"

"Yes," the man said, unconvincingly, looking directly, cheerfully, and politely, perhaps not to disappoint or deflate obtrusive questions.

"Thank you for allowing me to come in."

"Anytime."

There was a handshake and a good luck wish. On the way out, there was a brief hello to the gentleman lying on the bed nearest the door. He was fully dressed, yet seemed immobile. He, too, smiled and somehow seemed, perhaps, armed from fear. The sight of him was a message brought down from the mountaintop—

Thou Shalt Not Be Greedy, Thou Shalt Remember Thy Feet of Clay, Thou Shalt Be Thankful for Thy Life, Thou Shalt Loosen the Bonds That Bind Thee to Thyself.

Jo Linda led the way to the activities room and pointed to the antique coal oil lamps Naomi had given to Jo-Lin, reminder of the light that burned for Jesse in the early days. There were stacks of scrapbooks and a quiet search for a picture of Jesse and Naomi.

"If I find one, I'll send it to you," said Peggy Dyer, activity director.

"What do you remember about Jesse when he first came to room 129?"

"He opened his eyes, but he didn't recognize, he didn't respond. He didn't respond verbally or give eye contact."

Naomi?

"He would always calm down when she came in."

"How early would she come, how long would she stay?"

"She came about 10:30 and stayed until after 6:00 in the evening. He was up in a lounge chair type and she'd get him out of the room and wheel him around. She'd take him outside. She was a very independent lady; she liked to do for him."

"He was fed with a tube?"

"Yes."

Christmas Eve, 1982.

Naomi spent the night on the couch in the TV lounge, where the lead story from Salt Lake City was all about Barney Clark and his being up and walking around following his Jarvik-7 heart transplant, the first in the United States. Although Clark would live only a little more than three months more, the news accounts produced mixed feelings for Naomi Deane. She would have wished a new heart for Jesse, a chance to begin all over again, but she knew in her own heart that that was not to be. Jesse had defied the odds, and she would stay by his side as long as humanly possible. The next morning she read Christmas cards to him, but he did not respond and may not have known anything. But Naomi never stopped believing—she loved Jesse too much to admit defeat.

Jesse lived on as if to give life to *Hold April.*

> *Do not let April go but hold her tight,*
> *Month of eternal beauty and delight.*

Jesse lived through another birthday, his seventy-seventh—August 8, 1983—and Sam Piatt wrote another story. He quoted a nursing supervisor who said, "His condition hasn't changed much since he became a patient here last summer....He is aware of some things that are going on around him, and I believe he hears the voices of those speaking in the room. But some days he just seems to shut the rest of the world off—as if to say, "'This is my day.'"

Naomi Deane told Sam:

> *"I'll share with him some cards and letters from well-wishers...tell him of the phone calls he's received."* As for literary matters, *"I try to keep things together as Jesse would want me to, there are some things I don't know what to do with. I set them aside, and some days I just think that Jesse is going to come home and tell me what to do with them."*

In *Beyond Dark Hills* Jesse had written—

> *It was winter now, the winter of Time. The tobacco stubbles and the corn stubbles were white on the old fields. The woods were*

*naked and the wind whistled through the woods. The dark outlines of
the hills cut sharp against the cloudy January sky. The tall dark hills
looked barren and desolate. It was the land of tobacco, the land of
God, the land of oak trees, the land of beauty, the land of desolation,
the home of tragic living and the home of the sweetness of life. Great
dark hills, with life among them, with death among them. Great hills,
formed millions of years ago, that give us food, shelter, and warmth
in life and take us back to their bosom in the end.*

On one of the last days at Jo-Lin, the man from Troublesome Creek—
James Still, creator of *River of Earth* and "Heritage" in *Wolfpen Poems*—
came to say goodbye to the man from W-Hollow.

> *I shall not leave these prisoning hills*
> *Though they topple their barren heads to level earth....*
> *one with death rising to bloom again, I cannot go.*
> *Being of these hills I cannot pass beyond.*

James Still's last visit with Jesse is described by biographer Richardson:

"'Jesse, this is old Jim. I've come by to see you.'
"Jesse's eyelids moved, but he did not open his eyes."

Turning to look into the warmth of Naomi Deane, James Still must have
searched for and felt her understanding, the depth of her distress. After a
short visit, the quiet man from Troublesome Creek returned to his log
house in Knott County, Kentucky. James Still, confident in the critical
acclaim for his work, had been wounded by Jesse's extraordinary popular
acclaim—"Old Jim" nursing the hurt. Yet he too was comfortable with his
mortality, and he indicated this on one of the last times he sat at the table in
the front room of the log house on Dead Mare Branch and encouraged the
visiting reporter to go up to the loft and look at all the magazines in which
he had been published. James Still and Jesse Stuart—each in his own way
was destined to become a Kentucky treasure.

February 13, 1984.
Sam Piatt visited Jesse for the last time in Room 129.

*"How did he seem to you?"*

*"Well, he seemed really the way he had for a year. He was resting comfortably....I thought many times, what world is he in there? What is going on in his mind and can he hear her? Because Naomi Deane would bring the mail and that day she had something that she read to him."*

Sam watched as Naomi opened two batches totaling a hundred greeting cards from fifth- and sixth-grade Louisville students. She shared them with Jesse—as best she could.

*"I don't think she really allowed herself to give up hope. I think she maintained that hope that through some miracle he would recover."*

February 17, 1984.

At 4:40 p.m., attendants thought Jesse was sleeping. When they tried to turn him on the bed, they knew he had died. After a life of seventy-seven years—teaching, loving, almost non-stop writing and heart-pounding speeches to audiences roaring with cheers and laughter—Jesse Stuart was gone.

Sam Piatt wrote in a letter, February 21, 1984:

*His gallant heart stopped beating....Naomi Deane had been by his side through most of that day, but had left and was on her way home when death came. I had last visited with Jesse and Naomi Deane four days before he died. She talked then about final arrangements that Jesse wanted carried out. She was concerned that she might go first.*

The director's office at the Jo-Lin Health Center: "Can you remember anything about Naomi on the last day?"

"I do remember that she had just left and we had to call her back," said Jo Linda.

Naomi returned across the river to Jo-Lin, walked directly to room 129, and placed Jesse's hand in hers.

She wept.

After Dr. Max Wheeler made the formal pronouncement of death, Eddie Riggs arrived from his funeral home in Greenup, and Jesse's body was placed inside the ambulance. Naomi got into the front seat, for she was determined to be sure that her Jesse arrived safely—back home in Kentucky.

> *And he shall be like a tree*
> *planted by the rivers of water...*
>
> *Psalm 1*

*Shhhhhhh....*

It was cold outside on the southern side of the Ohio River, where Little Sandy River gave back all it had. There were a few whispers at first, but then a great quiet enveloped the old Methodist church on Main Street in Greenup. The pews were filled with Jesse's family and friends.

Children and their elders gathered in the community of bereavement, remembering the powerful voice that had sung for them in both good and difficult times. His was a huge presence that had risen, gone away, but returned home to live out his days among the Highlanders he loved.

Now he was no more but, in a deeper, exhilarating sense, he was still alive and for aye would be in books—like *Land of the Honey-Colored Wind*, *Songs of a Mountain Plowman*, and "Our Heritage."

> *We love this land we've always known*
> *That holds us and our dead—*
> *The rugged slopes with scattered stone*
> *That grow our daily bread.*

Jesse's casket was in place, closed so that only the memory of his craggy face remained. Now came the time for the living to look inward upon their selves, just as Jesse would have wanted it—nay, not a time of sorrow, but the opening of a pathway to a universe of joy.

The Reverend Julian Hammonds issued the call to worship at United Methodist Church at two o'clock, that afternoon of February 20, 1984.

> *Jesse would have wanted this to be a time of celebration. He lived a wonderful and magnificent life. We are here to honor a man who honored life. Jesse Stuart used his talents entrusted to him by God.*

*Jesse Stuart was a man of common touch with a very uncommon talent. He knew how to capture the seasons of life and nature. He wrote beautiful stories of everyday life. He sensed the beauty of life in elegant language.*

*Today is a celebration of triumph. There is no gloom or hopelessness here. Jesse knew that the kingdom of God is within you. He was a man of honor in all he did and in all he said. He was a man of high principle, you knew what he thought. Greenup County residents are lucky to have this treasure, this legacy Jesse Stuart left us.*

*He never knew a stranger.*

*There is no gloom here, for you see, our own Jesse made a request that we not share his writing and his poetry. What a beautiful man. It speaks so eloquently and so beautifully. And yet in his readings and in his comforts he often had Deane read to him a poem by John Burroughs, "The Summit of the Years."*

> *I have loved to feel the grass under my feet*
> *and sound of running streams by my side.*
> *The murmur of wind in the tree tops*
> *Has always been good music to me.*

The congregation rose and sang one of Jesse's favorite hymns, the timbre of the words stirring the hearts and souls of the faithful. It was the magnificent hymn binding up the wounds of all Christendom:

> *A mighty fortress is our God*
> *a bulwark never failing;*
> *our helper be amid the flood*
> *of mortal ills prevailing....*

Dr. Robert Wood, superintendent for the Ashland District, United Methodist Church, delivered the eulogy, the congregation on the edge of a moment as fragile as a bird cupped in a young boy's palms.

*What can one say to celebrate such a life as Jesse Stuart's, one who walked in our midst and lived his life as he was, and do the tremendous things which he did?*

*What can you say?*

*Our minds are boggled by his accomplishments. And yet, as we gather here we must have a bit of sadness—there's no way we can be rid of that.*

*And yet, Jesse Stuart would not want us overcome by our grief within. He would want us to do what he requested—to celebrate his life and to know about the things of eternity and the things of the Christian faith. How can one ever hope to express all that is upon our hearts?*

*We have come today, each one of us, in our own way to try—and each of us in our own way, to remember.*

*Some fourteen or maybe fifteen years ago while working with WKYH-TV in Hazard, Kentucky, I received a call from the station owner one day, asking that I come and do an interview. The interview was to be with Jesse Stuart.*

*And so I went.*

*And Jesse touched my life as he has touched your life and the lives of many other people. And I would like to share some of the impressions that I received—not only from that time, but from other times.*

*Jesse Stuart was a warm and outgoing person. And to know him a short while was like knowing him for a lifetime. For he was that easy to know. He put you at ease. I suppose I was to put him at ease that day in the interview—that's what an interviewer does. But that was not the case on that particular occasion. He put me at ease, and I felt like before the interview was over I had known Jesse Stuart for a long, long time, and I was grateful for the feeling.*

*He was a warm, friendly person who really, genuinely, liked people....His was a life of service to people. And his contribution will last forever, his contribution to the lives of people.*

*Jesse was an educator. He was quoted in the newspapers as having said, "I guess I will always be a teacher. I like the frontline of the classroom...." When I first met him I had read* Mr. Gallion's School. *I thought it would be good to know him like that, as principal...and after the interview that day I sort of included that in my heart. At last I had met that principal. Perhaps I had talked a bit to that principal, Jesse Stuart.*

*I would be remiss if I did not say that he was a Methodist. That's where we are, isn't it? He knew what Jesus meant when he said the kingdom of God is within you...Jesus within.*

*He was a man of character, he impressed me in this way. It stood out all around in what he did and what he said. He was honest. You knew he was genuine. You knew exactly where he stood, and you knew exactly what he thought—and that was good.*

*He had high principles. I had commented in the interview the fact that there was so much smut in some of the literature that was produced today, and I said unto him, "You have not used that," and his reply was quick, unrehearsed. He said, "You do not have to do that—if you're good."*

*And Jesse was good.*

*Jesse was good, and we all know that. He wished to add to people's lives and to be an example—he did and he was.*

*There are many ways to remember him and all of you have your own way.*

*He touched the lives of people from the highest to the lowest and was equally at home with all. Many of you are like my father-in-law, who read his books but never had the opportunity to meet him. And after Jesse's last stroke I visited with Dad and he said, "Well, our old buddy is in trouble, isn't he?"*

*"And I asked, 'Who's that?'"—We had several "old buddies," I guess.*

*And he said, "Why, Jesse Stuart, of course." He said, "I hope he makes it."*

*Well, I think Jesse would want me to say to you today, "I made it. My legs are strong. My breathing is easy, and I know the ultimate of all that I knew—I still love you, and God does too."*

*He will be missed.*

After the service at United Methodist Church in Greenup, where Little Sandy loses itself in the Ohio, six old buddies carried the heavy bronze casket  out the front door of the small, unpretentious church to the waiting hearse. Naomi Deane followed, her heart heavy with grief. But she'd fulfilled Jesse's wishes to the end.

The pallbearers were Thurman Darby and Judge Oscar Sammons, Jesse's classmates who graduated with him from Greenup High School in 1926; Bill Harrell, coach of the athletic teams at Greenup High School when Jesse was principal there; Richard Prince, the faithful nursing home helper, who came at four o'clock each afternoon to W-Hollow to help move Jesse into his wheelchair and roll him out where the squirrels played and the birds sang; Dr. Charles Conley, who made house calls at W-Hollow during the four years when Jesse was bedfast; and G. Sam Piatt, the newspaper reporter-friend, who "came to love Jesse and Naomi Deane like parents."

The long funeral procession crossed U.S. 23 and wound south on KY 1 from Greenup toward W-Hollow Road, and on past it to the turnoff leading up to Plum Grove Cemetery. In the car bearing the pallbearers, Thurman Darby nodded toward a wooded point behind some houses and said, "There was the path where Jesse came out of the woods on his walk to Greenup High School. It's about three or four miles back through the hills to where he lived."

> *He could have stayed back in those hills,* Sam Piatt thought to himself, *like so many have done—plowing, timbering, mending fences, and never have put a pen to paper. How poor that would have left us all. But he found the pathway out, willed his feet to follow it, and made his life count.*

Sam Piatt's memory came in a great rush like the wind that so often whipped through W-Hollow.

The funeral procession labored up the steep hill, and Piatt stared through the window of the pallbearers' car, remembering the day thirteen years before when he'd gone to W-Hollow to do his first story on the world-famous author Jesse Stuart. The questions and the answers now seemed to him to be a memorial.

> *After a while, we climbed into his little white Volkswagen and followed a logging road to the top of the ridges. It was the last week of April, and sunlight glittered on flowering dogwood.*

*He showed me Ol' Op's cabin, the setting for* The Good Spirit of Laurel Ridge. *He walked the woodland paths and ran his hands over the rough bark of hickory and oak trees and called them all by name. "This persimmon tree is loaded every fall," he said. "The 'possums really have a feast."*

*We gazed out from the ridge toward Greenup and the Ohio River, and I was able to see what he had so aptly put down on paper thirty years before.*

> *My land is fair for any eyes to see—*
> *Now look, my friends—look to the east and west!*
> *You see the purple hills far in the west—*
> *Hills lined with pine and gum and black oak tree—*
> *This land is mine, I sing of it to you—*
> *My land beneath the skies of white and blue.*
> *This land is mine, for I am part of it.*
> *I am the land, for it is part of me—*
> *We are akin and thus our kinship be!*
> *It would make me a brother to the tree!*

*Sonnet 4*
*Man with a Bull-Tongue Plow*

*As we headed back down into the valley, he pointed to a thirty-five degree slope, now covered with tall timber and saplings. "My father and I once cleared that hillside and planted corn along there."*

Sam Piatt's remembrances overflowed, knowing no surcease. A day in 1971 was as clear as an afternoon in 1984. Time was blended, just as Jesse said it would be—the beginning in the ending and the ending in the beginning. Now the burial of Jesse Stuart was as new as his birth, and Sam Piatt could not erase the memories, even if he tried.

The funeral cortege came to a halt at the top of the hill where Plum Grove Cemetery sits like a coverlet for the weary, a home welcoming all its wandering children, both the prodigal and the dutiful. It is a place to be visited often by those who read Jesse Stuart and see fragments of themselves.

The pallbearers removed the casket from the hearse, felt the smoothness of the handle grips, steadied their feet to be more sure they did not stumble, and carried the burden through the double chainlink gates, then proceeded the last few steps toward the south, to the open grave.

Naomi Deane had fulfilled each of Jesse's requests when he'd talked with her about the final arrangements. His wish of there being a "Celebration of Triumph" was carried out. He'd wanted as many friends as possible to share in that victory. It would not have bothered him in the least that there were so many cameras, microphones, and reporters' notebooks present. In this way, Jesse knew, those who could not attend the funeral and burial would be able to witness it from their homes and their workplaces.

Sam Piatt was a reporter to the end, but one who was able to revere Jesse as a friend. It would cause the journalist to break the bond, some would say the pretense, of "objectivity" and allow personal belief to flow inward. He would write of it in a letter the day after the burial:

> *Now, we who are Christians know that the grave is not our goal— that the body, indeed returns to dust, but the spirit to God who gave it. Jesse wrote much about death, and now he has unraveled the mystery that lies beyond the grave. Once he penned these lines:*
>
> > *Someday I shall return to earth and stone,*
> > *And grass and trees and briars and growing things.*
> > *And over me night winds shall make their moan.*
> > *And over me white dogwoods bloom in spring.*

Dr. Robert Wood read the first stanza of "What a Friend," and then the traditional words from "The Burial of the Dead:"

> *We therefore commit his body to the ground; earth to earth, ashes to ashes, dust to dust; in sure and certain hope of the Resurrection to eternal life.*

The Reverend Julian Hammonds prayed the benediction, then passed along the row of family members, consoling each one.

The wind was rising. There was a coldness blowing in, and it looked as if it might clabber up a rain, or spill a cloud of snow.

Naomi Deane rose from her chair, moved to the coffin and gently placed her right hand on it. Touching it ever so lightly, she spoke softly—

"Goodbye, Jesse."

She turned and walked away.

Jesse Stuart's life was celebrated at Plum Grove Cemetery, but in a new century, young and old readers will rediscover, or discover for the first time, the spirit and character of the man from W-Hollow. More important, they may see it as a celebration of themselves. That alone would have pleased Jesse. He'd know his life had really made a difference.

# JESSE WAS ANCHORED DEEP

*A valid spiritual life, in this world,*
*must have a practice and a practicality—*
*It must have a material result.*

Wendell Berry
*Standing on Earth*

*Gift!*

"What will happen to the land when we are gone?" Jesse had wondered aloud in the autumn of his life as he sat musing on his front porch in W-Hollow and looked out toward the drying pasture and the changing of the foliage guard in the wooded hills. A natural, spiritual heirloom should derive from a conscious, human decision. It should be unselfish. It should make fundamental sense. It should come from within and go forth to the universe.

So many serious questions blink in the woods, where white-tailed deer step warily through billions of fallen oak leaves, where wide-eyed bullfrogs croak up and down Shinglemill Run—"back where the hoot owls holler in the daytime"—where the good spirit of Old Op laughs past the sourwood trees, and Brer Rabbit's nose quivers in the sawbriars.

"What will happen to the wildlife? Where will the creatures find a home?" Jesse had wanted to know, the troubled words reported by G. Sam Piatt for the *Ashland Daily Independent*:

> *Developers already had expressed interest in the 1,000-acre farm,*
> *trying to entice him to sell portions of it. In his mind Stuart could see*

275

*bulldozers leveling the land, the great oak and gum and hickory trees being felled, and square, look-alike houses dotting the landscape.*

As early as 1953, Jesse had written to his professor, Dr. Crabb at Peabody College:

*I control all the head-waters of W-Hollow and almost half way down the stream because I have managed, a little at a time, to buy 600 acres (or more) of this land. I bought it because I loved this land. I used to work over it. My father used to work by the day for other farmers and I worked with him. Then we rented this land...all over the Hollow but never out of it. I live today within one mile of where I was born. Actually other people back in those days owned the land by deed but I owned it more than they did and now I have the paper deeds too. I can keep people from cutting the trees and destroying the land.*

*Right today in the beautiful low rolling Plum Grove hills, a surveyor and two helpers are marking off one-half acre lots (and they'll sell) on the old Jordan farm which joins me. A town is coming to that section and it is the land I possum hunted over as a boy. The last acre I bought there cost me $300. And I threw up my hands but bought it anyway. The other day I was offered, 18 months after getting it, $750 for this acre. But I didn't sell it. As I say, I'm getting fortified against the future. I see what is coming. And actually, it is hard to believe. As late as 1934, 92 acres of this land sold for $1025. This same place has sold for $30,000 or more, from 1949 to 53. It was sold off in lots and little acreages.*

*When Deane and I married we had kerosene lamps and burned wood in a cookstove and one fireplace. We made a dirt road to this house and built little wooden bridges across the streams. Three months of the year, we had to have frozen ground to drive in here. Today, we have a winter road, graveled....I bought the tile to get the state to build the W-Hollow road. Then we built the road to our home. We have electricity, all modern conveniences now....And this winter we got a heating system, hot-water, in our home. I've seen*

*every foot of hardroad come to this county, the county high schools*
*too and I'm 45. The work we've done here is beyond all the work*
*I've done in writing. We've made a Valley. We've got the forests, the*
*wild flowers, meadows where they should be on these acres.*

*Sincerely,*
*Your friend, your student, Jesse Stuart*

Wendell Berry's "The Gift of Good Land," an essay in his *Standing on Earth*, published in 1991 by Golgonooza Press, suggests a more thoughtful, conserving brotherhood that could embrace Jesse Stuart's idea of stewardship—and his decision to establish the Jesse Stuart Nature Preserve.

Jesse's land was valued at $1.2- $1.4 million. He had purchased, piece by piece, twenty-eight different tracts in W-Hollow, and his intention was to

*improve every acre and protect the wildlife....We love it...no gullies*
*now... I keep my land covered with grass and trees.*

Jesse would donate more than 700 acres for the Jesse Stuart Nature Preserve, land he'd worked a lifetime to accumulate, representing half the total appraised value, the other half derived from state and federal grants. It would not include the house and fourteen acres, which would remain private property. The gift was a deep-rooted decision, perhaps the culmination of a belief in Whitman's "When I give I give myself."

More than half a century later, Jane Stuart has made her parents' home her private residence, and she has carved out a distinctive life of her own. She holds a B.A. from Case Western Reserve University and a Ph.D. in Italian from Indiana University. She is a member of the Kentucky State Poetry Society and the Academy of American Poets. Her essay "This House and This World" appears in *Bloodroot: Reflections on Place by Appalachian Women Writers* published in 1998 by the University Press of Kentucky: "I have found a world at home....It's the eloquence of home that overwhelms me, and that I write about."

Jane Stuart has written books of poetry, short stories, and novels. She declined a request to visit with her in connection with the writing of this biography of her father. Jane says she has "found it best to respect my father's work quietly and...follow in my own footsteps."

Jesse and the Commonwealth of Kentucky would work together for the benefit of all—people, deer, frogs, owls, and all creatures calling W-Hollow "home." The time was right for such an arrangement—to delay might result in the destruction neither party wanted. It would happen because Jesse would will it to happen, the state of Kentucky would see the wisdom of it, and it would be done.

> *When Tomorrow has come*
> *And rain and Death*
> *Swish through the doorway*
> *Of the hold I have built against the wind*
> *And the hosts of the air,*
> *There will be but emptiness and night*
> *Since I am an atom and a builder.*
> *I have lived at the muddy root of life*
> *Deep set under the rock of time.*
> *And I did not know that now*
> *Is the time of all times;*
> *That today is yesterday,*
> *The inch of our future.*
>
> *Harvest of Youth*

Jesse had come to terms with inevitability, the certain, temple-pounding realization that there was no practical turning back to the bull-tongue plow days—they were as much a museum piece as the Nest Egg days of a hidden yesteryear. A nature preserve, therefore, would be a way to save natural habitats for the future—lasting homes for the Carolina wren, hoary mountain mint, and golden ragwort. The public would reap a new harvest of nature, increasing the likelihood of perpetuity. The outcome would require generosity. The gift must be unconditional.

Jesse could have amassed a plunderous fortune by wheeling and dealing with land developers—there might have been a country club, hunting lodge and liar's retreat, shopping center, Wal-Mart or K-Mart parking lots with asphalt and concrete smothering the wonders of Jesse's and Kentucky's W-Hollow world. It might have become a graveyard for busted Barbie dolls and bedraggled G.I. Joes—a giant landfill for the accumulated Space Age junk of the Ashland-Ironton-Catlettsburg industrial complex.

It might even have been a monastery for secret prayers.

He didn't want any of those outcomes, any more than he wanted stripminers to come in and level the hilltops in the name of "cheap" electrical power. Nor did he envision making his land a place for all-terrain vehicles, stock cars, skateboarders, horse races, or hordes of mindless, bargain-hunting Christmas shoppers. As for deer hunters, they'd have to hide, load, and draw down outside the boundaries of this protected place. Trophies and wall antlers would not be a commodity in the Jesse Stuart Nature Preserve.

"This land is as close to me as my skin. Many of my poems...have been written under its trees and in its fields," words Jesse dictated to Naomi and to be read for him on December 7, 1979, at Greenbo Lake State Resort Park as part of the formal dedication of the Jesse Stuart Nature Preserve. Jesse himself would not be able to attend, for he was no longer able to flail his arms and tell any more tall tales, weaving them and presenting them as he had almost forty years before from New York to California.

Steel-drivin' man!

Like John Henry, it was as if Jesse Stuart's energy had been boundless, measuring and manhandling the miles with magnum force, the same relentless way he plowed 'round the hills and shocked another year's worth of meager corn—daylight or full-moon bright, it didn't matter. He took his Kentucky straight in gulps, for he was not a city-sippin' man. And yet the day would come when the beanstalk would be burdened and bend before a great ice storm, tumbling to sloping ground.

Governor Julian Carroll, in the twilight of his political career, on that "red-letter day for Kentucky," stood by the hospital bed at W-Hollow and lightly touched Jesse's good right hand, spoke words of comfort and encouragement. The picture taken by photographer Jim Martin for the *Ashland Daily Independent* shows Naomi Deane being cordial yet diplomatic, protective between the governor and the poet—Jesse's eyes searching for meaning—mouth slack, agape with painfully-paced expectation. Dressed in neat pajamas, head and shoulders propped up with pillows, Jesse seemed so uncharacteristically immobile—entirely paralyzed on the left side, now only a fragment of his former self, the Jesse of the old barnstorming days gone, only a small piece of resilience and power remaining. No more hour-long speeches to thousands of adoring fans. No more flights and railway clickity-clacks across America. No more cruises on the Mediterranean or Caribbean. No more dandelions on the Acropolis, no more Mars Hill and Athens, Greece, where Jesse had his conversation with the gods:

> *The sun is going down. The hour is late. Winds are becoming stronger up here....Apollo's words were soft-wind, musical words that trembled like the leaves on the tree above me. They fingered the needles on the arms, hands, and fingers of the cypresses growing near the sacred water—on the site where the oracle used to be.*
>
> *"Now, may I ask what you do with your head and hands?"*
> *"I work with my hands on my land in a western world," I said.*
> *"Besides doing this, I am a poet."*
> *"First comes the poet," he said. "Then work with your hands!"*

Jesse understood the relationship of "work" and "writing"—bound together the way soil and water have a single mind. His genius reached to the sea as surely as Shinglemill Run passed beneath the Stuart house, a small stream of water with a sound as clear as sheep bells calling creatures to come home, reaffirmation that all God's prodigal sons and daughters can go home again.

Sundown was nigh.

The final agreement with the State of Kentucky for the Jesse Stuart Nature Preserve—714 acres, lands tenant-farmed by Mick and Martha and their five children, places where Jesse walked and wrote his 703 sonnets in *Man with a Bull-Tongue Plow*—would become a saved gift to the children of tomorrow. Gov. John Y. Brown and First Lady Phyllis George Brown came to W-Hollow to personally thank Jesse for the gift.

In the new century, in November 2003, it was possible to hike three miles of "moderately strenuous" trail—an area "for passive recreation and environmental education." The preserve, now owned by the people of the Commonwealth of Kentucky and managed by the Kentucky Nature

Preserves Commission, is designated a "Watchable Wildlife Site, for birdwatching, and literature study" as well as hiking.

The jagged piece of protected land stretches along county road 2433 from KY 1 to KY 2. At the junction of KY 1 and W-Hollow Road, there's a historical marker commemorating Jesse Stuart. He would have liked that, not only for himself and his own ego, but as a message to the world that other young people living in eastern Kentucky could excel, but first they would need to work and believe in *themselves*. Jesse's mother and father would never have dreamed such an honor would come to the little boy, a piece of themselves, born on that stormy day, August 8, 1906.

One and one-half miles west on W-Hollow Road there's a small parking lot for visitors to the Jesse Stuart Nature Preserve, which would have mystified Mick and Martha, who had worked so hard to clear the land and earn their living from it. There's no prominent sign, and the place could be easily missed. It's not a fancy entranceway, and a visitor might wonder if it shouldn't have a few dollars spent to make it look more inviting. With more than forty nature preserves in the Commonwealth and a huge statewide budget deficit, expenditures in behalf of hoot owls and Old Ops are not very likely.

The trail leading up and over Shinglemill Run to the top of Seaton Ridge cries out for knowledge and advance planning. No one should go there aimlessly, and hiking should not be undertaken casually or carelessly. A professional guide is recommended and, in the deer season, bright orange is a prudent color to wear (hunting is illegal, but enforcement is difficult and poaching happens). "Op's Cabin" appears on the preserve's map, but it has been severely vandalized and does not resemble "Old Op's cabin" as described and made famous by Jesse in *The Good Spirit of Laurel Ridge*.

Much of W-Hollow has changed in the past hundred years, much has stayed the same. In another century or two or three, the hollers will have reclaimed their pristine condition. It is easy to say, "The state's not doing anything, letting it grow up so wild," but such a charge misses the point of what a nature preserve is—exactly what the two words mean: nature saved as a gift to humanity.

The good spirit of Jesse walked the wooded miles when he was a struggling, ambition-driven youth, pioneer Stuart stock. Looking down from Seaton Ridge, the view of Little Sandy River snaking its way to the Ohio, the Mother River, is a reminder of the westerly movement of Kentucky's gathered water. Down on the eastern side of the ridge lies the town of Greenup, named for Christopher Greenup, the fourth governor of the Commonwealth, once praised as "the best qualified of the early Kentucky governors."

The eulogy for Christopher Greenup included the tribute "most useful man in Kentucky," according to *Kentucky Governors*, published by the University Press of Kentucky in 1985. One hundred years after the birth in a one-room log cabin, the same thing could be said of the "man from W-Hollow." Jesse Stuart's practical nature, his commonsense approach to teaching and writing, is a cornerstone for substantial structures, whether it be writing on education, soil conservation, or free enterprise.

His heritage endures.

Sam Piatt says Jesse enjoyed some precious moments of satisfaction with the way the Nature Preserve turned out. "It's going to be here for people to enjoy, birds are going to have trees to sing in," he told Sam.

The following year, in the summer of 1980, the new governor of Kentucky, John Y. Brown Jr., sent an emissary with a check representing Jesse's half of a $1.2-million agreement—$601,725!

It was a distant cry from the days when Jesse and his mother toiled for twenty-five cents a day, the bleak years when Jesse's father gouged out coal from the sides of the hills, drove railroad spikes, and planted the seeds of doubtful crops. Those were the years of dire poverty, when that word was another way of saying *sacrifice, endurance, and pride.*

Make no mistake, the large amount of money from Frankfort would be offset by a mountain of medical expenses. Without the windfall, Naomi Deane might one day have been hard put to pay for it all, which surely was counted among Jesse's greatest fears. Such an outcome eats at a good man's ego, disappoints his image of himself, and preys on his mind as he realizes he's slowly losing control. At times such as these, a savings account of humor can save a dreary day.

Jesse looked at the $601,725 check, smiled as much as his tired face would allow, and said to his reporter/friend—

*Here, Sam, take this down to Anderson's Grocery and*
*get it cashed—and git a couple of cigars!*

The Articles of Dedication for the Jesse Stuart Nature Preserve were accepted on December 7, 1979, but due to "an oversight" (according to the Jesse Stuart SNP Draft Management Plan) they were not recorded and had to be re-accepted on March 19, 1982. By this time Jesse was nearing the end of his life.

Credit goes to H. Edward Richardson and influential friends for providing leadership for the establishment of two connected entities: the Jesse Stuart Nature Preserve and the Jesse Stuart Foundation. Together, they saved the W-Hollow land for future generations and provided a home for Jesse's literary properties. Both were ambitious, worthy projects. The formations are described in Richardson's *Jesse: The Biography of an American Writer—Jesse Hilton Stuart* (McGraw-Hill, 1984).

*On January 17, 1980, Jesse assigned by contract publication*
*rights and titles of his literary works, both published and unpublish-*
*ed, to the Foundation for management by, and benefit to, the*
*Foundation and its many purposes and activities, as well as to the*
*Stuarts as long as both or either lives.*

In the year 2005, the nonprofit Jesse Stuart Foundation's mission remains: "Preserving the legacy of Jesse Stuart and the Appalachian way of life." The executive director is Dr. James M. Gifford, who has provided the leadership for acquiring of the old post office building in Ashland, the present location of the Foundation, and for developing the organization into "A Regional Press & Bookseller"—the "material result" of Jesse's generosity.

Many Appalachian writers, past and present, including of course Jesse Stuart, are having their work published and/or distributed by the Foundation. The roster of authors includes Harriette Arnow, Thomas Barnes, Ted Franklin Belue, Harry Caudill, Billy C. Clark, Thomas D. Clark, David and Lalie Dick, Wilma Dykeman, Allen W. Eckert, John Fox Jr., Danny Fulks, Janice Holt Giles, Loyal Jones, Glennis Stuart Lyles, George Ella Lyon, Sharyn McCrumb, Jim Wayne Miller, Lynwood Montell, Elizabeth Madox Roberts, and James Still.

Today, were it not for the Jesse Stuart Foundation and the Jesse Stuart

Nature Preserve, the heritage of the enduring naturalist who wrote "Nest Egg" might have been doomed to oblivion.

A painful loss has been averted—Jesse lives for the Commonwealth.

# EPILOGUE

*Oh, my children, where air we going on this mighty river of earth,*
*a-borning, begetting, and a-dying—*
*the living and the dead riding the waters?*
*Where air it sweeping us?...*

James Still
*River of Earth*

*Peace.*

She rests beside Jesse.

Naomi Deane Norris Stuart died on Tuesday, June 22, 1993, at King's Daughters' Medical Center in Ashland, Kentucky. She had suffered a stroke in 1986 and had spent most of 1987 in a health care facility in Florida. But she lived her final years in her home in W-Hollow.

"I love it and would live nowhere else," she once told James M. Gifford, director of the Jesse Stuart Foundation.

Quiet spoken and gracious, Naomi Deane remembered, "Jesse was surprised when I suggested that we take a lunch and walk to this spot one cold Sunday. It was April 16, my birthday, the year after we were married. He was pleased when I suggested that we make this our home...a home filled with loving memories."

James Gifford recalled his last visit with Naomi Deane:

> *On June 2* [1993], *I visited with Mrs. Stuart in her home. I always enjoyed presenting her with new books, and I had driven out to W-Hollow that day to give her a copy of our new reprint of* Hie to the Hunters. *While there, I asked her what she considered her greatest*

*accomplishment.*

*"She thought for a minute and said— 'Going to college and teaching.'"*

It was a humble, telling answer, one that Jesse would have applauded. Despite his overweening public manner, Jesse respected his wife for her individuality. The fact that she didn't say her greatest accomplishment was being the wife of a world-famous author was a sign of her love for her profession as a teacher.

Naomi Deane Norris Stuart's days as a student at Morehead State Teachers College, later to become Morehead State University, were filled with dreams of being a help for Appalachian youth. Not in her wildest flights of fantasy did she imagine that she'd marry and stand alongside one of Kentucky's most famous writers, travel around the world with him, bear their child, and live to see the completion of a Jesse Stuart Room in the Camden-Carroll Library on the MSU campus—all this and crowned by years of bountiful classroom teaching.

The walls of the room at Morehead State are filled with pictures bespeaking family, creativity, education, and W-Hollow.

Next to the Jesse Stuart Room is the James Still Room, with pictures of Still's log house on Little Carr Creek. Hence after passing on, two old rivals have been reinstated as companions lighting the way for others to follow.

Included among the treasures in the Jesse Stuart Room is the actual bull-tongue plow, built in 1930 by Fred Holbrook with hatchet, ax and handsaw, and sold to Jesse's father for six dollars.

On the bookshelves are first-edition copies of each of Jesse's books, all inscribed to Naomi Deane.

*The Man with a Bull-Tongue Plow*'s inscription reads:

*October 14, 1934*
*W-Hollow*

*Deane Norris you and I have gone together,*
*we walked together when the moon was full;*
*when winds were sobbing in the mountain heather—*

*Deane Norris, you were straight and beautiful,*
*and I was proud to walk beside of you.*
*You were as pretty as a willow tree*
*when its sharp leaves turn silver in the wind.*
*We have gone out and danced the night together—*
*swinging to rhythms of the violin—*
*you neatly patterned as a willow tree.*
*Your auburn hair so naturally was curled*
*with softness of a blossom first unfurled,*
*your eyes were dew-drops in the early morn*
*the sun left hanging to the blades of corn.*

William Boozer wrote in the *Nashville Banner*, "The years together of Naomi Deane and Jesse Stuart make an inspiring love story that will live forever....And many there are who never expect to look upon his kind again."

Jesse Hilton Stuart and Naomi Deane Norris Stuart lived and died and live again in a whirl of everlasting time and flowing water—Heaven-sent moisture beginning as Cedar Riffles on the Greenup County shoulder of the Appalachian Highlands, ending in the vastness of the Caribbean Sea.

With the building of each new cloud formation, the purified water comes home again.

On Friday, June 25, 1993, Naomi Deane was reunited with Jesse. They're eternally at rest in Plum Grove Cemetery, downstream from W-Hollow.

# AFTERWORD

## by Thomas D. Clark

Among the ranks of Kentucky authors, none is more worthy of a searching biography than Jesse Stuart, and none presents his biographer with a greater interpretive challenge—that of unraveling the factual and spiritual dynamics of a complex personality. David Dick has been diligent in his search for factual, but more important is his effort to strip out and identify the contrasting and often contradictory strands of Stuart's life and writings. To do so has required a deep bonding with his subject.

Dick has been a compassionate biographer, searching indefatigably for the inner spiritual nuances that buoyed Stuart's overflowing imagination. But perhaps his greatest contribution is to help us understand Jesse Stuart's attachment to his native place—W-Hollow in northeastern Kentucky—and to the deeply ingrained folkways and traditions of that place that shaped him both as a man and as a writer. On the one hand they served Stuart as a continuing source of inspiration, but Dick perceives also the relentless grip of the lingering frontier land that provided him an insulative blanket of refuge.

Wisely, Dick has given his subject free rein to lope in and out of his biography. Posthumously, Jesse Stuart speaks out, loud and clear, as he did in life. Collectively the Stuart letters provide penetrating insight into the soul of a man who teetered on the borderline between an arrest stage of adolescence and literary maturity.

Viewed from the pinnacle of the American literary canon, Jesse Stuart must be identified as an individual detached from the main current of the latter half of the twentieth century. An anomaly of his writings is the fact that he came of literary age in an era when a host of southern regional writers were ardently creating a fresh literary identity for their land. Measured against the offerings of the famous Vanderbilt Agrarians and New Critics whom he once hoped to emulate, Jesse Stuart appears as a virtual cipher, a near fugitive in another time and place.

No doubt in time to come other Stuart biographers will weigh the turnings of life in a primitive agrarian environment. They will appraise

Jesse Stuart and his writings by various literary and human standards. None, however, can deny their subject's success in carving out a distinctive niche in the great panorama of American literature.

In writing Stuart's biography, David Dick has been generous in spirit and space. He has presented a regional author with the candor of Clio but also with a jovian judiciousness. There may be drifting around "out there" a cache of fugitive facts that may someday enlarge our insights into Jesse Stuart, man and author, but this seems unlikely at present. David Dick has blazed a bold literary path to the W-Hollow door of a prodigious author, a man who held tenaciously to the handle of a bull-tongue with one hand and with the other, a pen constantly overflowing with promise.

# A Chronological List of Jesse Stuart's Books

1. *Harvest of Youth*. Howe, Oklahoma: The Scroll Press, 1930. Poems

2. *Man with a Bull-Tongue Plow*. New York: E.P. Dutton, 1934. Poems

3. *Head o' W-Hollow*. New York: E.P. Dutton, 1936. Short stories

4. *Beyond Dark Hills*. New York: E.P. Dutton, 1938. Autobiographical

5. *Tim: A Story*. Cincinnati: *The Little Man Magazine*, 1939. Novelette

6. *Trees of Heaven*. New York: E.P. Dutton, 1940. Novel

7. *Men of the Mountains*. New York: E.P. Dutton, 1941. Short stories

8. *Taps for Private Tussie*. New York: E.P. Dutton, 1943. Novel

9. *Album of Destiny*. New York: E.P. Dutton, 1944. Poems

10. *Mongrel Mettle*. New York: E.P. Dutton, 1944. Novel

11. *Foretaste of Glory*. New York: E.P. Dutton, 1946. Novel

12. *Tales from the Plum Grove Hills*. New York: E.P. Dutton, 1946. Short stories

13. *The Thread That Runs So True*. New York: Charles Scribner's Sons, 1949. Autobiographical

14. *Clearing in the Sky and Other Stories*. New York: McGraw Hill, 1950. Short stories

15. *Hie to the Hunters*. New York: Whittlesey House of McGraw-Hill, 1950. Novel

16. *Kentucky Is My Land*. New York: E.P. Dutton, 1952. Poems

17. *The Beatinest Boy*. New York: Whittlesey House of McGraw Hill, 1953. Juvenile novel

18. *The Good Spirit of Laurel Ridge*. New York: McGraw Hill, 1953. Novel

19. *A Penny's Worth of Character*. New York: Whittlesey House of McGraw Hill, 1954. Juvenile novel

20. *Red Mule*. New York: Whittlesey House of McGraw-Hill, 1955. Juvenile novel

21. *The Year of My Rebirth*. New York: McGraw-Hill, 1956. Autobiographical

22. *Plowshare in Heaven*. New York: McGraw-Hill, 1958. Short stories

23. *God's Oddling*. New York: McGraw-Hill, 1960. Biography

24. *Huey, the Engineer*. James E. Beard: St. Helena, California, 1960. Novelette

25. *The Rightful Owner*. New York: McGraw-Hill, 1960. Juvenile novel

26. *Andy Finds a Way*. New York: Whittlesey House of McGraw-Hill, 1961. Juvenile novel

27. *Hold April*. New York: McGraw-Hill, 1962. Poems

28. *A Jesse Stuart Reader: Stories and Poems Selected and Introduced by Jesse Stuart.* New York: McGraw-Hill, 1963. Poems, essays, short stories

29. *Save Every Lamb.* New York: McGraw-Hill, 1964. Short stories

30. *Daughter of the Legend.* New York: McGraw-Hill, 1965. Novel

31. *A Jesse Stuart Harvest.* New York: Laurel-Leaf Library of Dell Publishing, 1965. Short stories

32. *My Land Has a Voice.* New York: McGraw-Hill, 1966. Short stories

33. *A Ride with Huey the Engineer.* New York: McGraw-Hall, 1966. Juvenile novel

34. *Mr. Gallion's School.* New York: McGraw-Hill, 1967. Autobiographical fiction

35. *Rebels with a Cause.* Murray, Kentucky: Murray State University, 1967. Essay

36. *Strength from the Hills: The Story of Mick Stuart, My Father.* New York: Pyramid Books, 1968. (Abridgment of *God's Oddling*). Biography

37. *Stories by Jesse Stuart.* New York: McGraw-Hill, 1968. Short stories

38. *Come Gentle Spring.* New York: McGraw-Hill, 1969. Short stories

39. *Old Ben.* New York: McGraw-Hill, 1970. Juvenile novel

40. *Seven by Jesse.* Terre Haute: Indiana Council of Teachers of English, 1970. Short Stories

41. *To Teach, To Love.* Cleveland: Word Publishing, 1970. Autobiographical

42. *Autumn Lovesong.* Kansas City, Missouri: Hallmark Publishing, 1971. Poems

43. *Come Back to the Farm.* New York: McGraw-Hill, 1971. Short stories

44. *Come to My Tomorrowland.* Nashville: Aurora Publishing, 1971. Juvenile novel

45. *Dawn of Remembered Spring.* New York: McGraw-Hill, 1972. Poems and short stories

46. *Tennessee Hill Folk.* Nashville: Vanderbilt University Press, 1972. Appalachian photographs by Joe Clark with narrative essay by Jesse Stuart

47. *The Land Beyond the River.* New York: McGraw-Hill, 1973. Novel

48. *32 Votes Before Breakfast.* New York: McGraw-Hill, 1974. Short stories

49. *My World.* Lexington, Kentucky: University Press of Kentucky, 1975. Autobiographical

50. *Up the Hollow from Lynchburg.* New York: McGraw-Hill, 1975. Appalachian photographs by Joe Clark with text by Jesse Stuart.

51. *The World of Jesse Stuart.* New York: McGraw Hill, 1975. Poems

52. *The Only Place We Live.* Sauk City, Wisconsin: Wisconsin House, 1976. (Co-authored by Jesse Stuart, August Derleth, and Robert E. Gard) Poems

53. *The Seasons of Jesse Stuart*. Danbury, Connecticut: Archer Editions Press, 1976. Poems

54. *Honest Confession of a Literary Sin*. Detroit: W-Hollow Books, 1977. Essay

55. *Dandelion on the Acropolis*. Lynnville, Tennessee: Archer Editions Press, 1978. Travel journal

56. *The Kingdom Within*. New York: McGraw-Hill, 1979. Autobiographical fiction

57. *Lost Sandstones and Lonely Skies and Other Essays*. Lynnwood, Tennessee: Archer Editions Press, 1979. Essays

58. *If I Were Seventeen Again and Other Essays*. Lynnwood, Tennessee: Archer Editions Press, 1980. Essays

59. *Land of the Honey-Colored Wind*. Morehead, Kentucky: Jesse Stuart Foundation, 1981. Poems and Short Stories

60. *The Best-Loved Short Stories of Jesse Stuart*. New York: McGraw Hill, 1982. Short stories

61. *Songs of a Mountain Plowman*. Morehead, Kentucky: Jesse Stuart Foundation and Morehead State Appalachian Development Center, 1986. Poems

62. *Cradle of the Copperheads*. New York: McGraw-Hill, 1988. Autobiographical Fiction

63. *Split Cherry Tree*. Ashland, Kentucky: Jesse Stuart Foundation, 1990. Novelette

64. *New Harvest: Forgotten Stories of Kentucky's Jesse Stuart (Collected and edited by David Palmore)*. Ashland, Kentucky: Jesse Stuart Foundation, 2003. Short stories

## TEXTBOOKS CO-EDITED BY JESSE STUART

1. Outlooks Through Literature. Scott Foresman Educational Publishers, 1964.

2. *Short Stories For Discussion*. New York: Charles Scribner's Sons Publishers, 1965.